D0395710

Jane Irwin
Storyteller

Jane Irwin and Jeff Berndt
Co-Creators

Front cover calligraphy by Jeff Berndt and Maryvonne Sarfati.

Interior cover photograph courtesy of John Hall, used with permission.

Cover design and layout by Paul Sizer of Café Digital Studios. www.paulsizer.com

"Wave Over Wave" Lyrics by Jim Payne and Janis Spence, Music by Jim Payne SOCAN © SingSong Inc.

All stories, characters and images are copyright 1996-2007 Jane Irwin and Fiery Studios, unless otherwise specified. All rights reserved. No part of this book may be reproduced or utilized in any form or by any means, electronic or mechanical, including photocopying, recording, or by any information storage and retrieval system, without written permission except in the case of reprints in the context of reviews.

Published by Fiery Studios, PO Box 51595, Kalamazoo, Michigan 49005.
fierystudios@hotmail.com www.vogelein.com

First Printing, August 2007. Printed in the USA by Malloy Incorporated. www.malloy.com

ISBN 978-0-9743110-1-2 (0-9743110-1-4).

Vögelein

OLD GHOSTS

Jane Irwin

Foreword by
Barbara Lien-Cooper
and
Dr. Park Cooper

Fiery Studios

For Martin Blake Linell,
known to us as Blake Mason

1978 - 2001

"Because those kids
need to know that
there are gentle men."

Foreword

The human creative spirit is a fragile thing, like dragonfly wings or the springs and gears of clockwork.

When we're lucky, we get some idiosyncratic, beautiful, personal comics from that fragile creative spirit that says that *this* story has to be told; the spirit that says, "Go out. Connect with one person, a thousand, a million, as long as someone reads and feels and understands." That's success.

Now, the best works in comics make you *feel* something. Excitement that good won over evil. Horror because the zombies just keep on coming. Laughter at the world's absurdity. Then there's some comics like *Vögelein*. Comics that tug at your heart—not trying to jerk tears nor get a Pavlovian response of shock, but instead are trying to show us a little bit of what it's really like to be humane and compassionate.

One doesn't need to have read the previous volume of *Vögelein* to enjoy this one—if you haven't, let me catch you up—Vögelein is a clockwork creation who's really alive, a windup fairy with wings who can feel all the things we can feel, and fly to boot. She has a couple of human friends who can wind her up in her back, where she can't reach. That's it. That's all you really need, not that you *shouldn't* find the first volume as well.

But in this volume, the second in a continuing series, Jane gives those who did read the first volume some closure about things that they didn't know they needed it for—can Vögelein learn to fend for herself against the humans of the city? Can she come to terms with all the regrets of her past? Can she learn to be a braver and more centered 21st century fairy?

It's a book of little moments, as when Vögelein tells about the death of someone close to her, or the moments when she rests in Jane's better-than-ever cityscapes, or even when Jane chooses, instead of telling us, to show us the fears or compassions of *Vögelein*'s supporting characters.

Vögelein's one of those comics that teaches us what it's like to be human, which is ironic considering it's about a clockwork fairy. It's an all-ages fairy tale that adults will appreciate as much as children. It's rare. It's beautiful. It's from someone's heart.

It's a gift that Jane Irwin offers you.

It's a comic with its own unique voice, its own unique vision, its own unique worldview.

The comics world is just a little better place for having *Vögelein* in it.

— Barbara Lien-Cooper and Dr. Park Cooper,
writers, Dabel Brothers'/Marvel's *Half Dead*
and Wicker Man Studios' *Gun Street Girl*
www.wickermanstudios.com

So či del o berš, del o časo.

"What a year may not bring, an hour might."

-- Vlax Romani proverb,
translation by Dr. Ian Hancock
from his book *We are the Romani People*

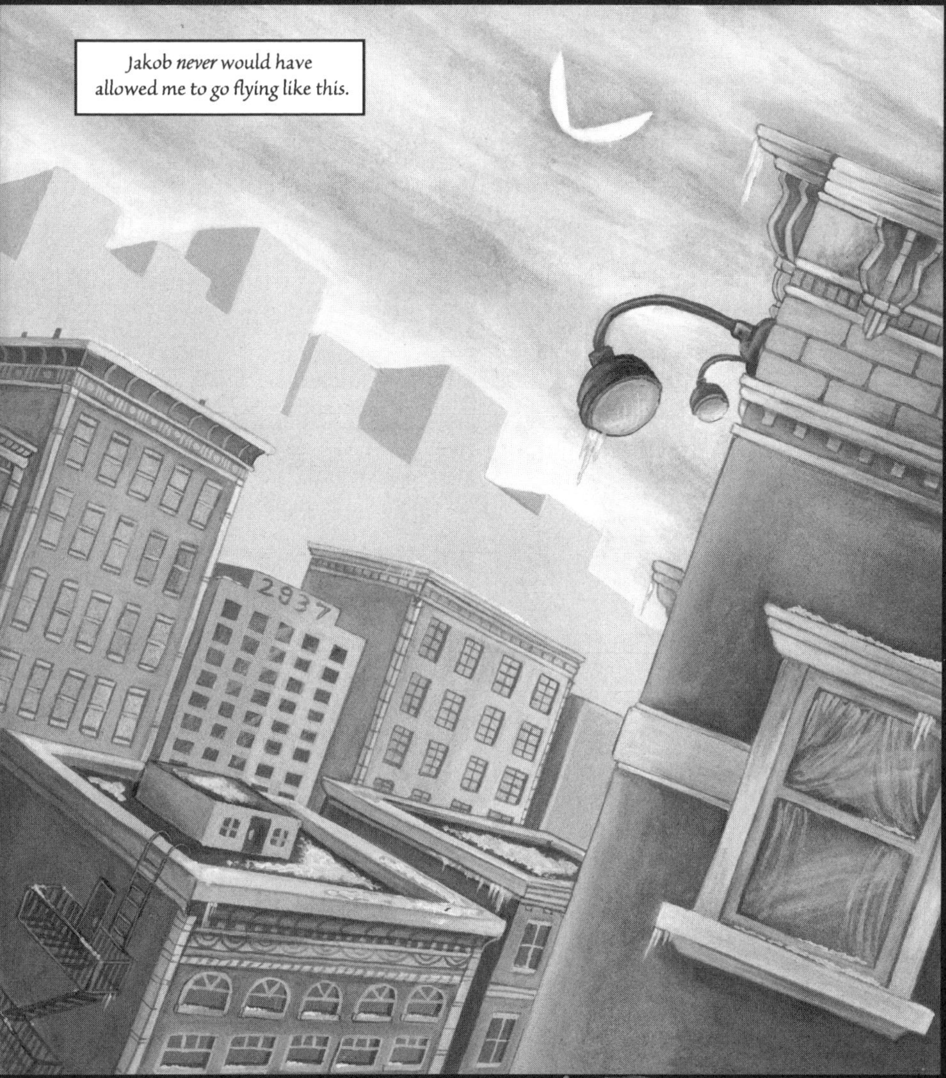
Jakob *never* would have allowed me to go flying like this.

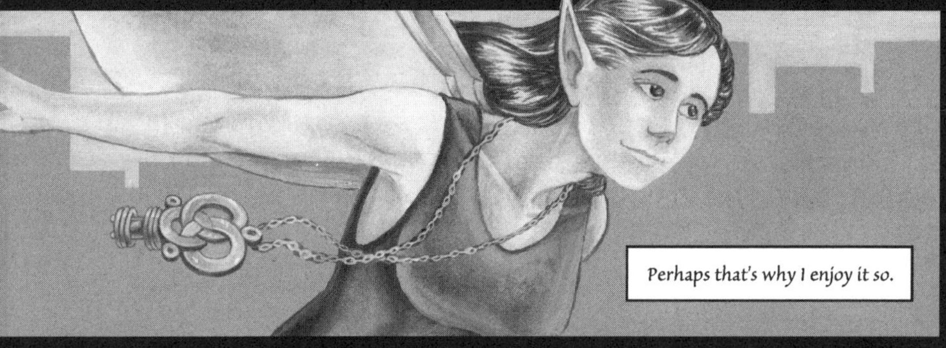
Perhaps that's why I enjoy it so.

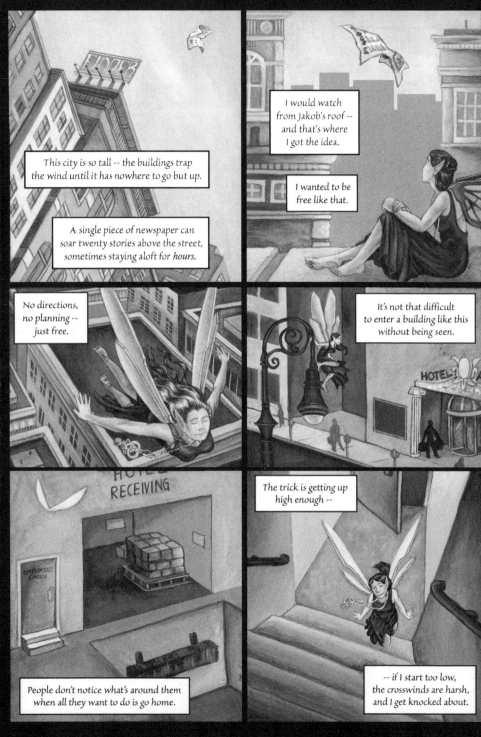

This city is so tall -- the buildings trap the wind until it has nowhere to go but up.

A single piece of newspaper can soar twenty stories above the street, sometimes staying aloft for *hours.*

I would watch from Jakob's roof -- and that's where I got the idea.

I wanted to be free like that.

No directions, no planning -- just free.

It's not that difficult to enter a building like this without being seen.

People don't notice what's around them when all they want to do is go home.

The trick is getting up high enough --

-- if I start too low, the crosswinds are harsh, and I get knocked about.

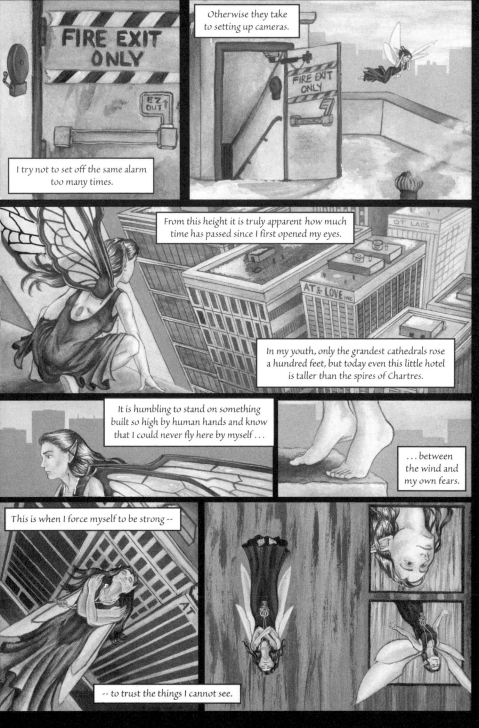

Otherwise they take to setting up cameras.

FIRE EXIT ONLY

EZ OUT

I try not to set off the same alarm too many times.

FIRE EXIT ONLY

From this height it is truly apparent how much time has passed since I first opened my eyes.

GT LABS

AT & LOVE inc

In my youth, only the grandest cathedrals rose a hundred feet, but today even this little hotel is taller than the spires of Chartres.

It is humbling to stand on something built so high by human hands and know that I could never fly here by myself . . .

. . . between the wind and my own fears.

This is when I force myself to be strong --

-- to trust the things I cannot see.

15

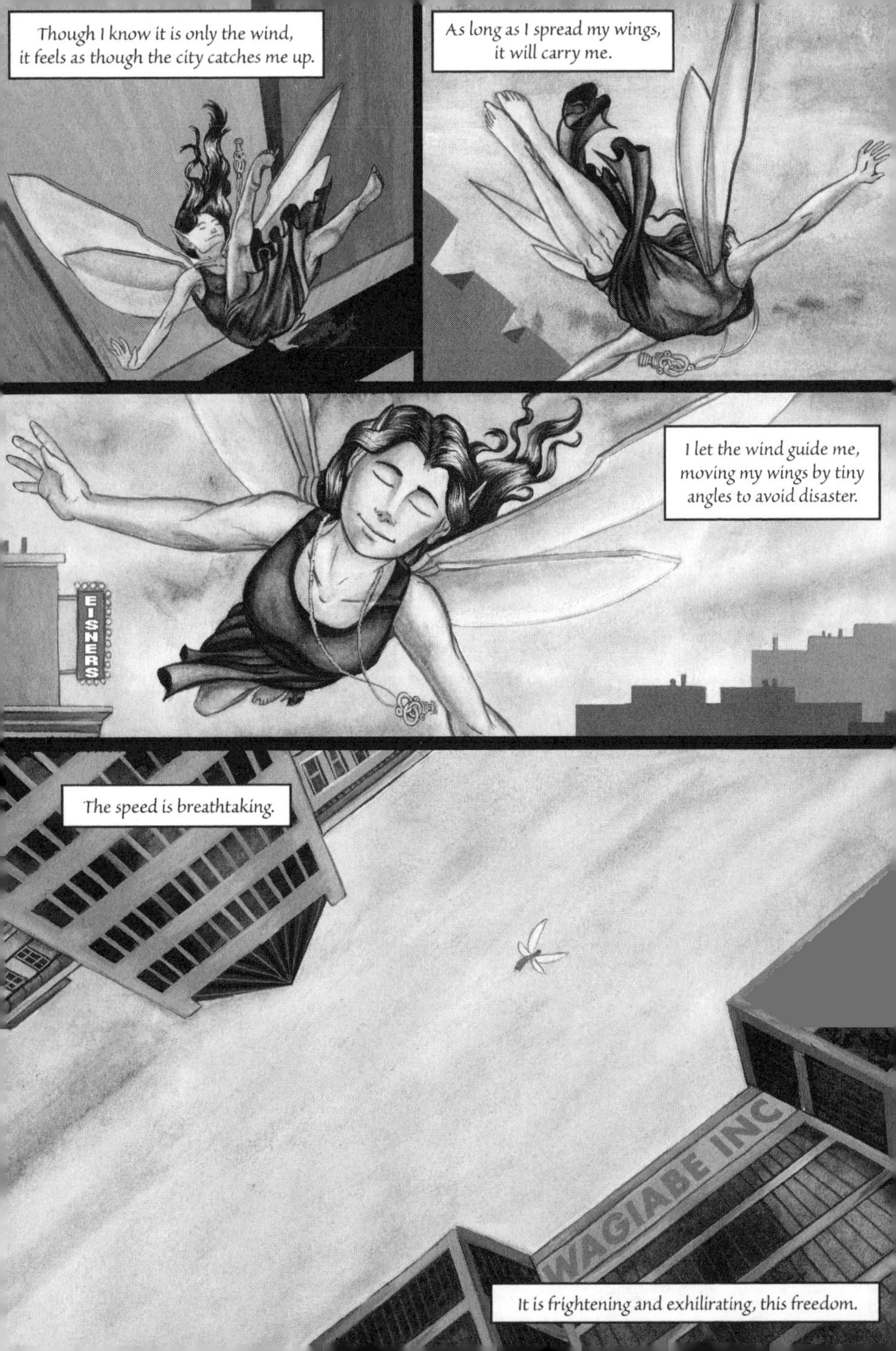
Though I know it is only the wind, it feels as though the city catches me up.
As long as I spread my wings, it will carry me.
I let the wind guide me, moving my wings by tiny angles to avoid disaster.
EISNERS
The speed is breathtaking.
WAGIABE INC
It is frightening and exhilirating, this freedom.

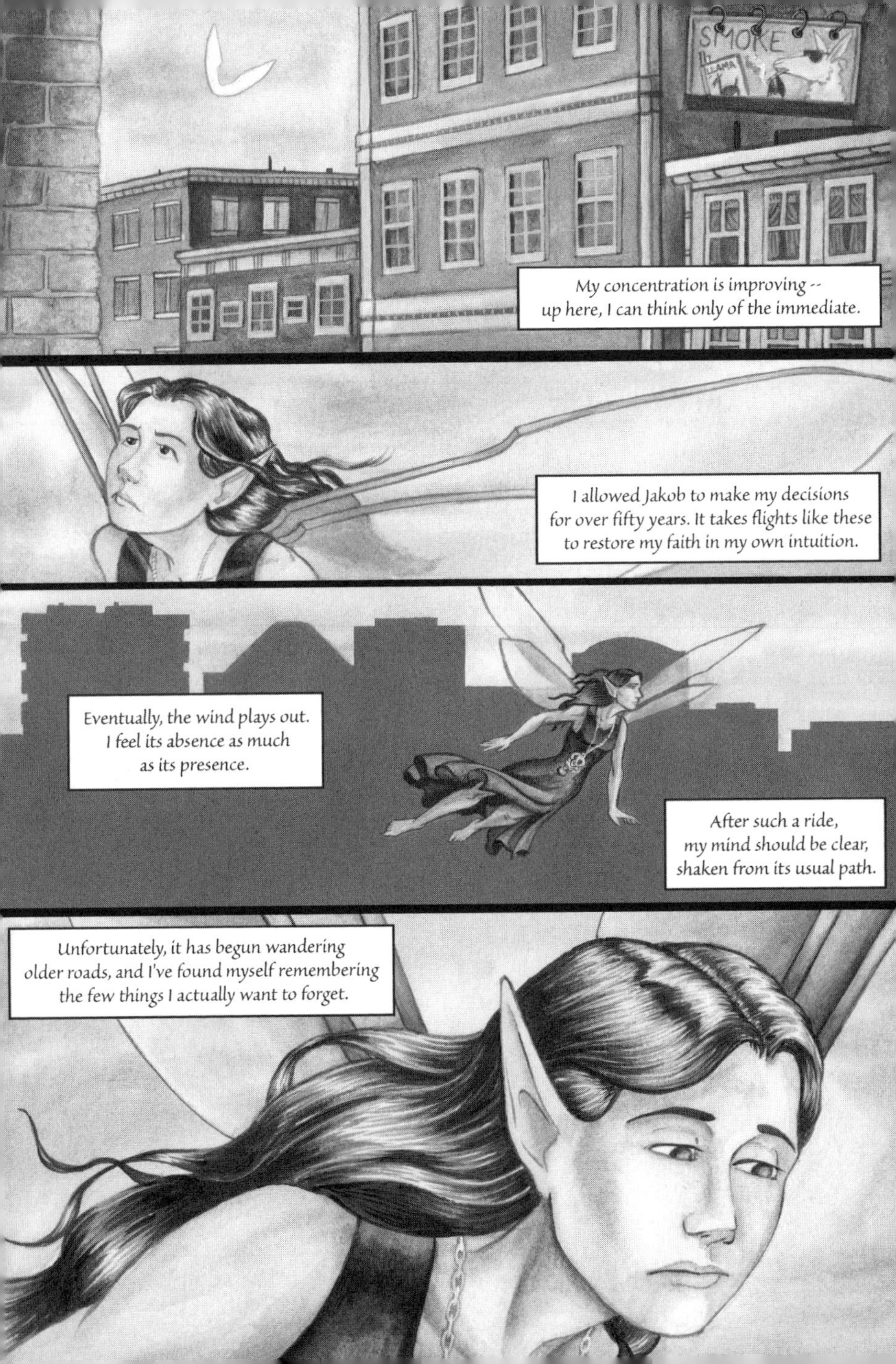
SMOKE
LLAMA
My concentration is improving -- up here, I can think only of the immediate.
I allowed Jakob to make my decisions for over fifty years. It takes flights like these to restore my faith in my own intuition.
Eventually, the wind plays out. I feel its absence as much as its presence.
After such a ride, my mind should be clear, shaken from its usual path.
Unfortunately, it has begun wandering older roads, and I've found myself remembering the few things I actually want to forget.

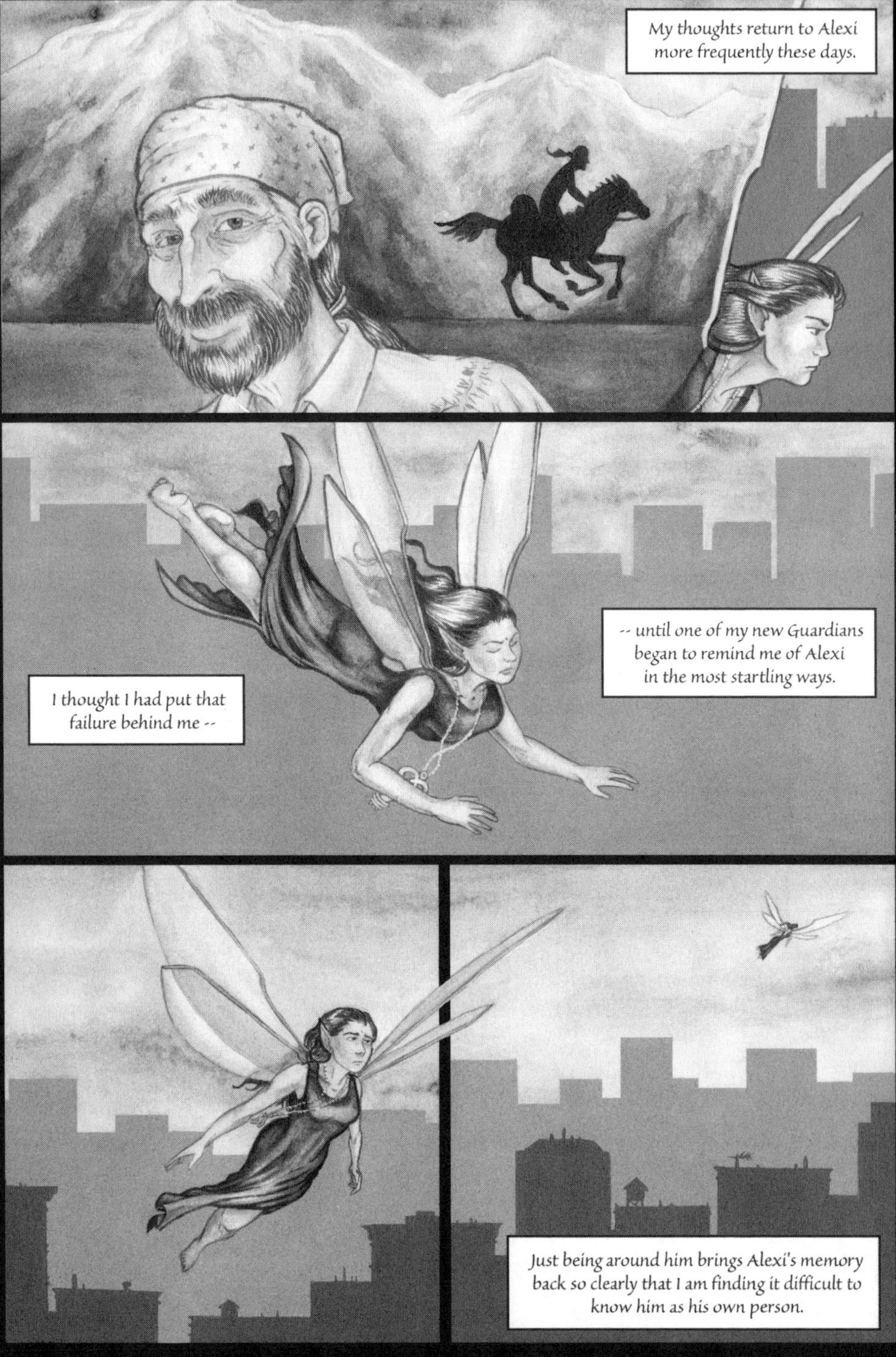
My thoughts return to Alexi more frequently these days.
I thought I had put that failure behind me --
-- until one of my new Guardians began to remind me of Alexi in the most startling ways.
Just being around him brings Alexi's memory back so clearly that I am finding it difficult to know him as his own person.

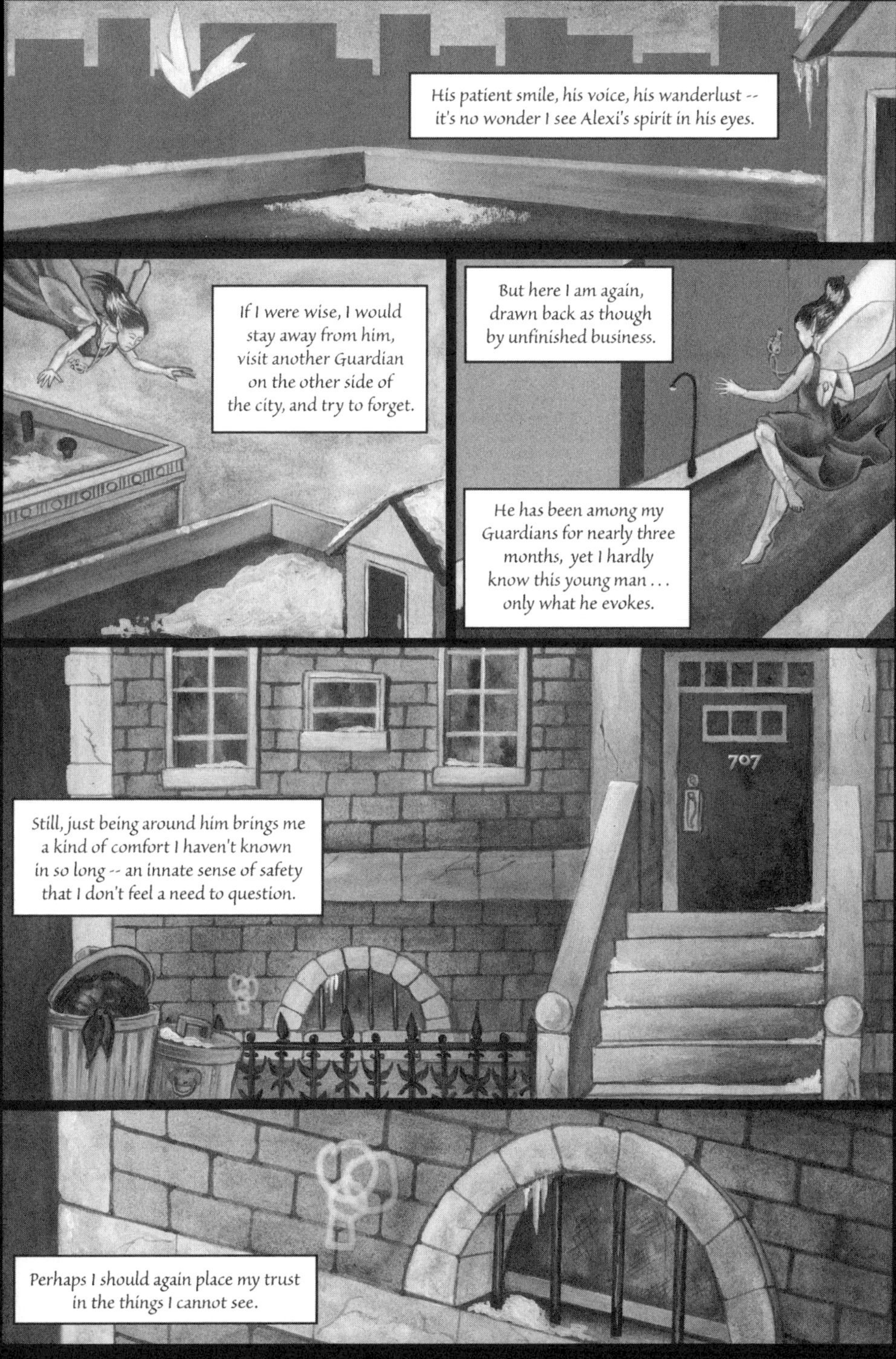
His patient smile, his voice, his wanderlust -- it's no wonder I see Alexi's spirit in his eyes.
If I were wise, I would stay away from him, visit another Guardian on the other side of the city, and try to forget.
But here I am again, drawn back as though by unfinished business.
He has been among my Guardians for nearly three months, yet I hardly know this young man . . . only what he evokes.
Still, just being around him brings me a kind of comfort I haven't known in so long -- an innate sense of safety that I don't feel a need to question.
707
Perhaps I should again place my trust in the things I cannot see.

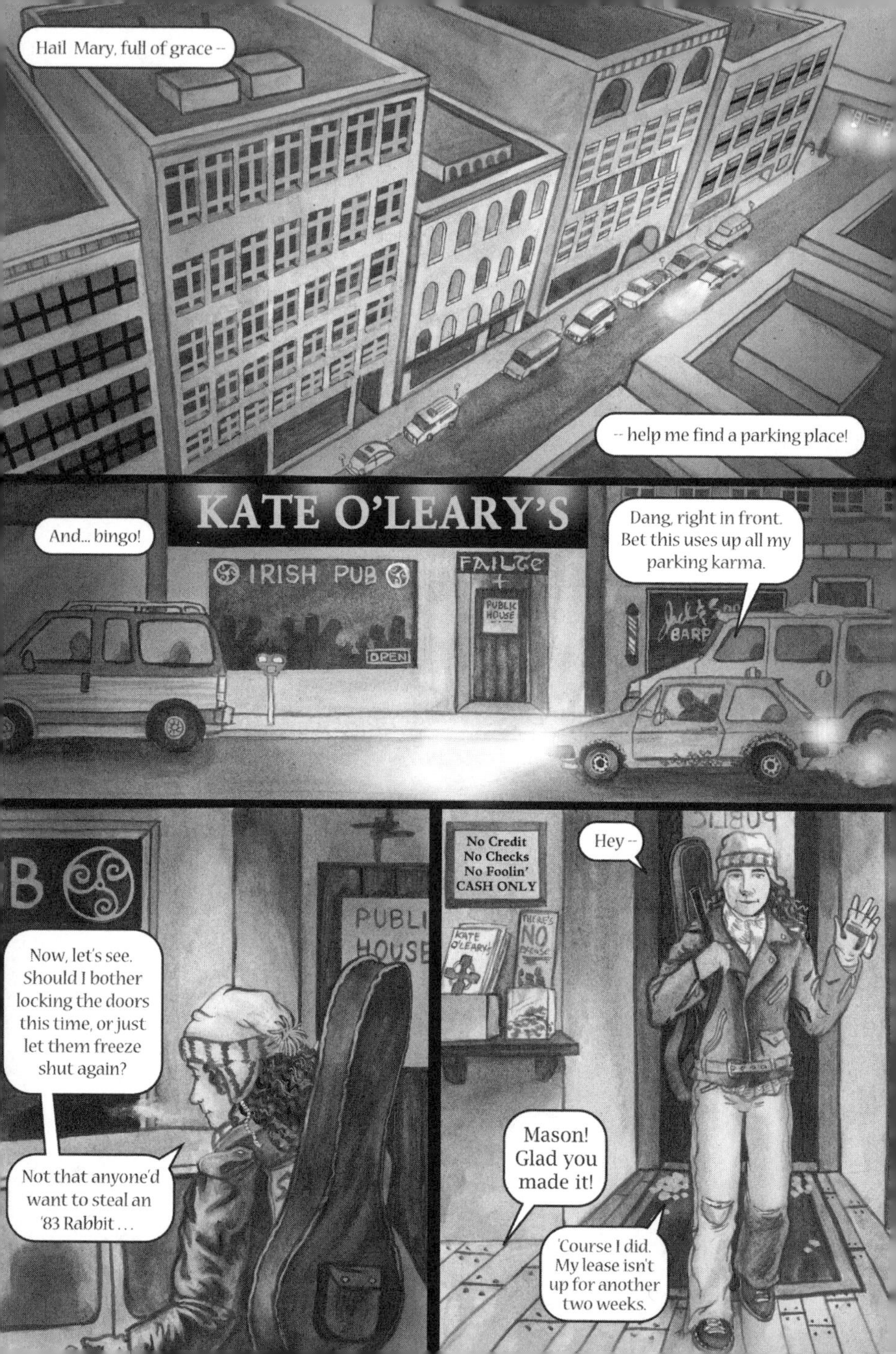

Hail Mary, full of grace --
-- help me find a parking place!
KATE O'LEARY'S
And... bingo!
IRISH PUB
FAILTE
PUBLIC HOUSE
OPEN
Dang, right in front. Bet this uses up all my parking karma.
BARP
PUBLIC HOUSE
Now, let's see. Should I bother locking the doors this time, or just let them freeze shut again?
Not that anyone'd want to steal an '83 Rabbit . . .
No Credit
No Checks
No Foolin'
CASH ONLY
Hey --
Mason! Glad you made it!
'Course I did. My lease isn't up for another two weeks.

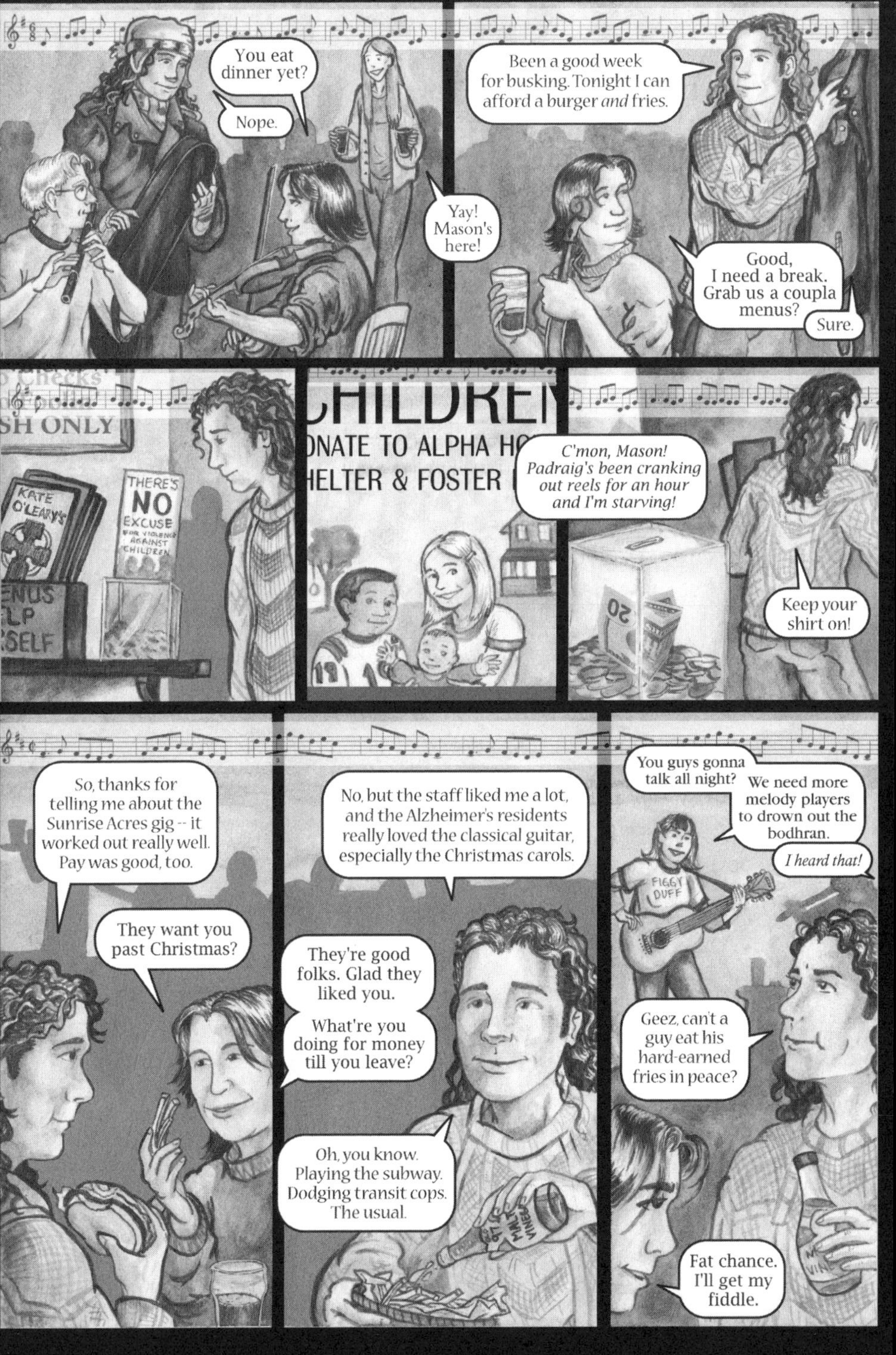
You eat dinner yet?
Nope.
Yay! Mason's here!
Been a good week for busking. Tonight I can afford a burger *and* fries.
Good, I need a break. Grab us a coupla menus?
Sure.
SH ONLY
KATE O'LEARY'S
THERE'S NO EXCUSE FOR VIOLENCE AGAINST CHILDREN
CHILDREN
ONATE TO ALPHA HO
HELTER & FOSTER
C'mon, Mason! Padraig's been cranking out reels for an hour and I'm starving!
Keep your shirt on!
So, thanks for telling me about the Sunrise Acres gig -- it worked out really well. Pay was good, too.
They want you past Christmas?
No, but the staff liked me a lot, and the Alzheimer's residents really loved the classical guitar, especially the Christmas carols.
They're good folks. Glad they liked you.
What're you doing for money till you leave?
Oh, you know. Playing the subway. Dodging transit cops. The usual.
MALT VINEGAR
You guys gonna talk all night?
We need more melody players to drown out the bodhran.
I heard that!
FIGGY DUFF
Geez, can't a guy eat his hard-earned fries in peace?
Fat chance. I'll get my fiddle.

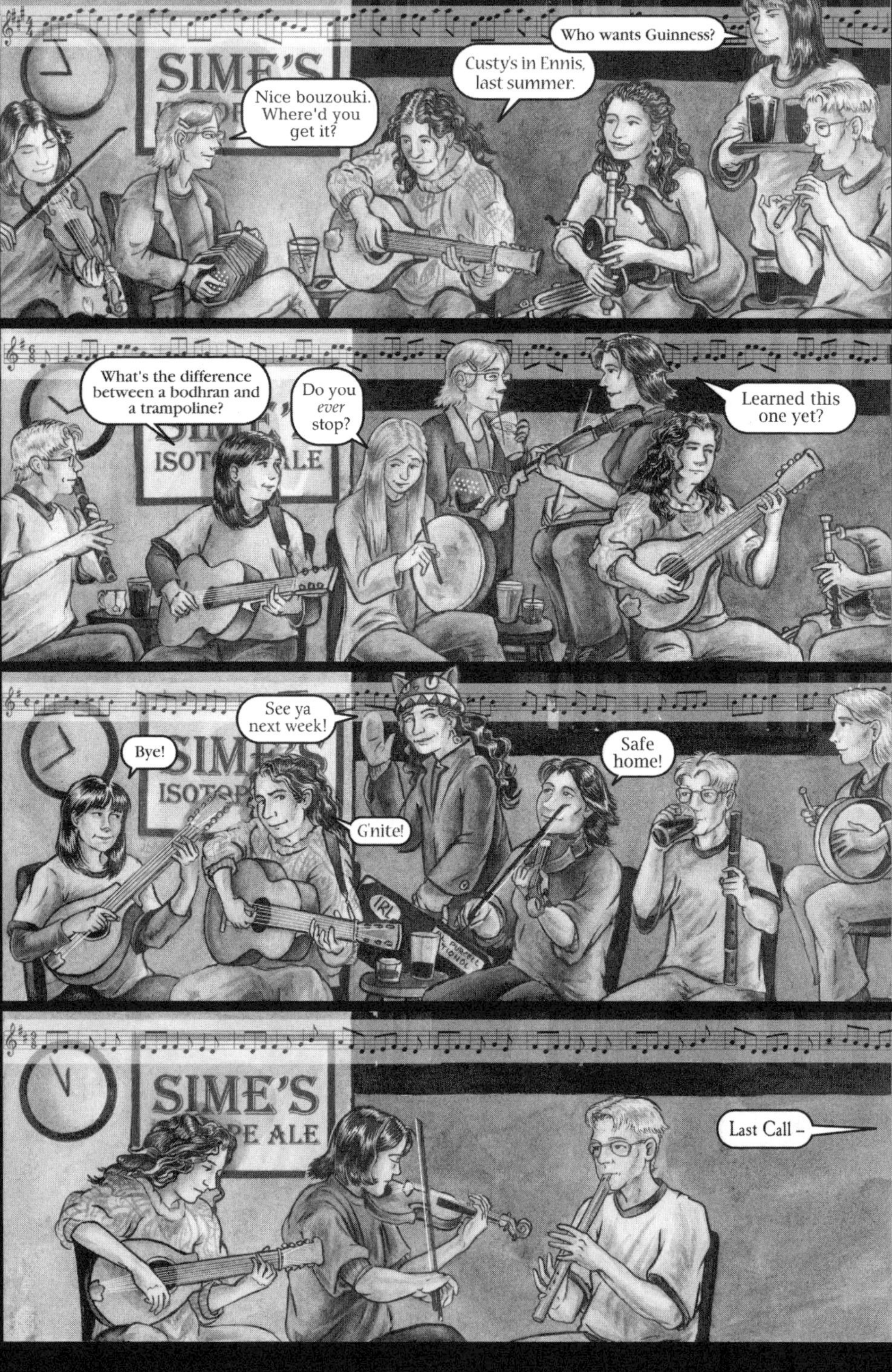
SIME'S
Nice bouzouki. Where'd you get it?
Custy's in Ennis, last summer.
Who wants Guinness?
What's the difference between a bodhran and a trampoline?
Do you *ever* stop?
Learned this one yet?
SIME'S ISOTOPE ALE
See ya next week!
Bye!
G'nite!
Safe home!
Last Call –
SIME'S
PE ALE

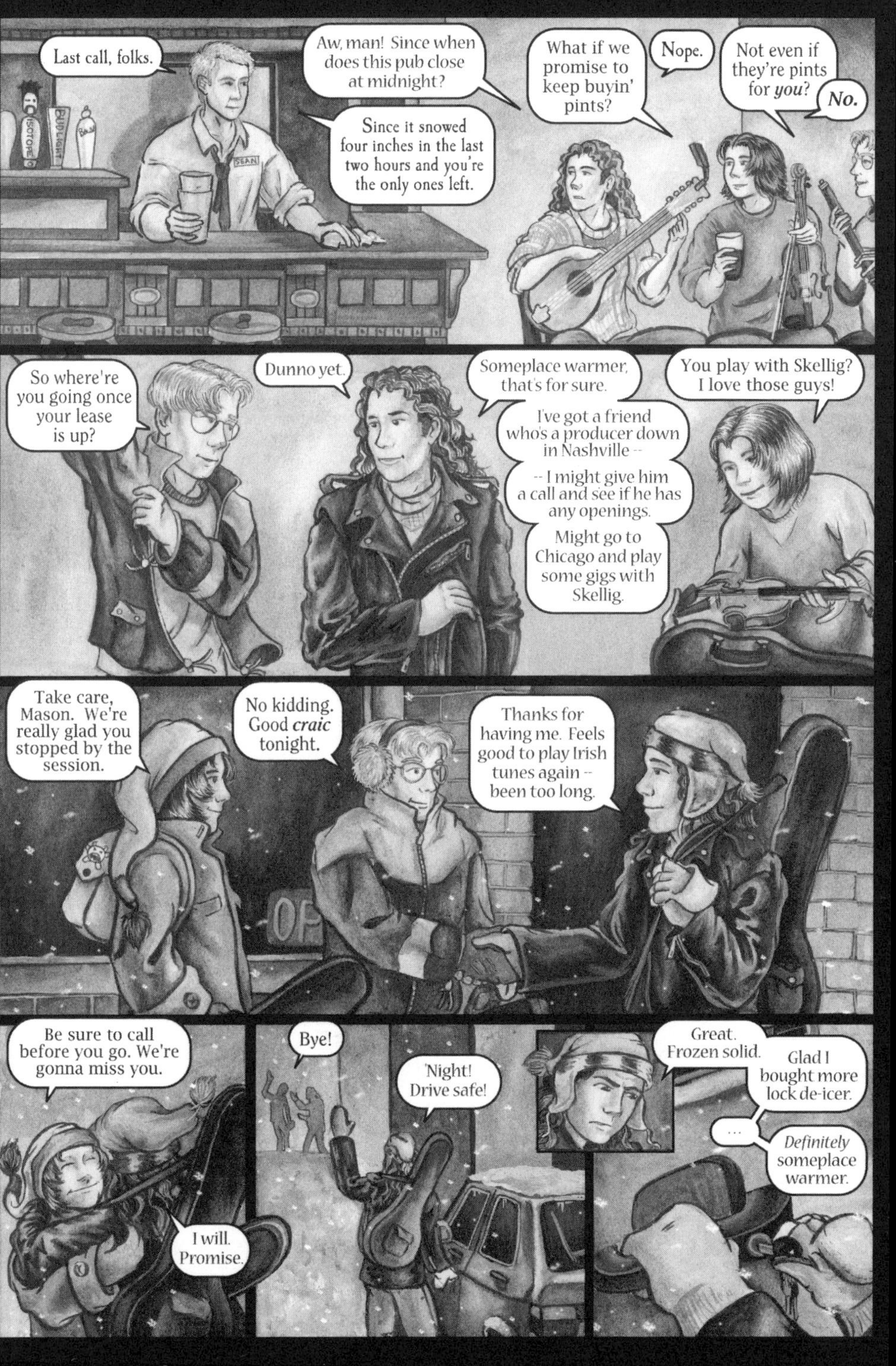
Last call, folks.
Aw, man! Since when does this pub close at midnight?
Since it snowed four inches in the last two hours and you're the only ones left.
What if we promise to keep buyin' pints?
Nope.
Not even if they're pints for *you*?
No.
So where're you going once your lease is up?
Dunno yet.
Someplace warmer, that's for sure.
I've got a friend who's a producer down in Nashville --
-- I might give him a call and see if he has any openings.
Might go to Chicago and play some gigs with Skellig.
You play with Skellig? I love those guys!
Take care, Mason. We're really glad you stopped by the session.
No kidding. Good ***craic*** tonight.
Thanks for having me. Feels good to play Irish tunes again -- been too long.
Be sure to call before you go. We're gonna miss you.
I will. Promise.
Bye!
'Night! Drive safe!
Great. Frozen solid.
Glad I bought more lock de-icer.
...
Definitely someplace warmer.

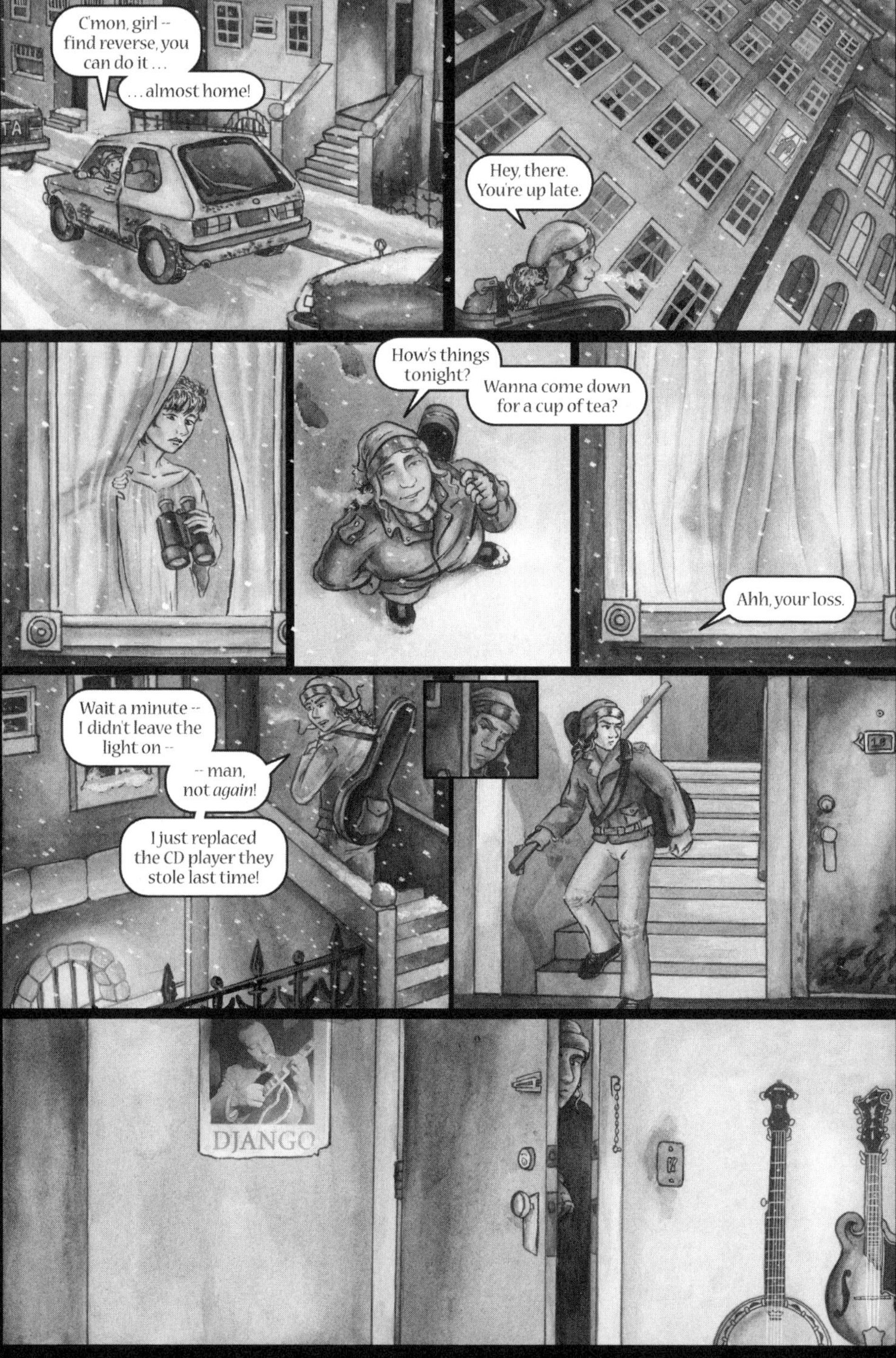

C'mon, girl -- find reverse, you can do it ...
... almost home!
Hey, there. You're up late.
How's things tonight?
Wanna come down for a cup of tea?
Ahh, your loss.
Wait a minute -- I didn't leave the light on --
-- man, not *again*!
I just replaced the CD player they stole last time!
DJANGO

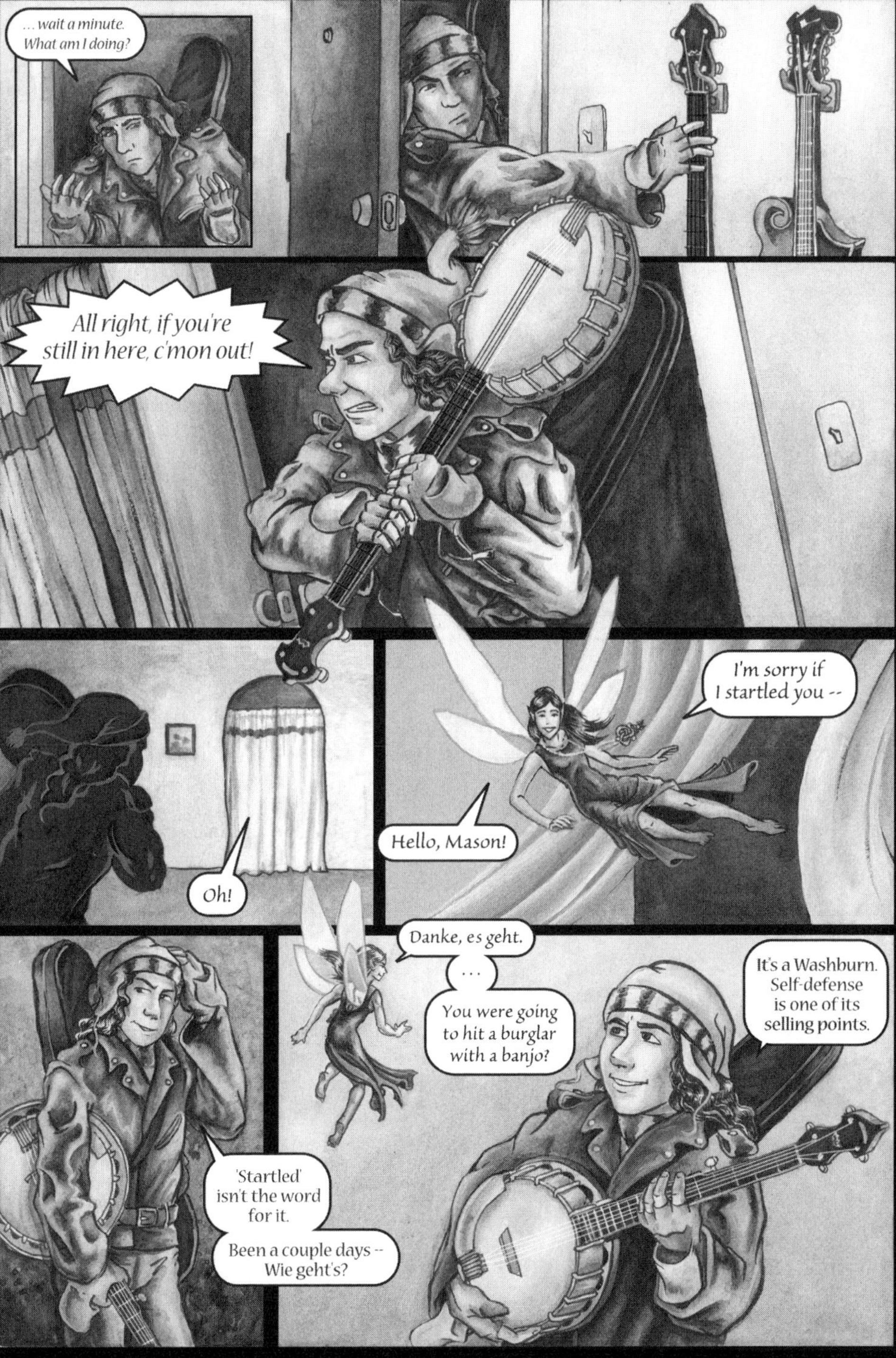
... wait a minute. What am I doing?
All right, if you're still in here, c'mon out!
Oh!
I'm sorry if I startled you --
Hello, Mason!
'Startled' isn't the word for it.
Been a couple days -- Wie geht's?
Danke, es geht.
...
You were going to hit a burglar with a banjo?
It's a Washburn. Self-defense is one of its selling points.

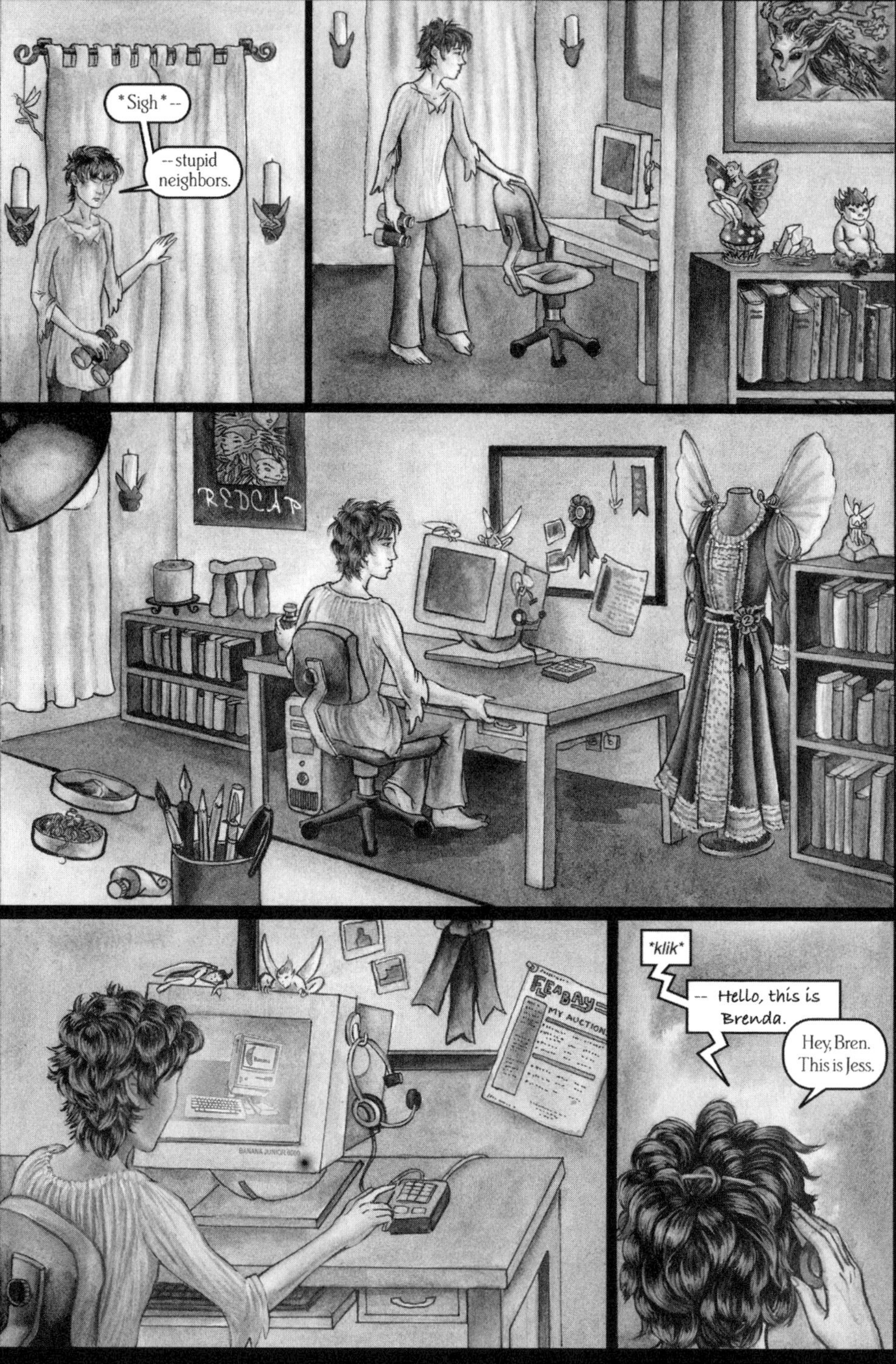
* Sigh * --
-- stupid neighbors.
REDCAP
FLEABAY
MY AUCTIONS
BANANA JUNIOR 6000
klik
-- Hello, this is Brenda.
Hey, Bren. This is Jess.

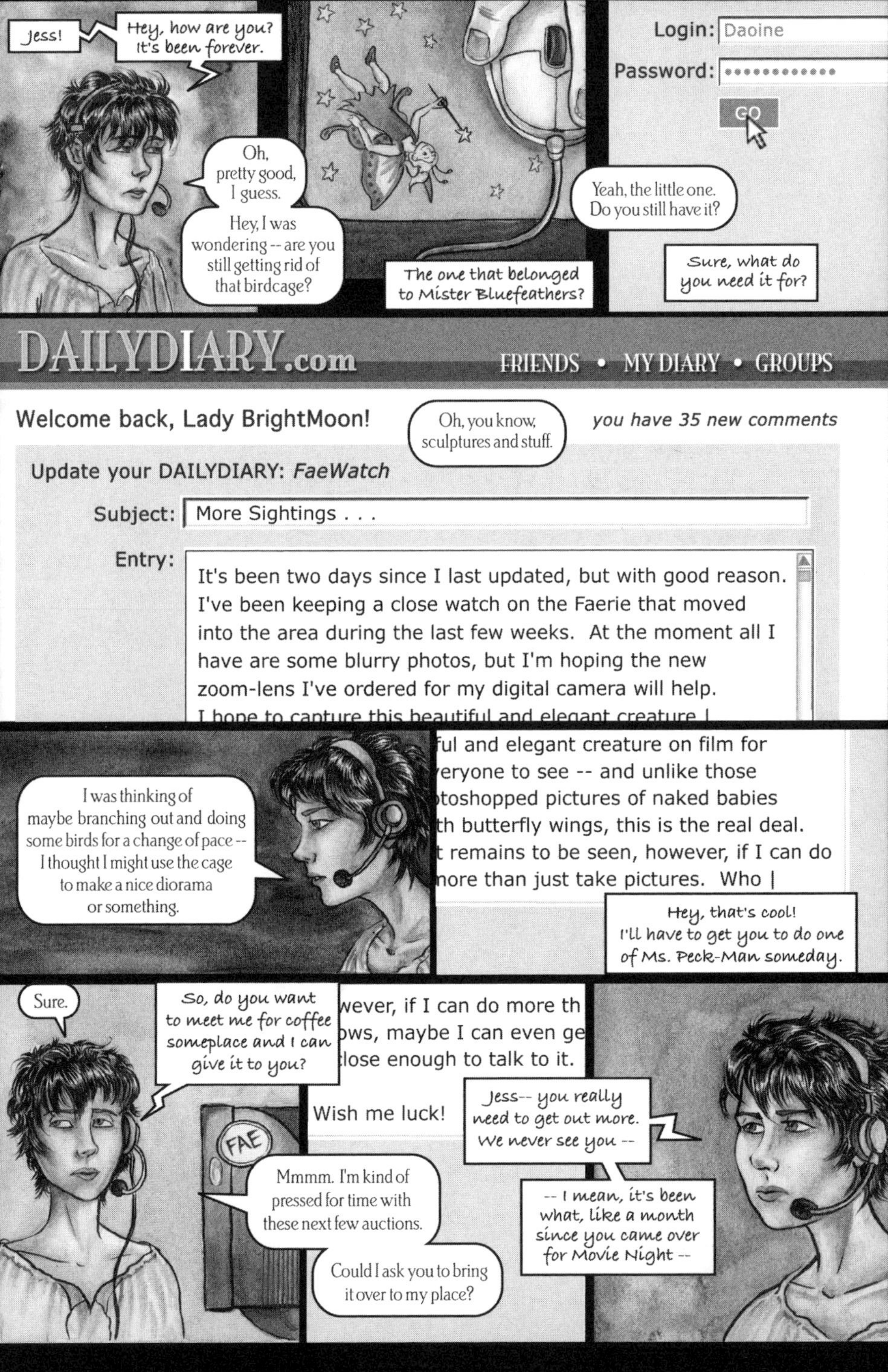
Jess!
Hey, how are you? It's been forever.
Oh, pretty good, I guess.
Hey, I was wondering -- are you still getting rid of that birdcage?
The one that belonged to Mister Bluefeathers?
Login: Daoine
Password:
GO
Yeah, the little one. Do you still have it?
Sure, what do you need it for?
DAILYDIARY.com
FRIENDS • MY DIARY • GROUPS
Welcome back, Lady BrightMoon!
Oh, you know, sculptures and stuff.
you have 35 new comments
Update your DAILYDIARY: FaeWatch
Subject: More Sightings . . .
Entry:
It's been two days since I last updated, but with good reason. I've been keeping a close watch on the Faerie that moved into the area during the last few weeks. At the moment all I have are some blurry photos, but I'm hoping the new zoom-lens I've ordered for my digital camera will help. I hope to capture this beautiful and elegant creature |
I was thinking of maybe branching out and doing some birds for a change of pace -- I thought I might use the cage to make a nice diorama or something.
ful and elegant creature on film for
eryone to see -- and unlike those
otoshopped pictures of naked babies
th butterfly wings, this is the real deal.
t remains to be seen, however, if I can do
nore than just take pictures. Who |
Hey, that's cool! I'll have to get you to do one of Ms. Peck-Man someday.
Sure.
So, do you want to meet me for coffee someplace and I can give it to you?
wever, if I can do more th
ows, maybe I can even ge
lose enough to talk to it.
Wish me luck!
FAE
Mmmm. I'm kind of pressed for time with these next few auctions.
Could I ask you to bring it over to my place?
Jess-- you really need to get out more. We never see you --
-- I mean, it's been what, like a month since you came over for Movie Night --

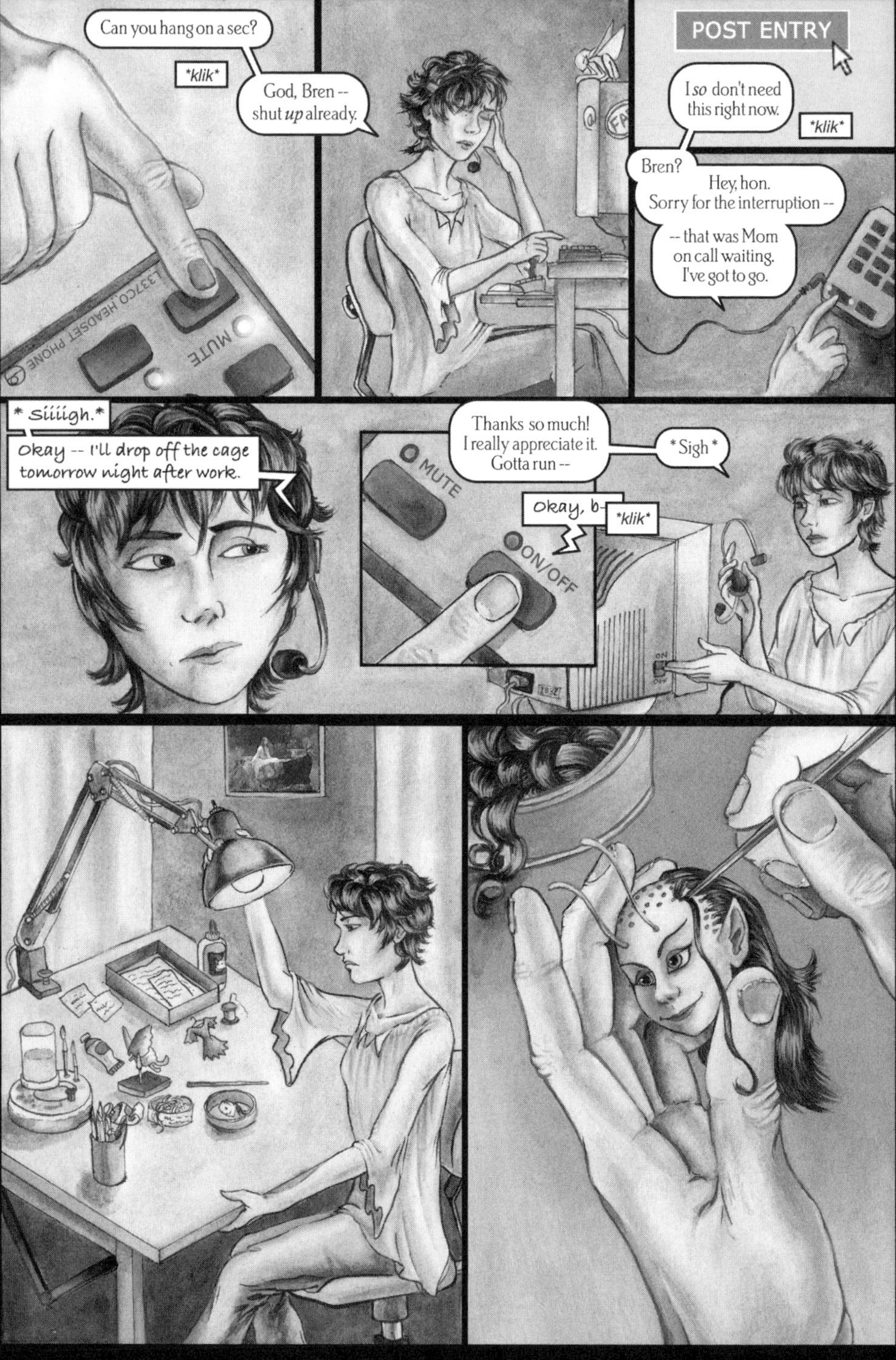
Can you hang on a sec?
klik
L337CO. HEADSET PHONE
MUTE
God, Bren -- shut *up* already.
POST ENTRY
I *so* don't need this right now.
klik
Bren?
Hey, hon. Sorry for the interruption --
-- that was Mom on call waiting. I've got to go.
* Siiiigh.*
Okay -- I'll drop off the cage tomorrow night after work.
MUTE
ON/OFF
Thanks so much! I really appreciate it. Gotta run --
* Sigh *
Okay, b-
klik

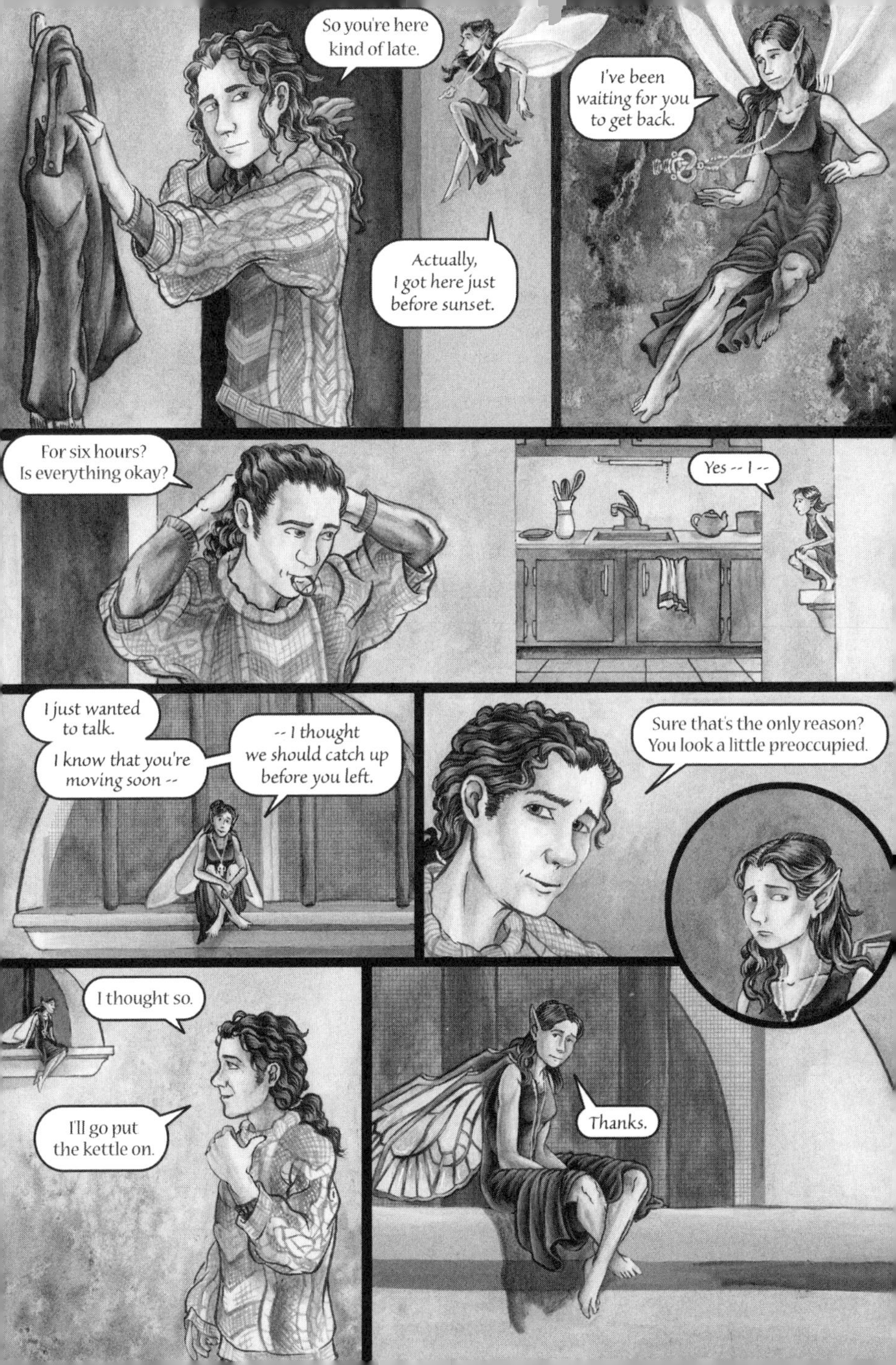
So you're here kind of late.
I've been waiting for you to get back.
Actually, I got here just before sunset.
For six hours? Is everything okay?
Yes -- I --
I just wanted to talk.
I know that you're moving soon --
-- I thought we should catch up before you left.
Sure that's the only reason? You look a little preoccupied.
I thought so.
I'll go put the kettle on.
Thanks.

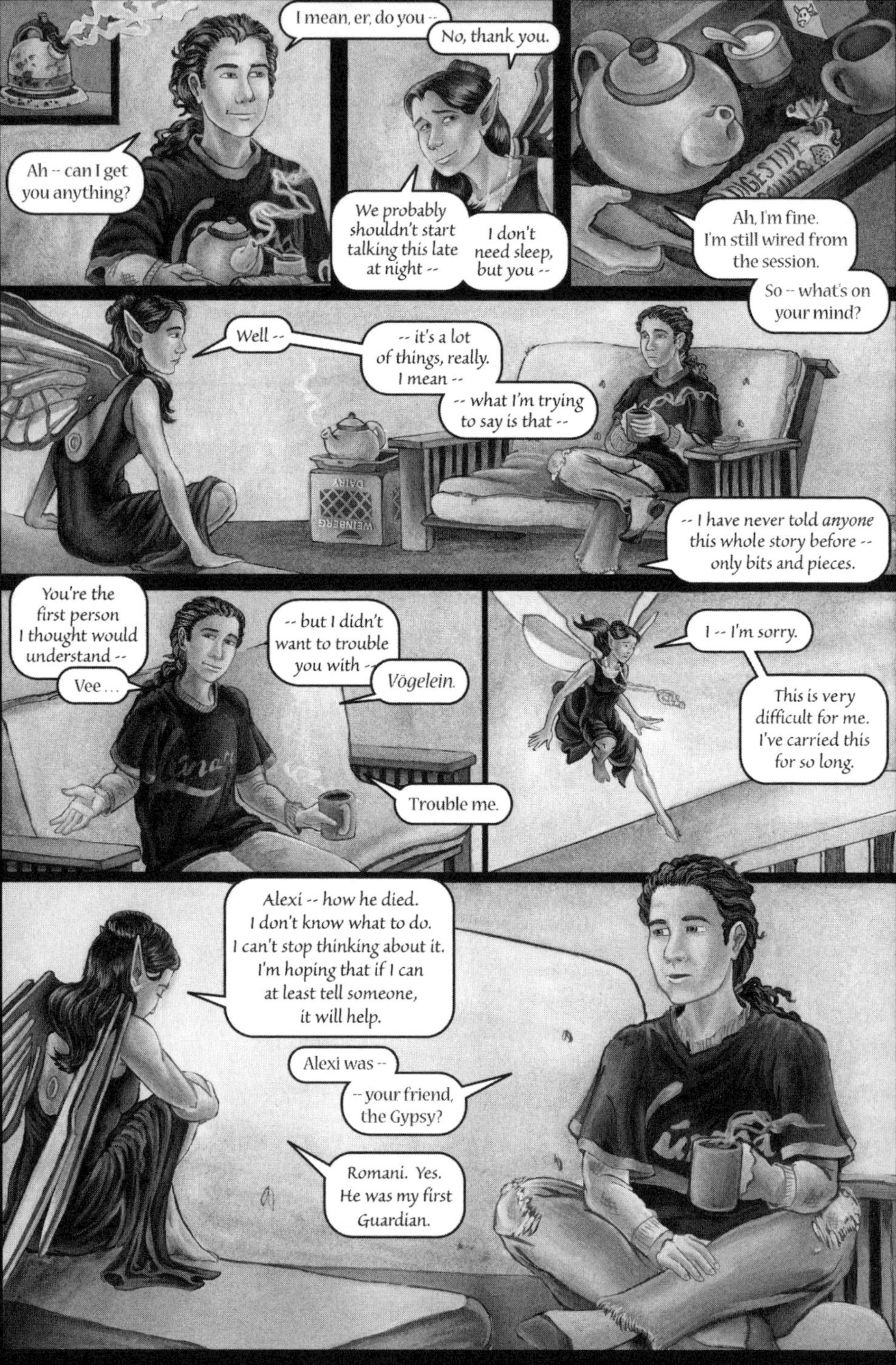
Ah -- can I get you anything?
I mean, er, do you --
No, thank you.
We probably shouldn't start talking this late at night --
I don't need sleep, but you --
Ah, I'm fine. I'm still wired from the session.
So -- what's on your mind?
Well --
-- it's a lot of things, really. I mean --
-- what I'm trying to say is that --
-- I have never told *anyone* this whole story before -- only bits and pieces.
You're the first person I thought would understand --
-- but I didn't want to trouble you with --
Vee ...
Vögelein.
Trouble me.
I -- I'm sorry.
This is very difficult for me. I've carried this for so long.
Alexi -- how he died. I don't know what to do. I can't stop thinking about it. I'm hoping that if I can at least tell someone, it will help.
Alexi was --
-- your friend, the Gypsy?
Romani. Yes. He was my first Guardian.

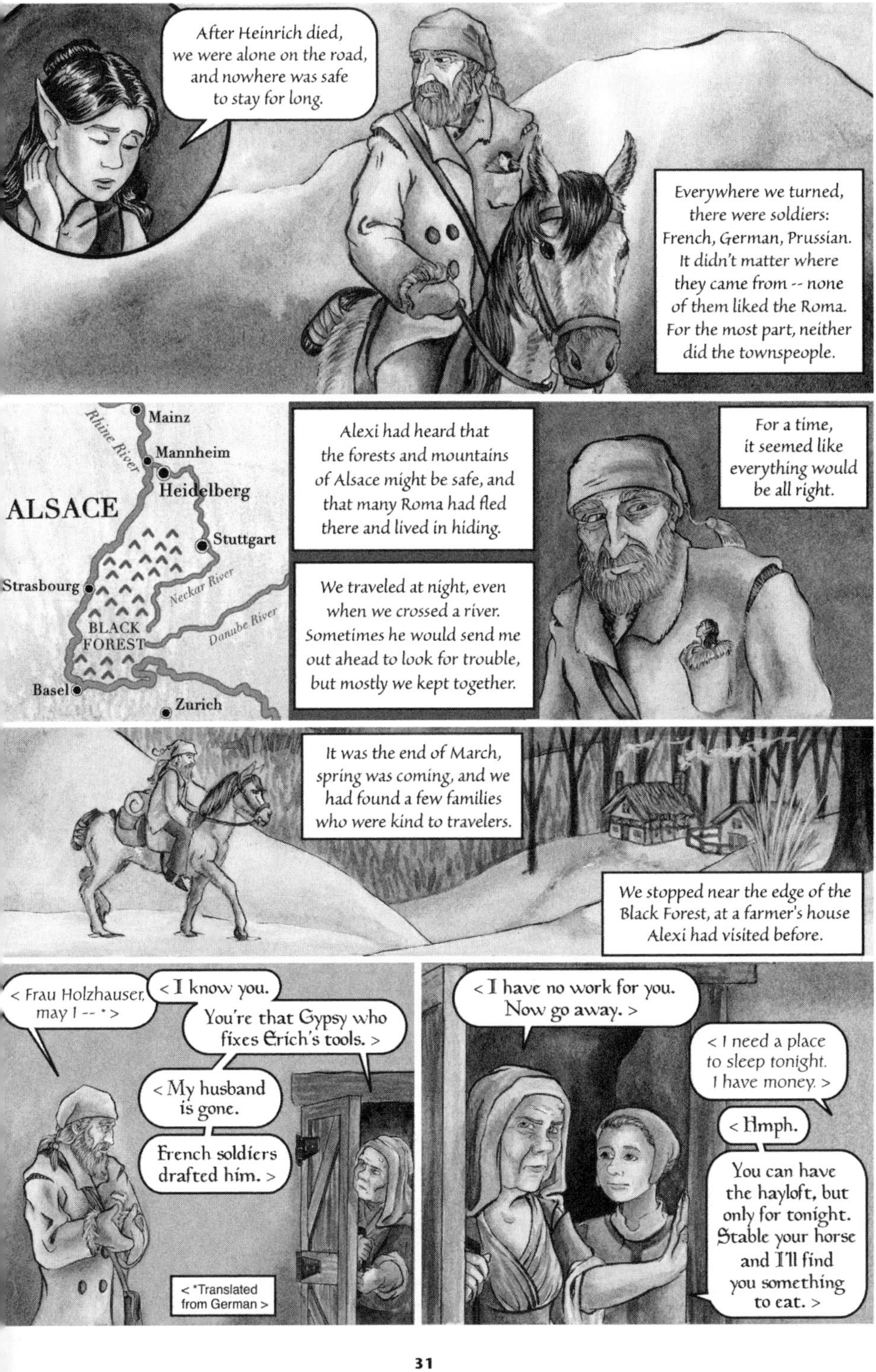
After Heinrich died, we were alone on the road, and nowhere was safe to stay for long.
Everywhere we turned, there were soldiers: French, German, Prussian. It didn't matter where they came from -- none of them liked the Roma. For the most part, neither did the townspeople.
Mainz
Rhine River
Mannheim
Heidelberg
ALSACE
Stuttgart
Strasbourg
Neckar River
Danube River
BLACK FOREST
Basel
Zurich
Alexi had heard that the forests and mountains of Alsace might be safe, and that many Roma had fled there and lived in hiding.
We traveled at night, even when we crossed a river. Sometimes he would send me out ahead to look for trouble, but mostly we kept together.
For a time, it seemed like everything would be all right.
It was the end of March, spring was coming, and we had found a few families who were kind to travelers.
We stopped near the edge of the Black Forest, at a farmer's house Alexi had visited before.
< Frau Holzhauser, may I -- * >
< I know you.
You're that Gypsy who fixes Erich's tools. >
< My husband is gone.
French soldiers drafted him. >
< *Translated from German >
< I have no work for you. Now go away. >
< I need a place to sleep tonight. I have money. >
< Hmph.
You can have the hayloft, but only for tonight. Stable your horse and I'll find you something to eat. >

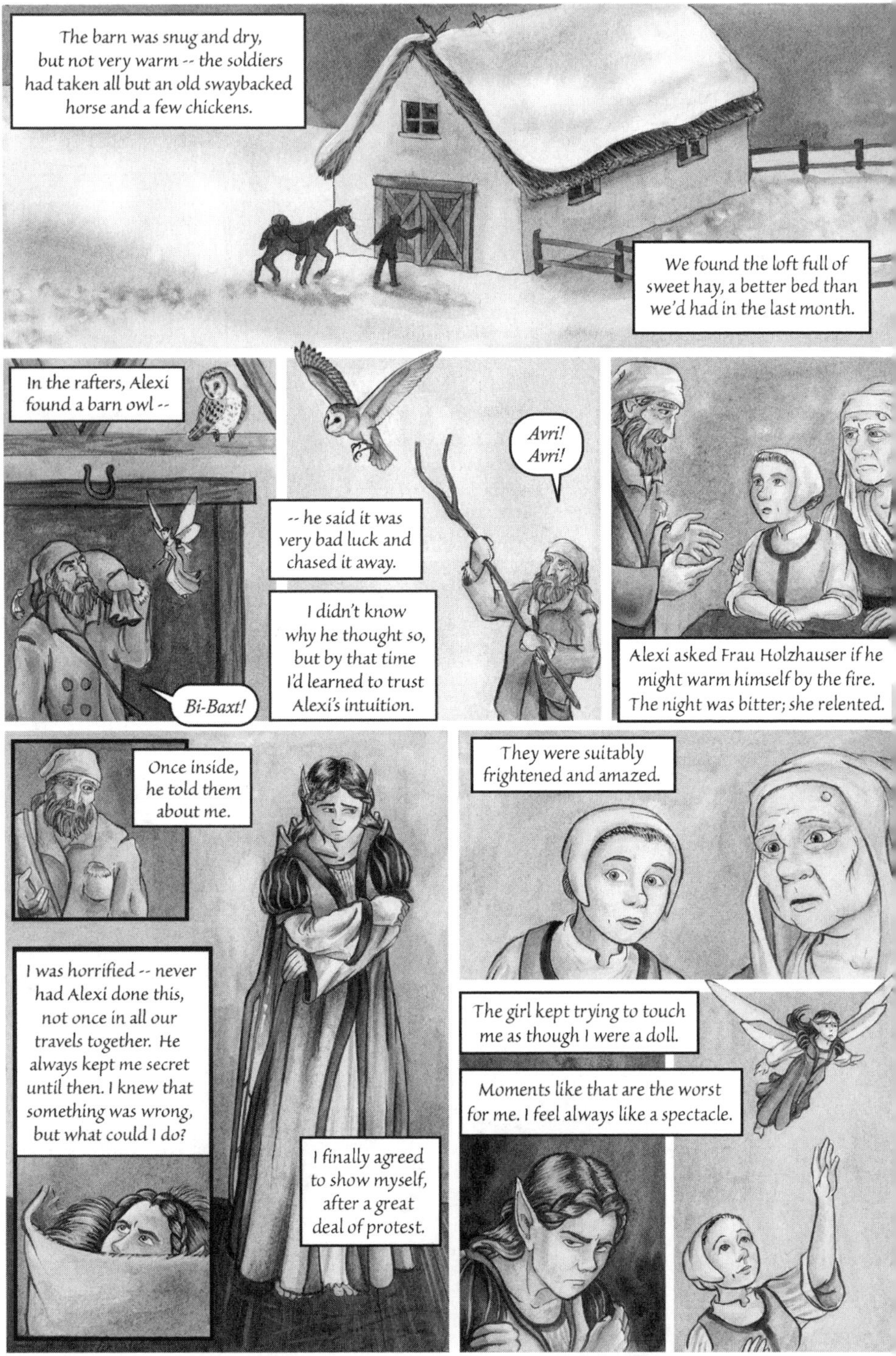
The barn was snug and dry, but not very warm -- the soldiers had taken all but an old swaybacked horse and a few chickens.
We found the loft full of sweet hay, a better bed than we'd had in the last month.
In the rafters, Alexi found a barn owl --
Bi-Baxt!
-- he said it was very bad luck and chased it away.
I didn't know why he thought so, but by that time I'd learned to trust Alexi's intuition.
Avri! Avri!
Alexi asked Frau Holzhauser if he might warm himself by the fire. The night was bitter; she relented.
Once inside, he told them about me.
I was horrified -- never had Alexi done this, not once in all our travels together. He always kept me secret until then. I knew that something was wrong, but what could I do?
I finally agreed to show myself, after a great deal of protest.
They were suitably frightened and amazed.
The girl kept trying to touch me as though I were a doll.
Moments like that are the worst for me. I feel always like a spectacle.

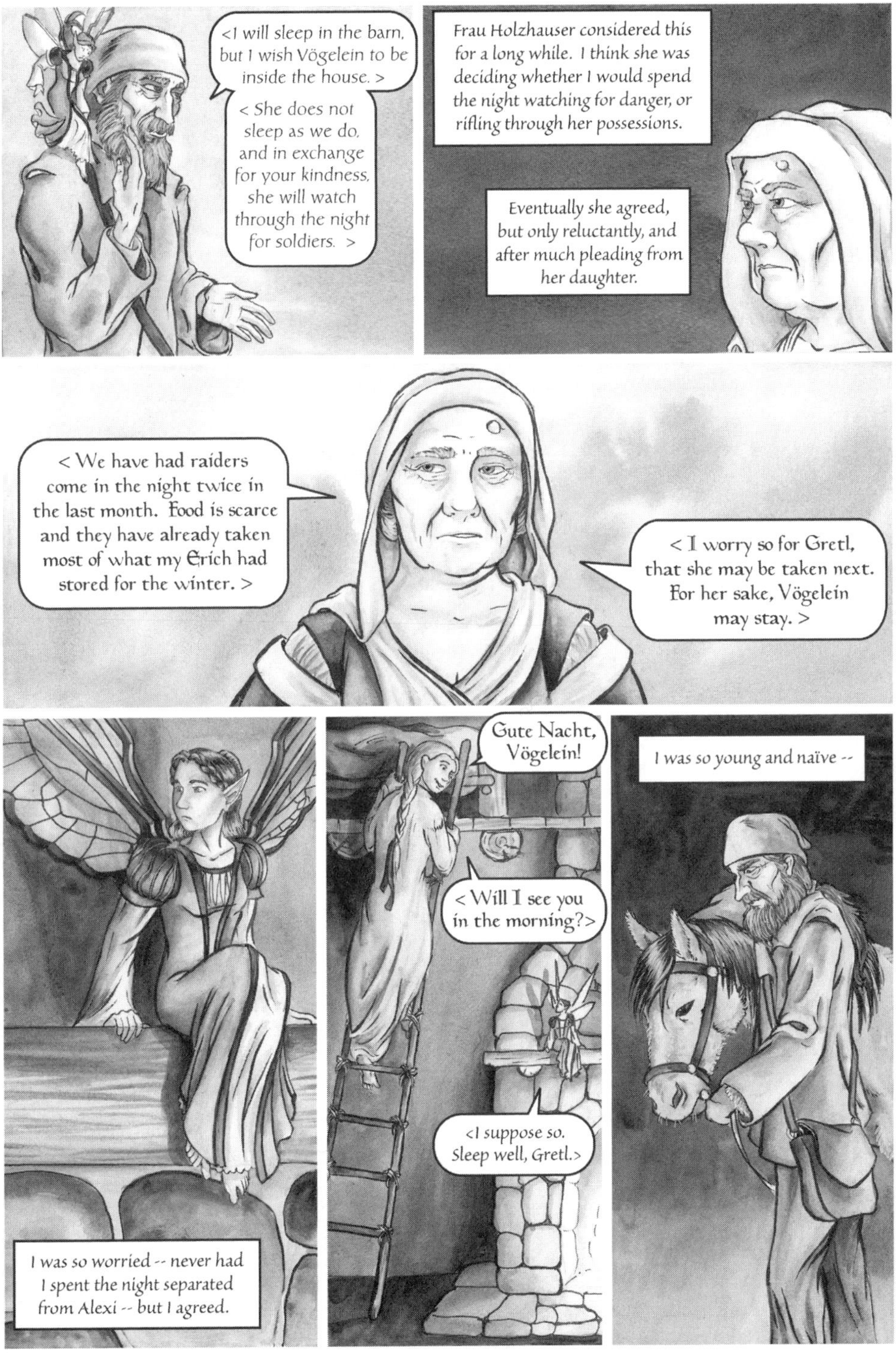

<I will sleep in the barn, but I wish Vögelein to be inside the house. >
< She does not sleep as we do, and in exchange for your kindness, she will watch through the night for soldiers. >
Frau Holzhauser considered this for a long while. I think she was deciding whether I would spend the night watching for danger, or rifling through her possessions.
Eventually she agreed, but only reluctantly, and after much pleading from her daughter.
< We have had raiders come in the night twice in the last month. Food is scarce and they have already taken most of what my Erich had stored for the winter. >
< I worry so for Gretl, that she may be taken next. For her sake, Vögelein may stay. >
I was so worried -- never had I spent the night separated from Alexi -- but I agreed.
Gute Nacht, Vögelein!
< Will I see you in the morning?>
<I suppose so. Sleep well, Gretl.>
I was so young and naïve --

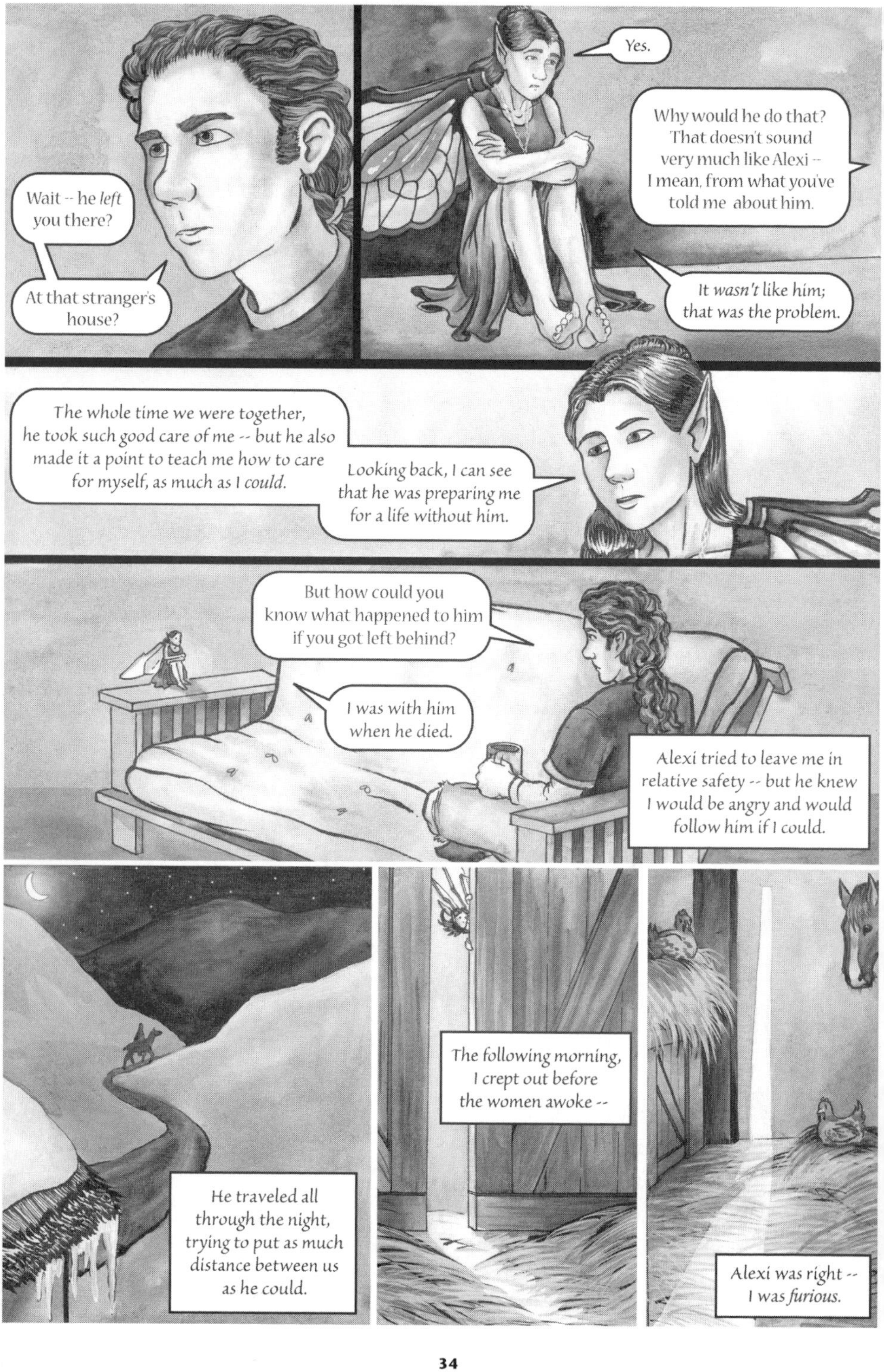
Wait -- he *left* you there?
At that stranger's house?
Yes.
Why would he do that? That doesn't sound very much like Alexi -- I mean, from what you've told me about him.
It *wasn't* like him; that was the problem.
The whole time we were together, he took such good care of me -- but he also made it a point to teach me how to care for myself, as much as I *could.*
Looking back, I can see that he was preparing me for a life without him.
But how could you know what happened to him if you got left behind?
I was with him when he died.
Alexi tried to leave me in relative safety -- but he knew I would be angry and would follow him if I could.
He traveled all through the night, trying to put as much distance between us as he could.
The following morning, I crept out before the women awoke --
Alexi was right -- I was *furious.*

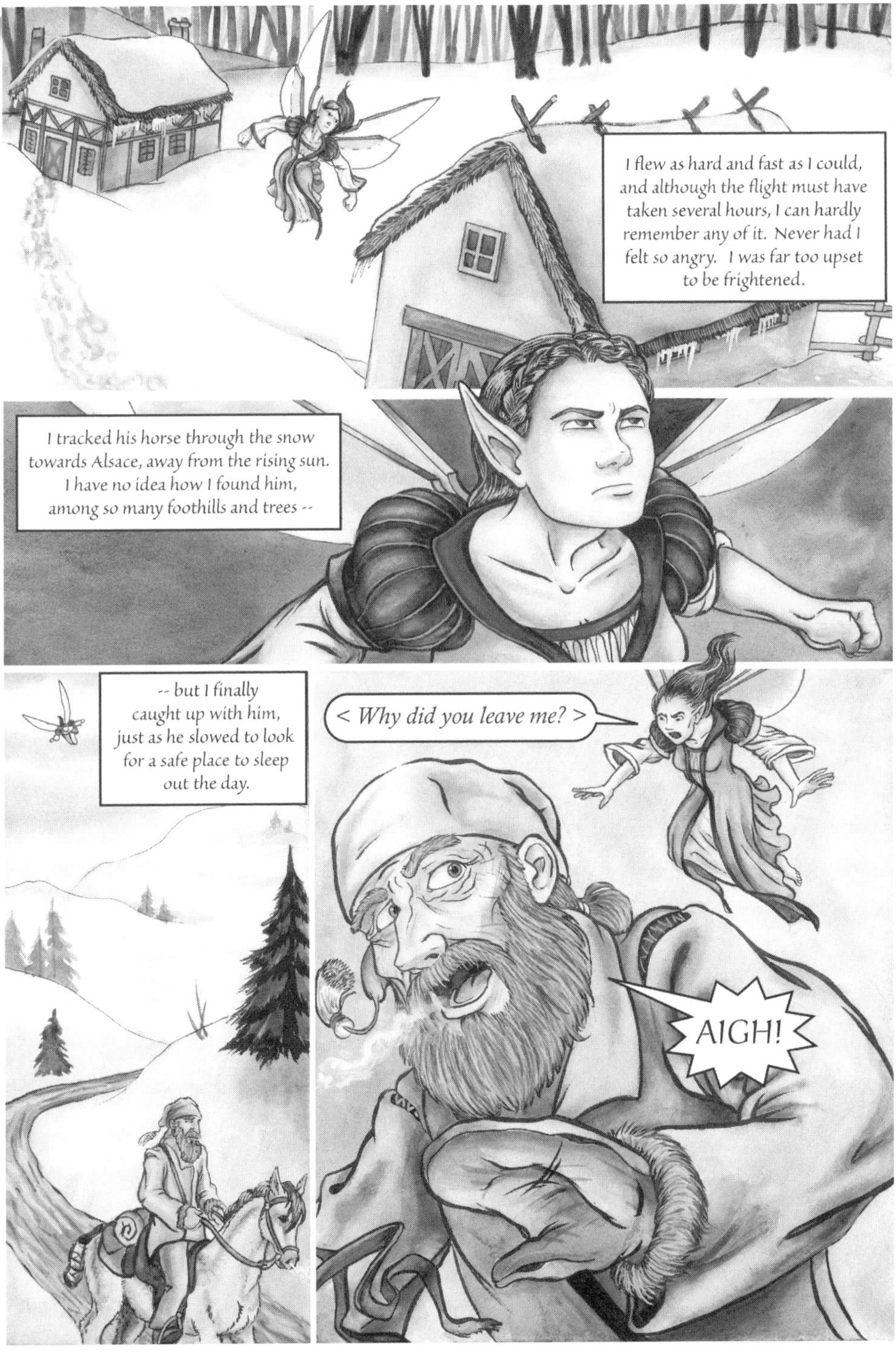
I flew as hard and fast as I could, and although the flight must have taken several hours, I can hardly remember any of it. Never had I felt so angry. I was far too upset to be frightened.
I tracked his horse through the snow towards Alsace, away from the rising sun. I have no idea how I found him, among so many foothills and trees --
-- but I finally caught up with him, just as he slowed to look for a safe place to sleep out the day.
< Why did you leave me? >
AIGH!

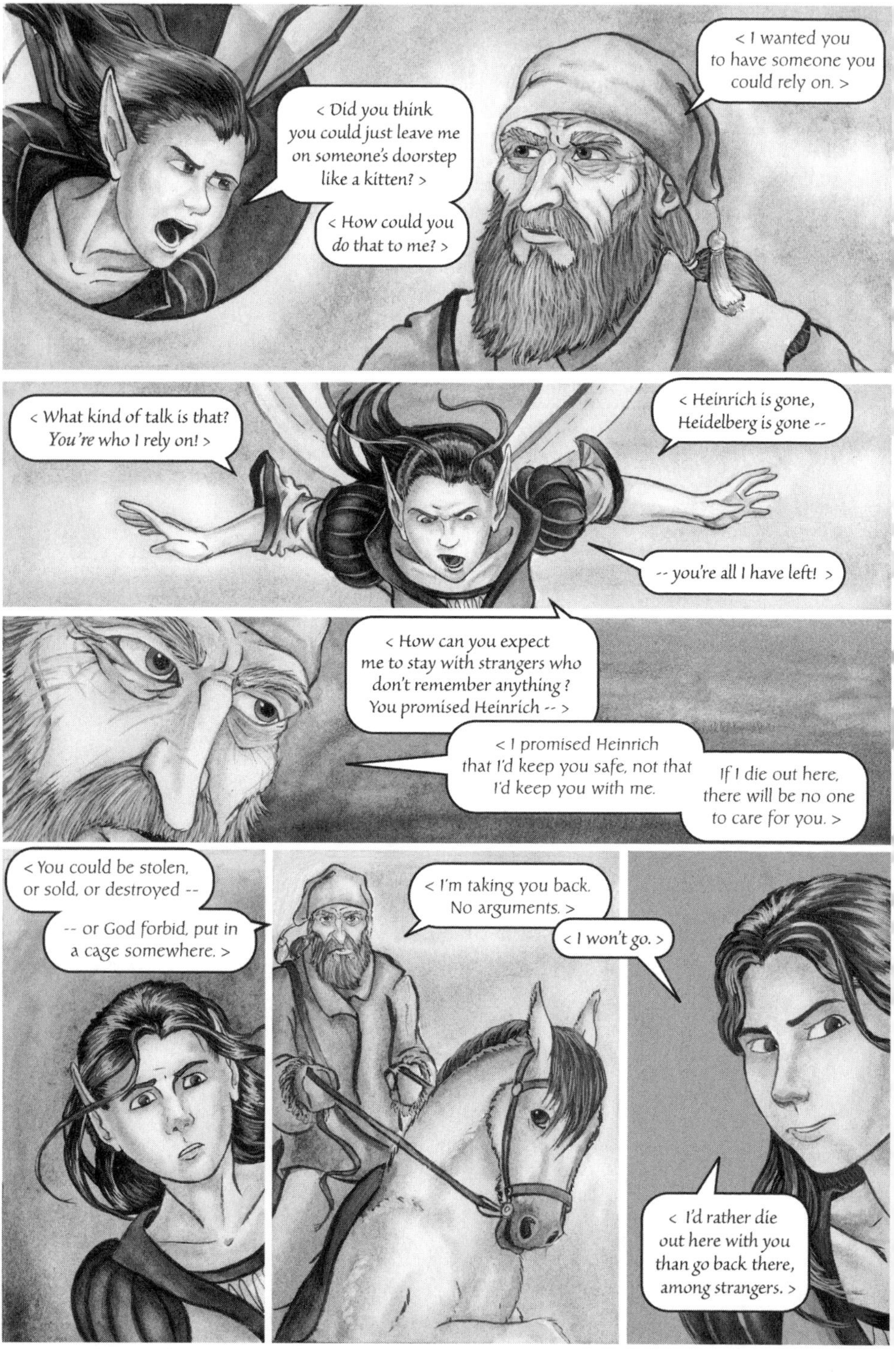

< Did you think you could just leave me on someone's doorstep like a kitten? >
< How could you do that to me? >
< I wanted you to have someone you could rely on. >
< What kind of talk is that? *You're* who I rely on! >
< Heinrich is gone, Heidelberg is gone --
-- you're all I have left! >
< How can you expect me to stay with strangers who don't remember anything ? You promised Heinrich -- >
< I promised Heinrich that I'd keep you safe, not that I'd keep you with me.
If I die out here, there will be no one to care for you. >
< You could be stolen, or sold, or destroyed --
-- or God forbid, put in a cage somewhere. >
< I'm taking you back. No arguments. >
< I won't go. >
< I'd rather die out here with you than go back there, among strangers. >

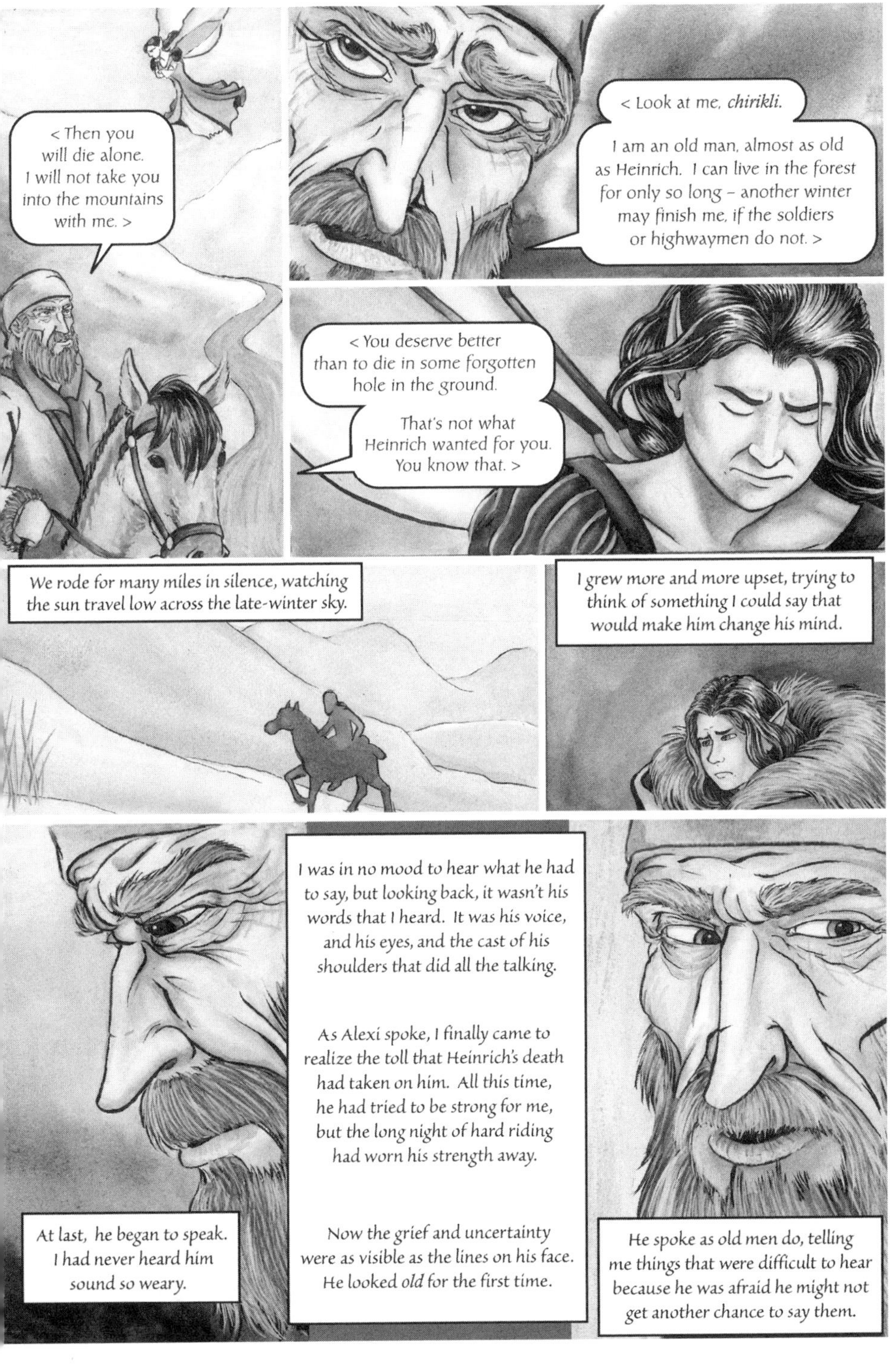

< Then you will die alone. I will not take you into the mountains with me. >
< Look at me, *chirikli.*
I am an old man, almost as old as Heinrich. I can live in the forest for only so long – another winter may finish me, if the soldiers or highwaymen do not. >
< You deserve better than to die in some forgotten hole in the ground.
That's not what Heinrich wanted for you. You know that. >
We rode for many miles in silence, watching the sun travel low across the late-winter sky.
I grew more and more upset, trying to think of something I could say that would make him change his mind.
At last, he began to speak. I had never heard him sound so weary.
I was in no mood to hear what he had to say, but looking back, it wasn't his words that I heard. It was his voice, and his eyes, and the cast of his shoulders that did all the talking.
As Alexi spoke, I finally came to realize the toll that Heinrich's death had taken on him. All this time, he had tried to be strong for me, but the long night of hard riding had worn his strength away.
Now the grief and uncertainty were as visible as the lines on his face. He looked *old* for the first time.
He spoke as old men do, telling me things that were difficult to hear because he was afraid he might not get another chance to say them.

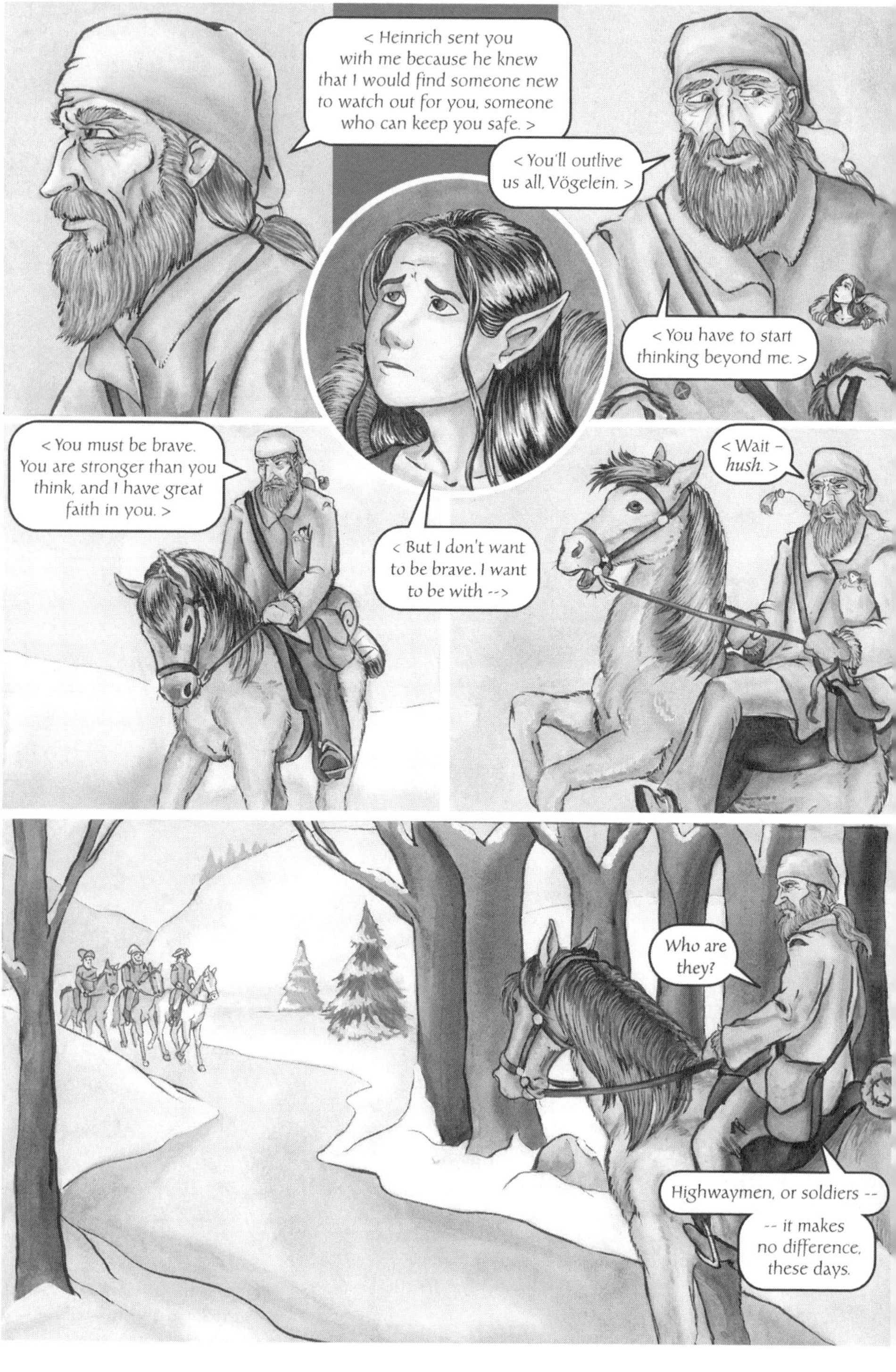

< Heinrich sent you with me because he knew that I would find someone new to watch out for you, someone who can keep you safe. >
< You'll outlive us all, Vögelein. >
< You have to start thinking beyond me. >
< You must be brave. You are stronger than you think, and I have great faith in you. >
< But I don't want to be brave. I want to be with -- >
< Wait - *hush.* >
Who are they?
Highwaymen, or soldiers --
-- it makes no difference, these days.

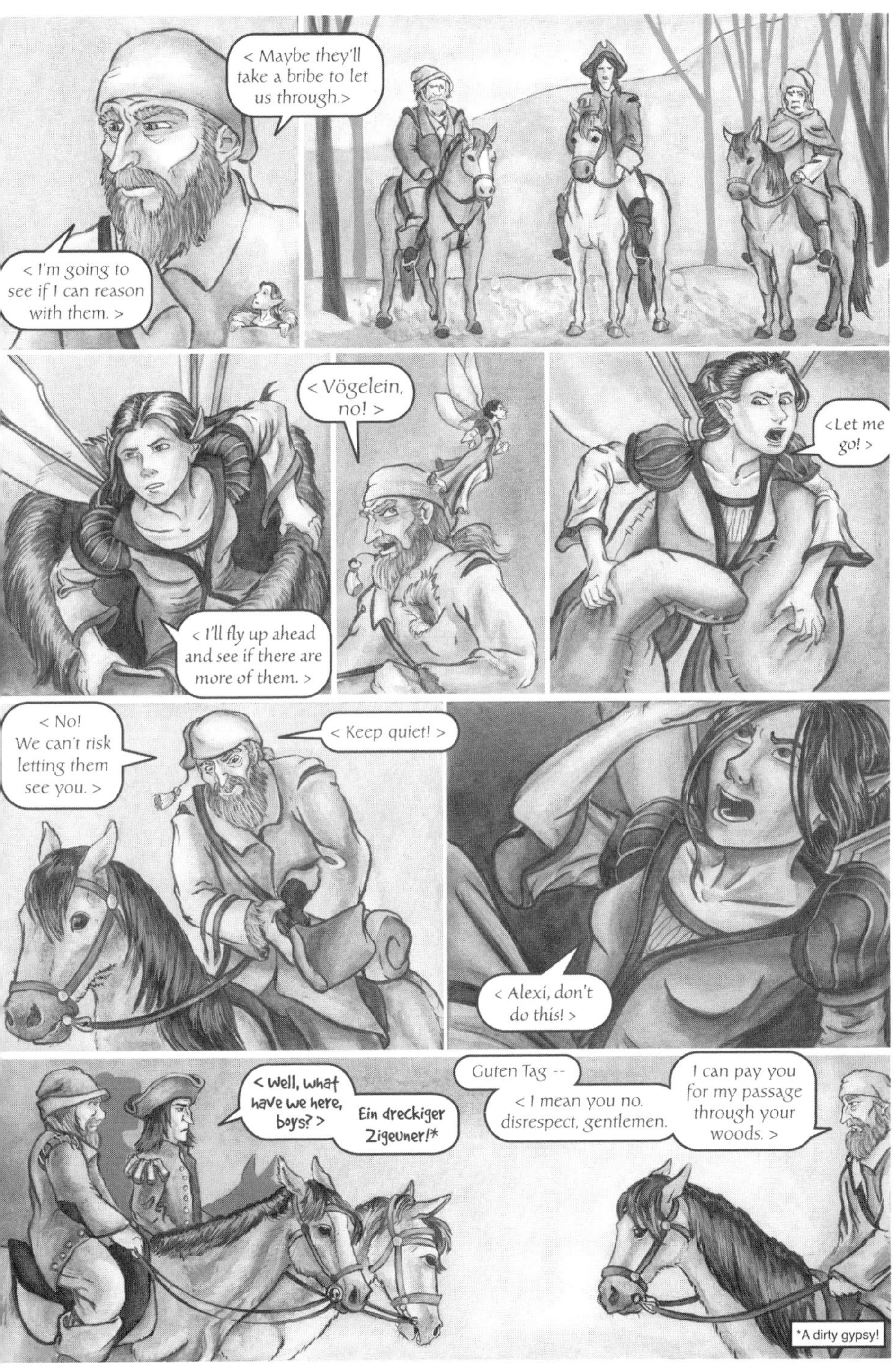
< Maybe they'll take a bribe to let us through.>
< I'm going to see if I can reason with them. >
< I'll fly up ahead and see if there are more of them. >
< Vögelein, no! >
<Let me go! >
< No! We can't risk letting them see you. >
< Keep quiet! >
< Alexi, don't do this! >
< Well, what have we here, boys? >
Ein dreckiger Zigeuner!*
Guten Tag --
< I mean you no. disrespect, gentlemen.
I can pay you for my passage through your woods. >
*A dirty gypsy!

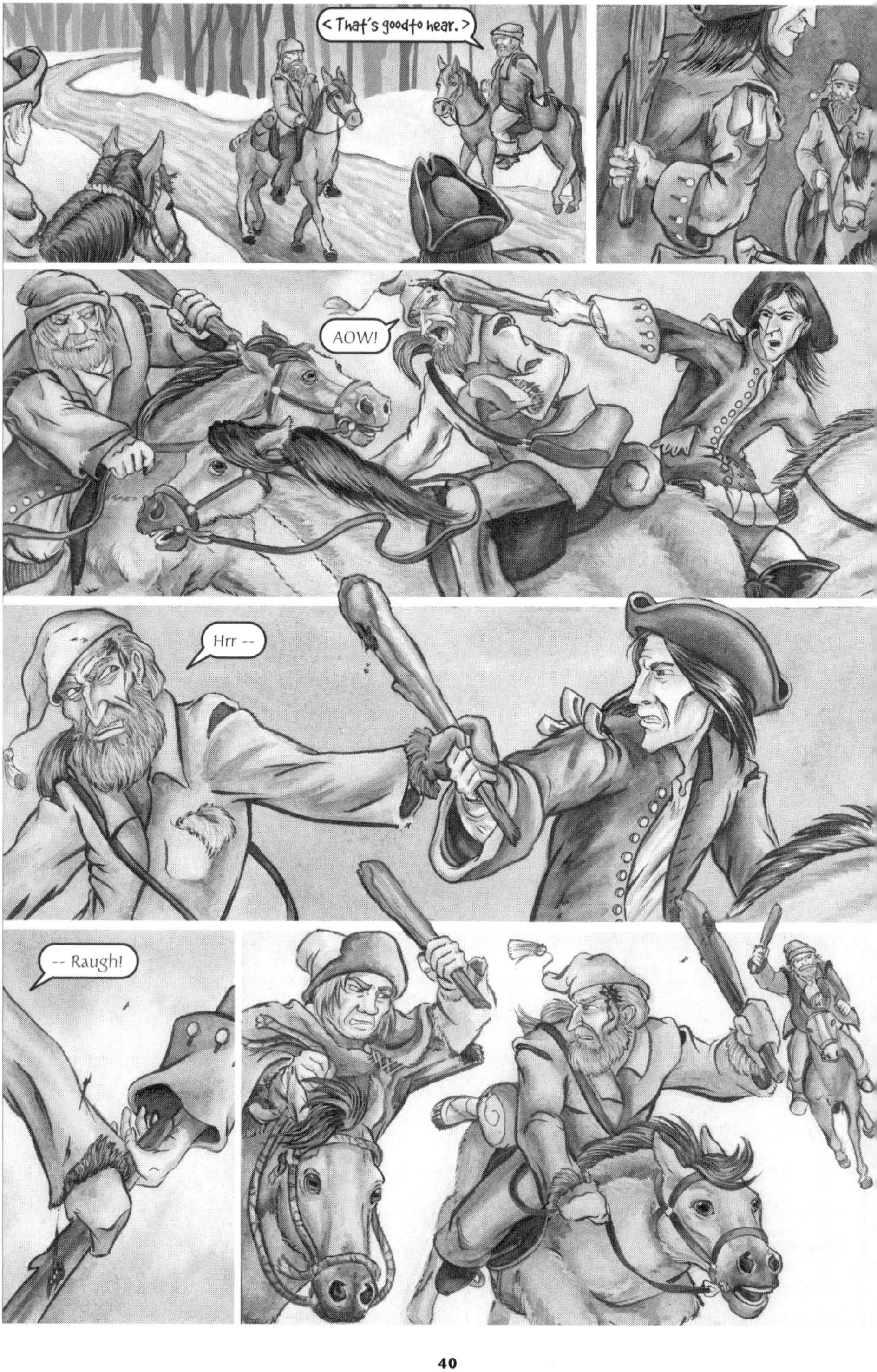
< That's good to hear. >
AOW!
Hrr --
-- Raugh!

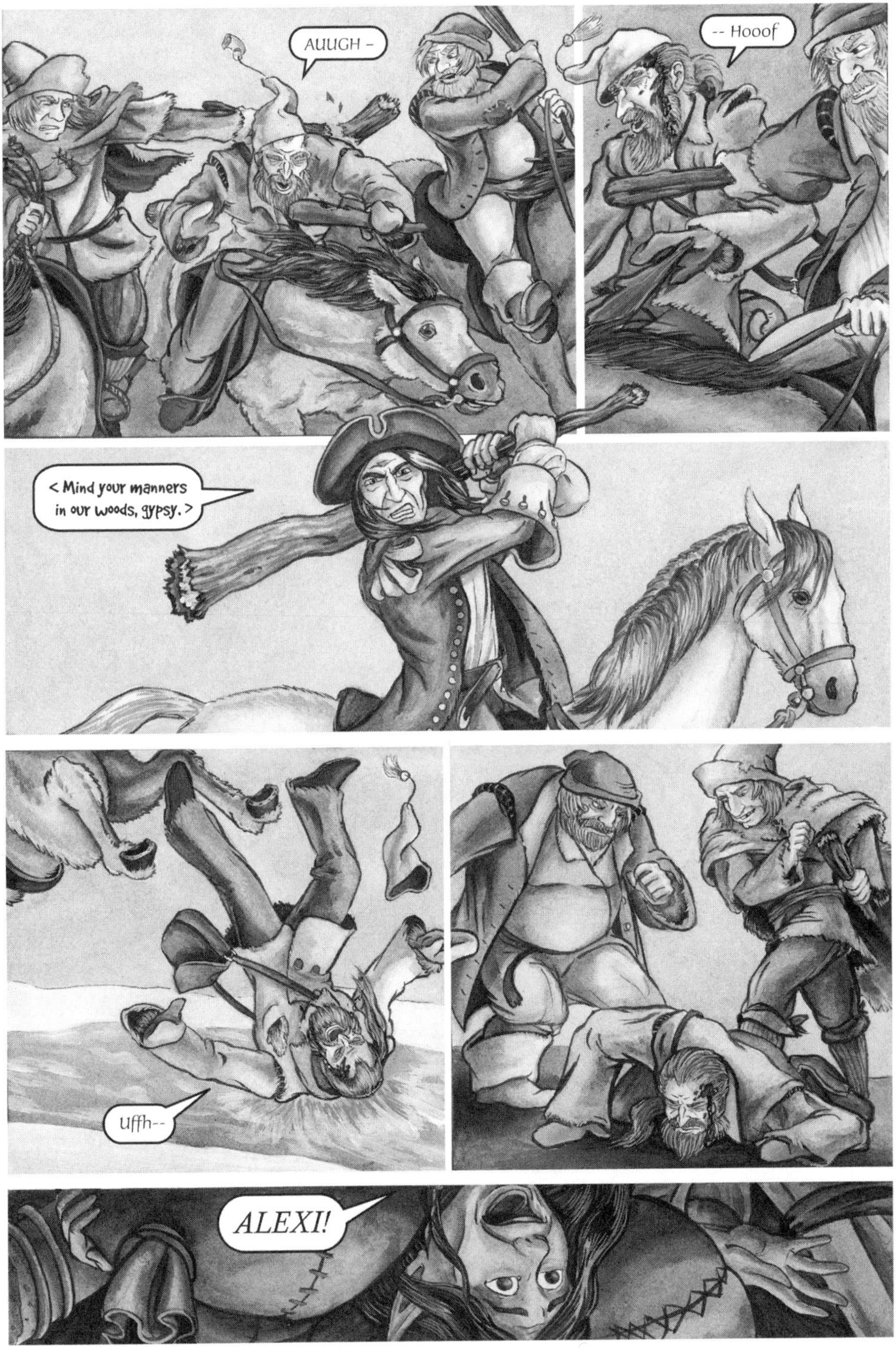
AUUGH –
-- Hooof
< Mind your manners in our woods, gypsy. >
Uffh--
ALEXI!

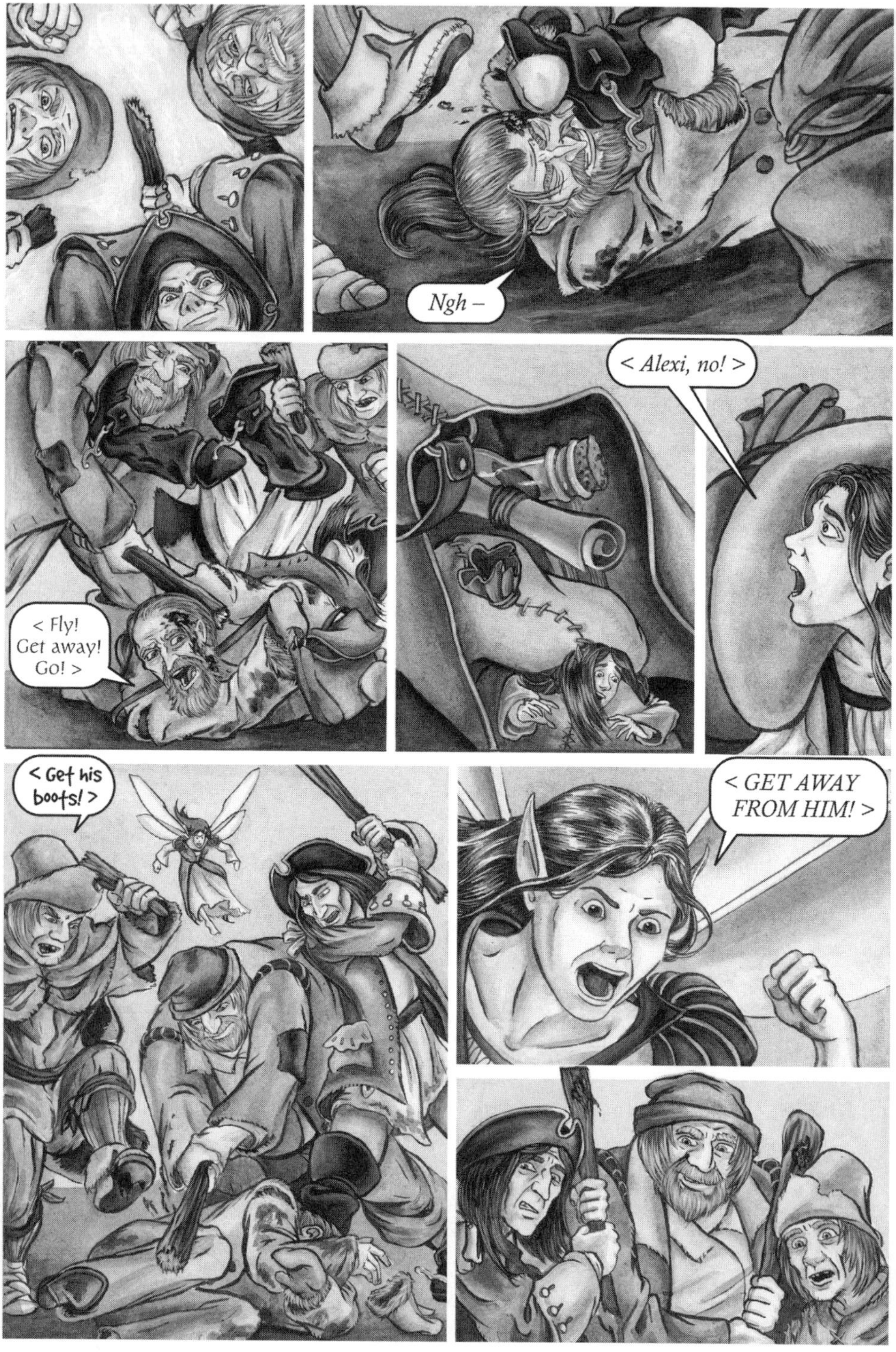

Ngh –
< Fly! Get away! Go! >
< Alexi, no! >
< Get his boots! >
< GET AWAY FROM HIM! >

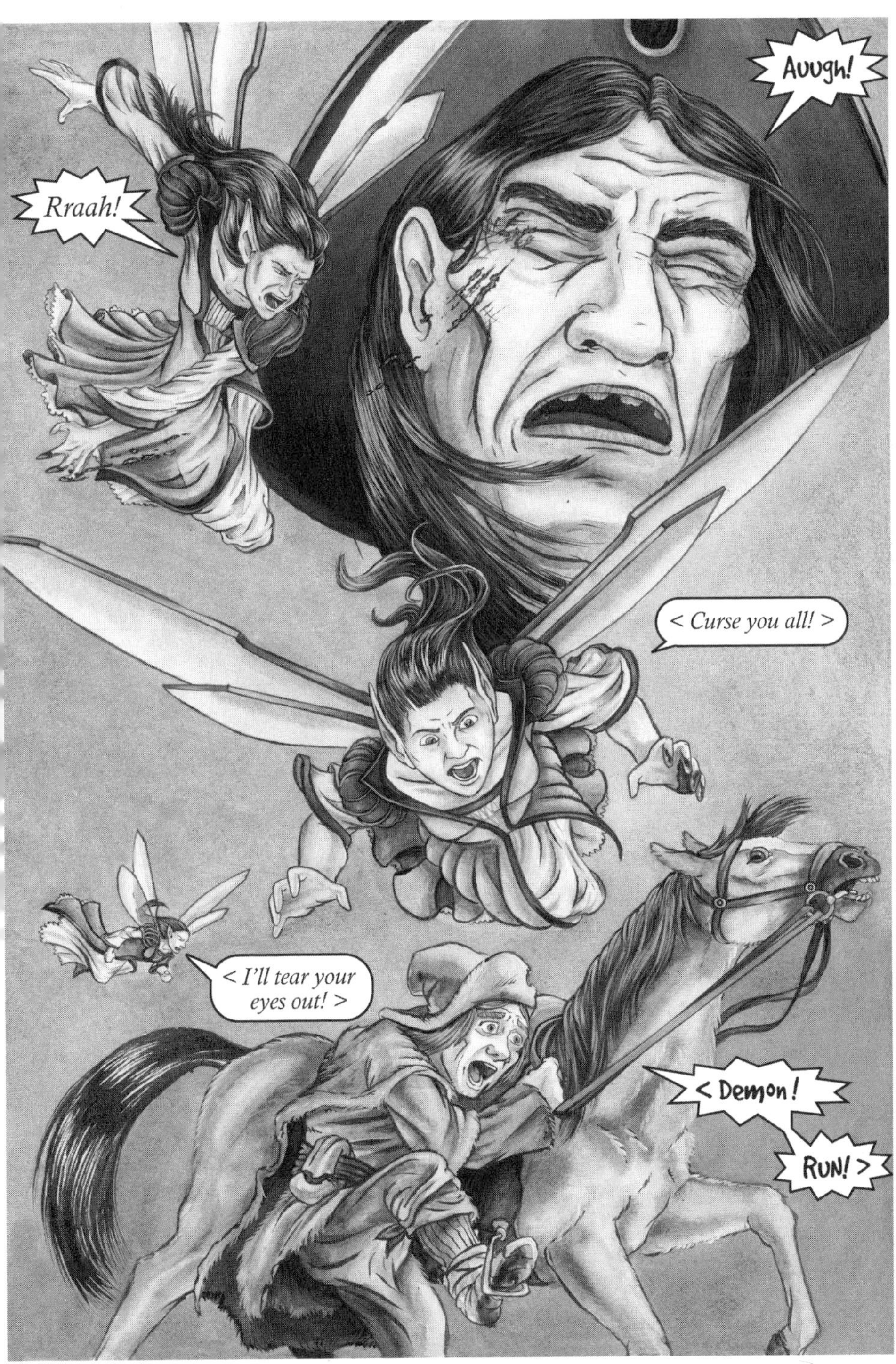
Auugh!
Rraah!
< Curse you all! >
< I'll tear your eyes out! >
< Demon!
RUN! >

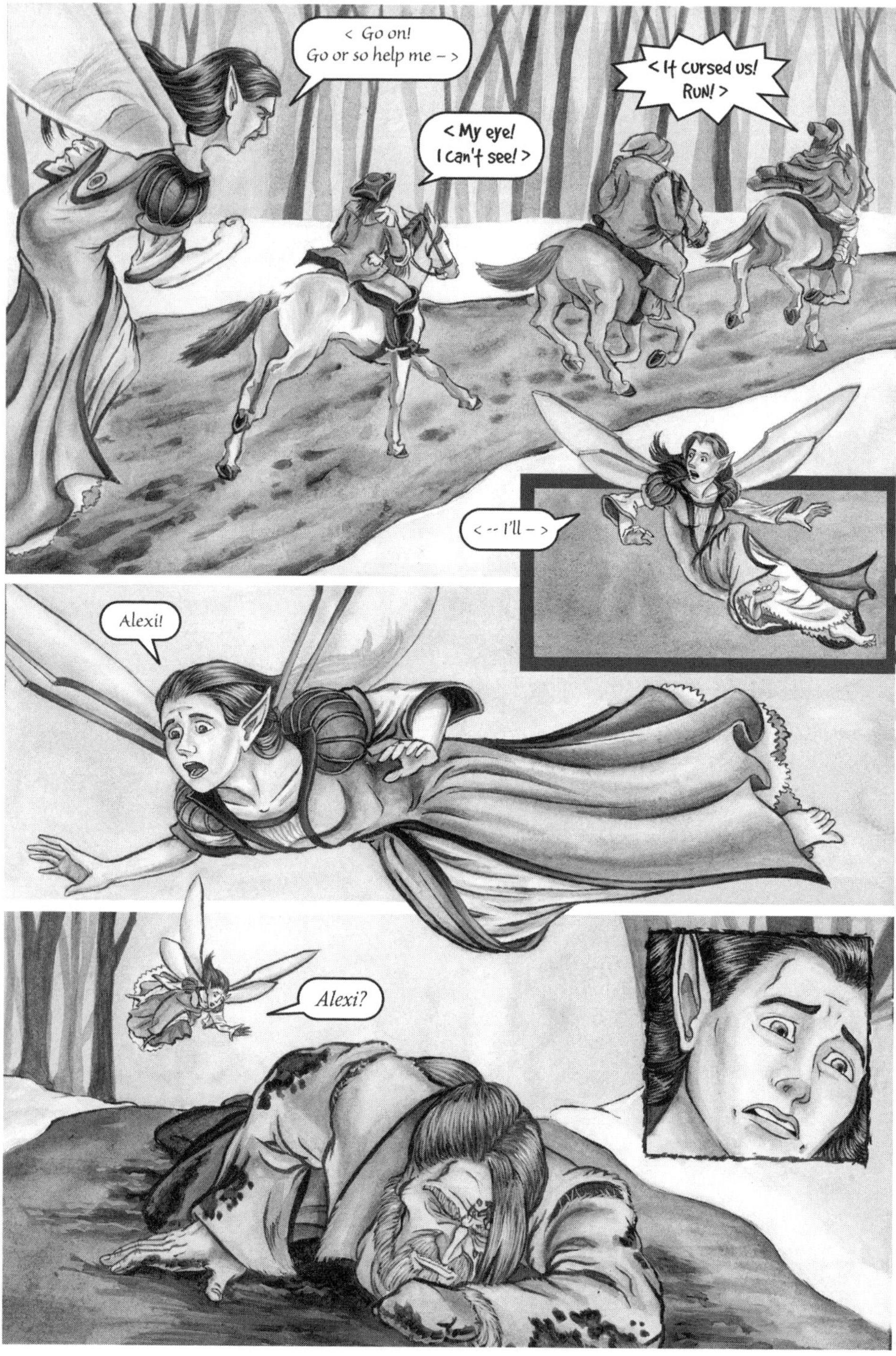

< Go on! Go or so help me – >
< It cursed us! RUN! >
< My eye! I can't see! >
< -- I'll – >
Alexi!
Alexi?

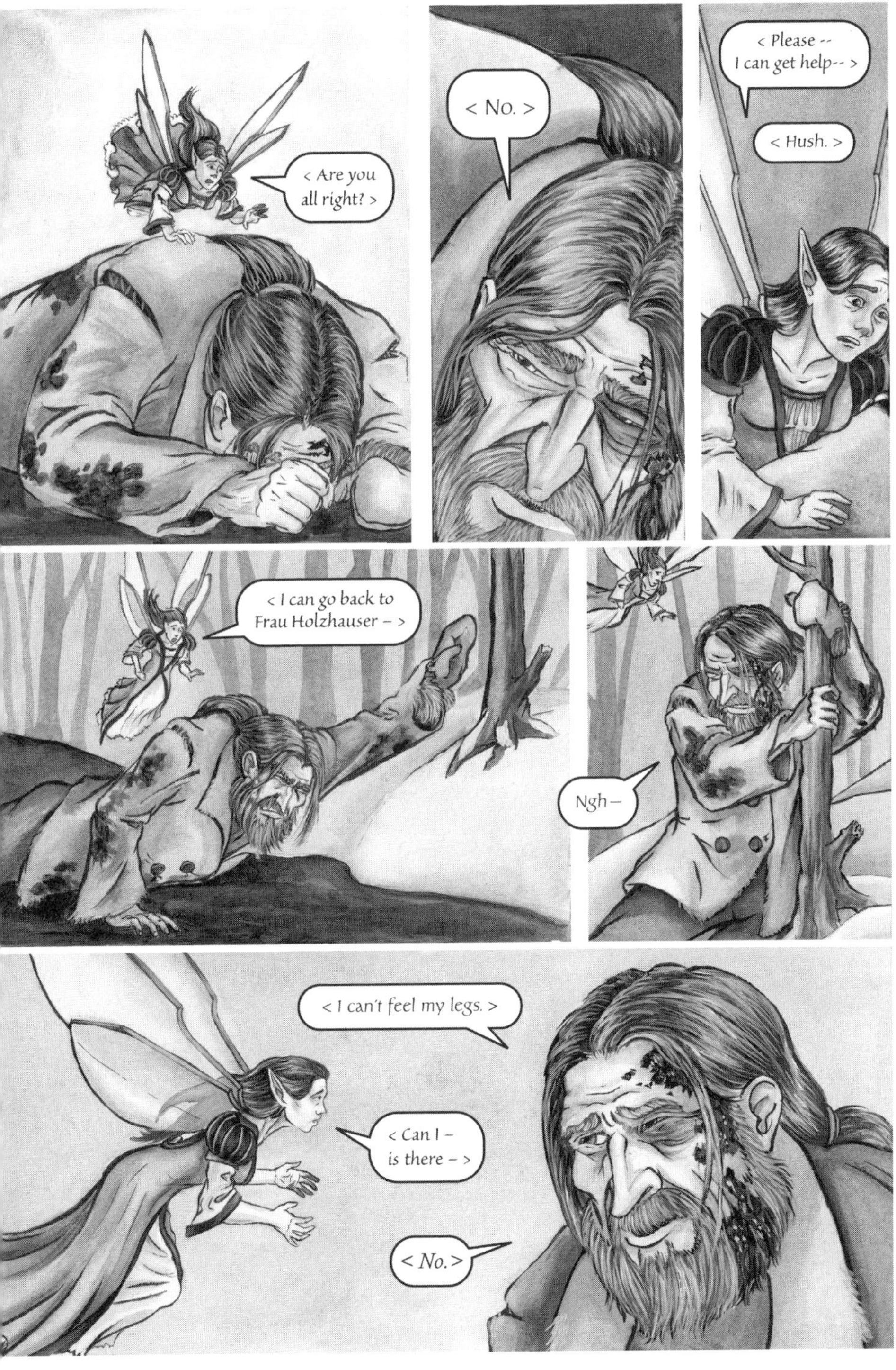
< Are you all right? >
< No. >
< Please -- I can get help-- >
< Hush. >
< I can go back to Frau Holzhauser – >
Ngh–
< I can't feel my legs. >
< Can I – is there – >
< No.>

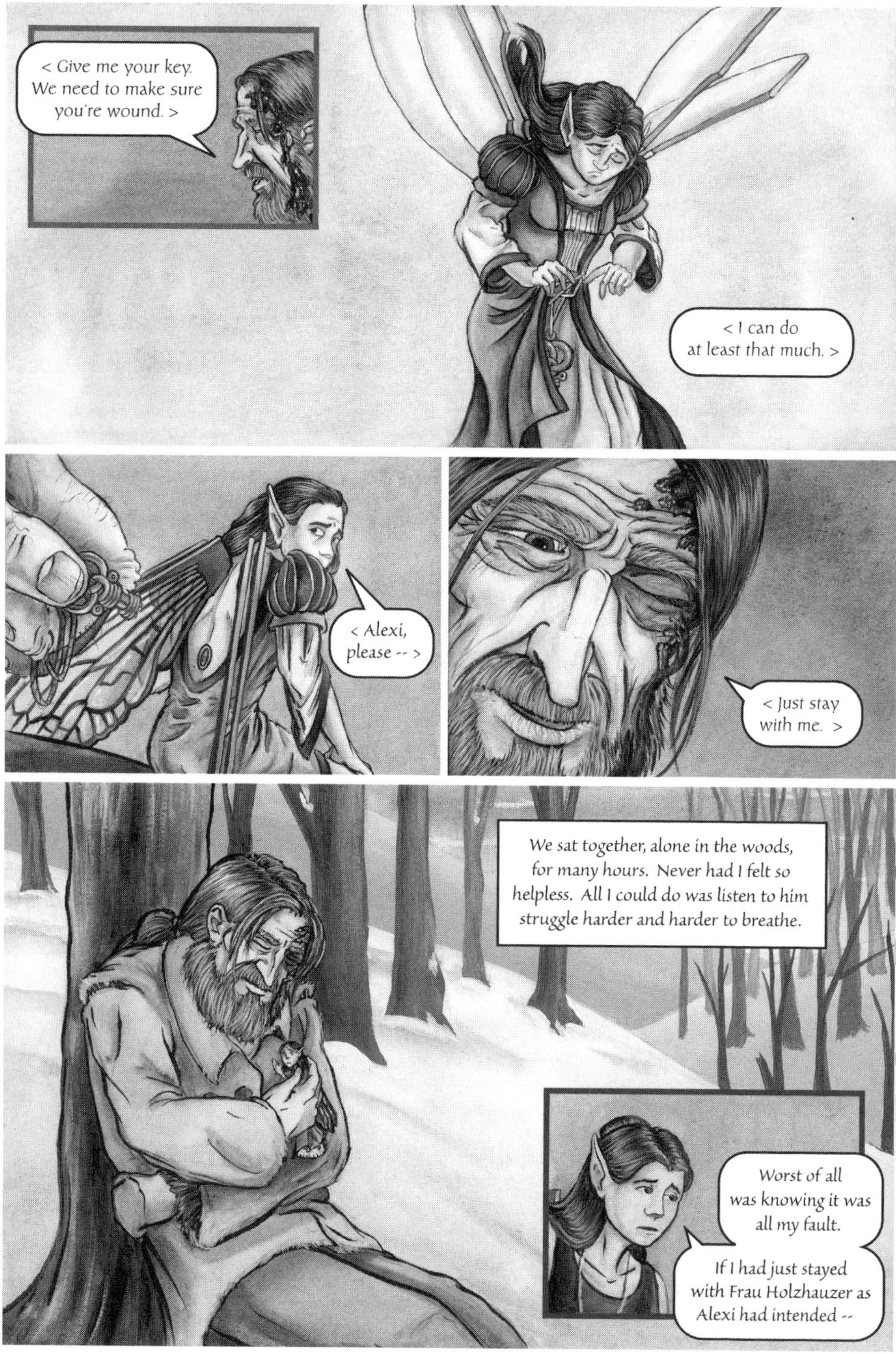

< Give me your key. We need to make sure you're wound. >
< I can do at least that much. >
< Alexi, please -- >
< Just stay with me. >
We sat together, alone in the woods, for many hours. Never had I felt so helpless. All I could do was listen to him struggle harder and harder to breathe.
Worst of all was knowing it was all my fault.
If I had just stayed with Frau Holzhauzer as Alexi had intended --

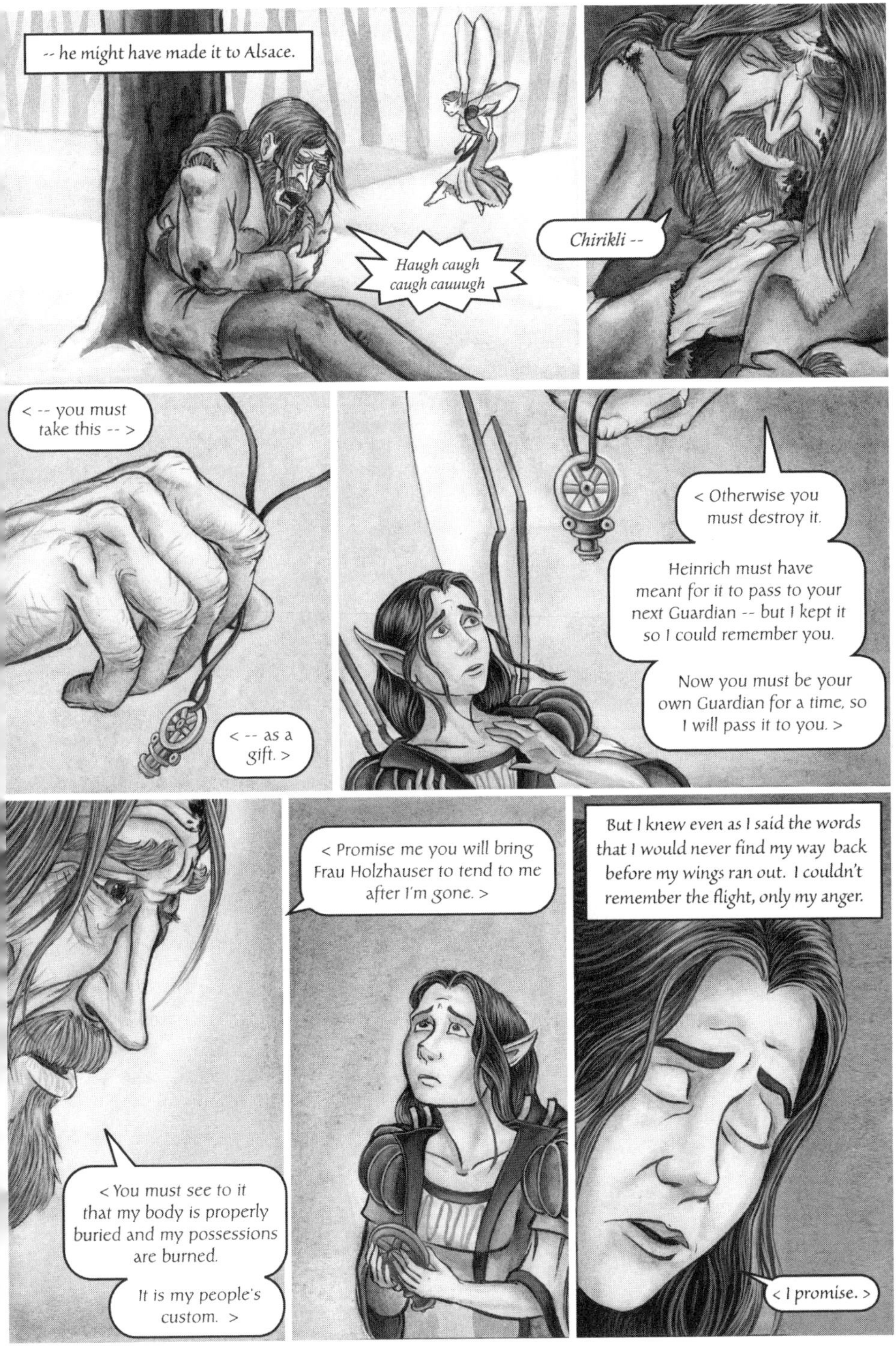
-- he might have made it to Alsace.
Haugh caugh caugh cauuugh
Chirikli --
< -- you must take this -- >
< -- as a gift. >
< Otherwise you must destroy it.
Heinrich must have meant for it to pass to your next Guardian -- but I kept it so I could remember you.
Now you must be your own Guardian for a time, so I will pass it to you. >
< You must see to it that my body is properly buried and my possessions are burned.
It is my people's custom. >
< Promise me you will bring Frau Holzhauser to tend to me after I'm gone. >
But I knew even as I said the words that I would never find my way back before my wings ran out. I couldn't remember the flight, only my anger.
< I promise. >

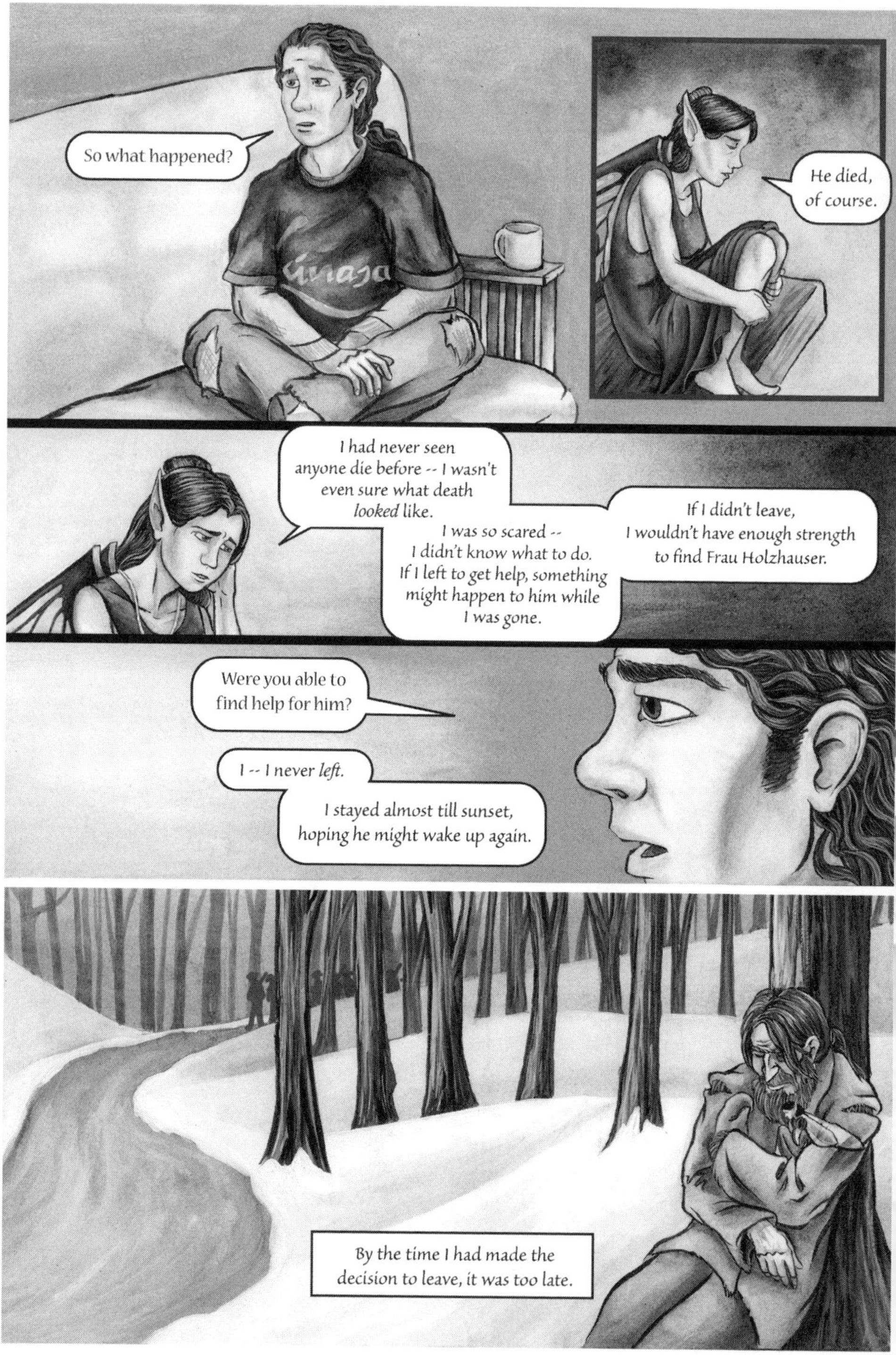
So what happened?
He died, of course.
I had never seen anyone die before -- I wasn't even sure what death *looked* like.
I was so scared -- I didn't know what to do. If I left to get help, something might happen to him while I was gone.
If I didn't leave, I wouldn't have enough strength to find Frau Holzhauser.
Were you able to find help for him?
I -- I never *left*.
I stayed almost till sunset, hoping he might wake up again.
By the time I had made the decision to leave, it was too late.

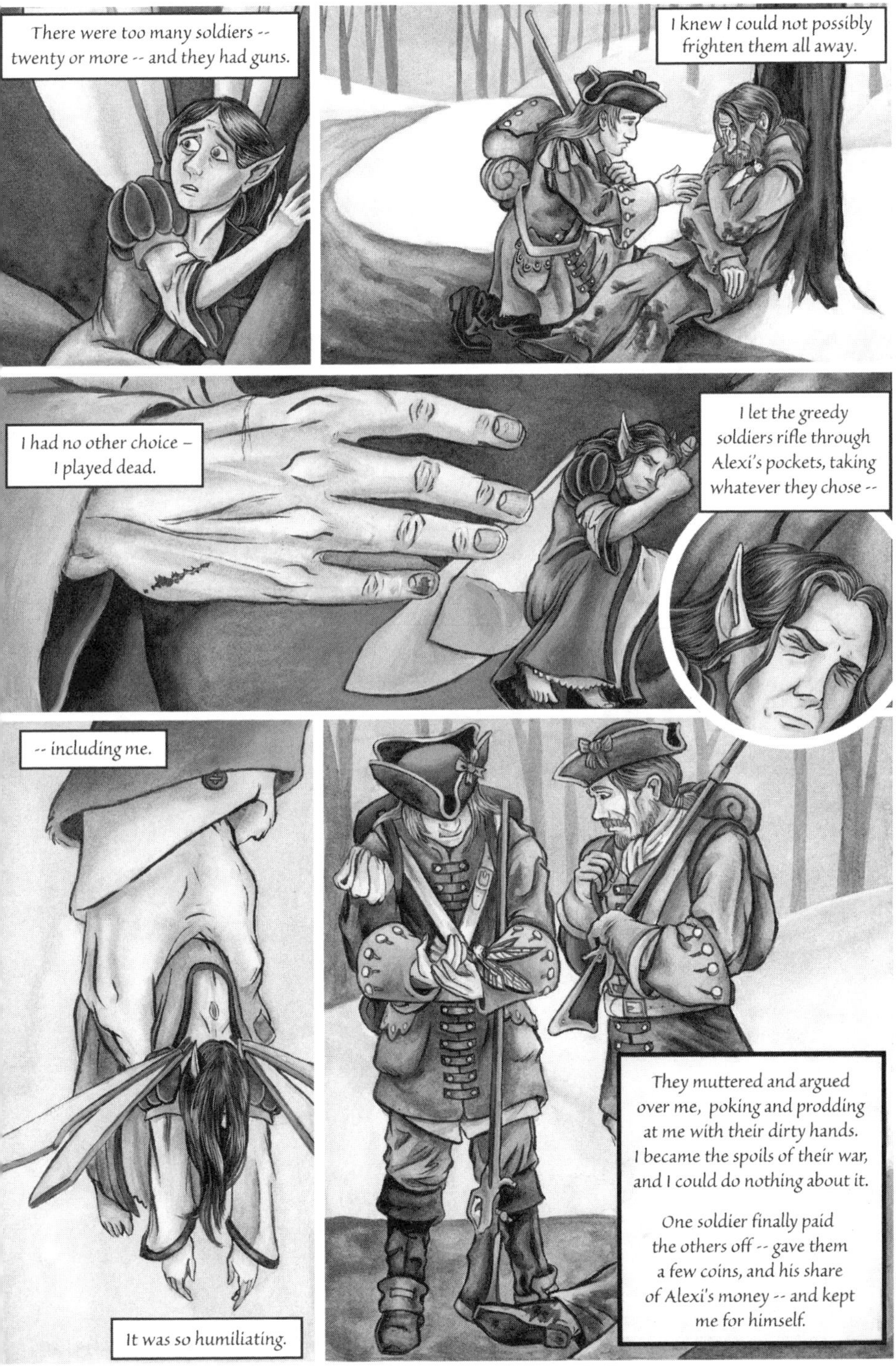
There were too many soldiers -- twenty or more -- and they had guns.
I knew I could not possibly frighten them all away.
I had no other choice – I played dead.
I let the greedy soldiers rifle through Alexi's pockets, taking whatever they chose --
-- including me.
It was so humiliating.
They muttered and argued over me, poking and prodding at me with their dirty hands. I became the spoils of their war, and I could do nothing about it.
One soldier finally paid the others off -- gave them a few coins, and his share of Alexi's money -- and kept me for himself.

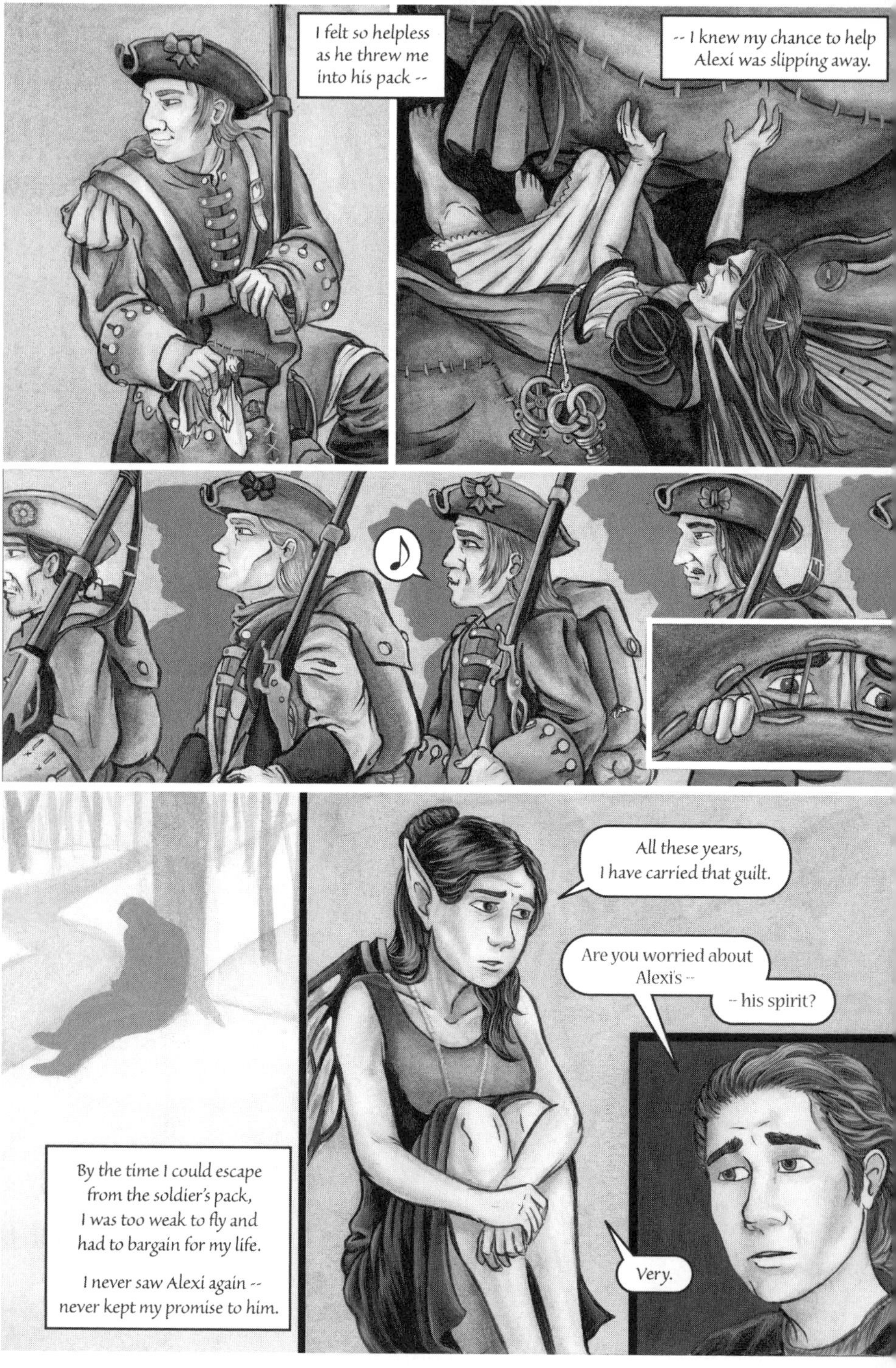
I felt so helpless as he threw me into his pack --
-- I knew my chance to help Alexi was slipping away.
♪
All these years, I have carried that guilt.
By the time I could escape from the soldier's pack, I was too weak to fly and had to bargain for my life.
I never saw Alexi again -- never kept my promise to him.
Are you worried about Alexi's --
-- his spirit?
Very.

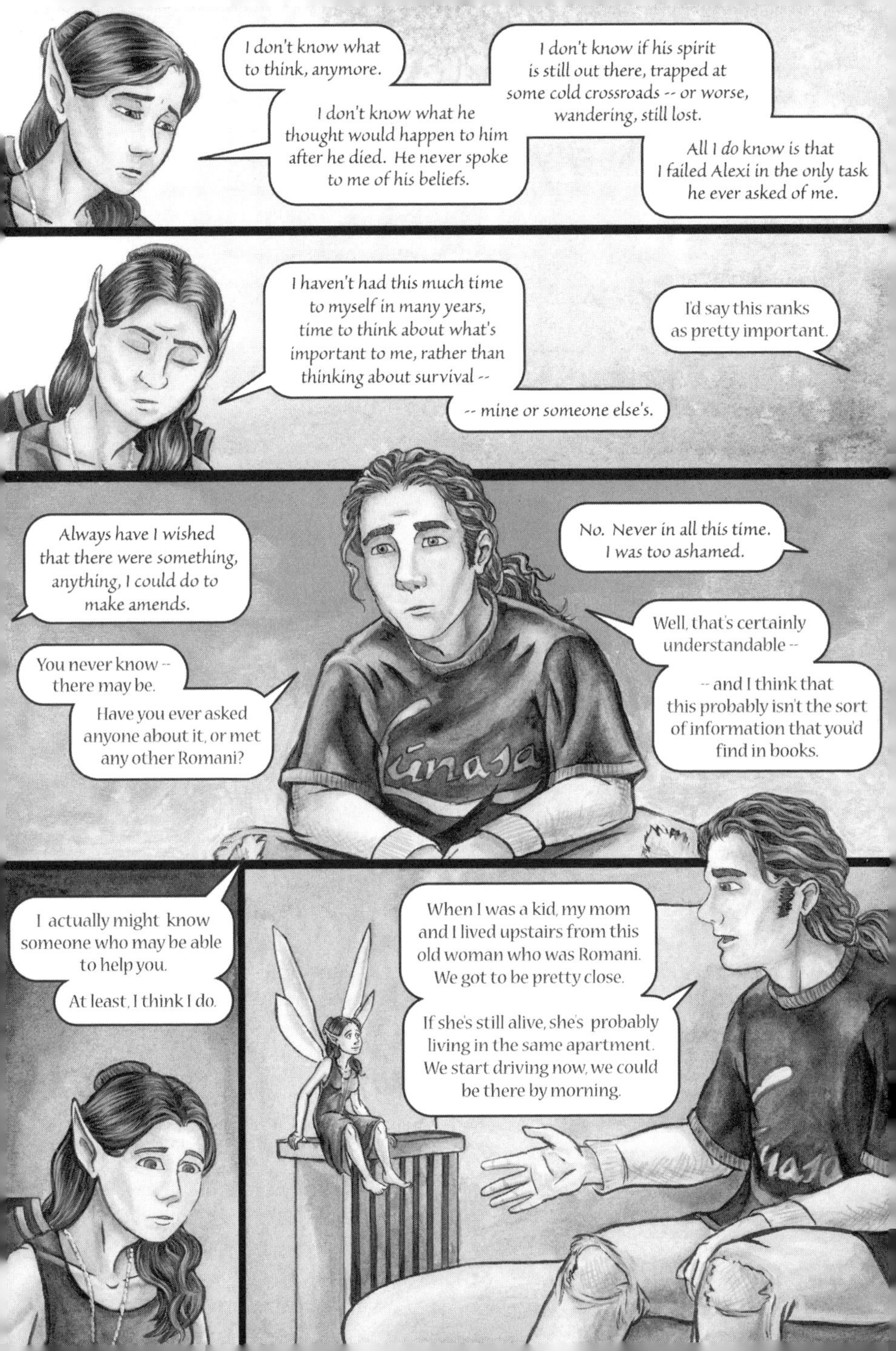

I don't know what to think, anymore.
I don't know what he thought would happen to him after he died. He never spoke to me of his beliefs.
I don't know if his spirit is still out there, trapped at some cold crossroads -- or worse, wandering, still lost.
All I *do* know is that I failed Alexi in the only task he ever asked of me.
I haven't had this much time to myself in many years, time to think about what's important to me, rather than thinking about survival --
-- mine or someone else's.
I'd say this ranks as pretty important.
Always have I wished that there were something, anything, I could do to make amends.
You never know -- there may be.
Have you ever asked anyone about it, or met any other Romani?
No. Never in all this time. I was too ashamed.
Well, that's certainly understandable --
-- and I think that this probably isn't the sort of information that you'd find in books.
I actually might know someone who may be able to help you.
At least, I think I do.
When I was a kid, my mom and I lived upstairs from this old woman who was Romani. We got to be pretty close.
If she's still alive, she's probably living in the same apartment. We start driving now, we could be there by morning.

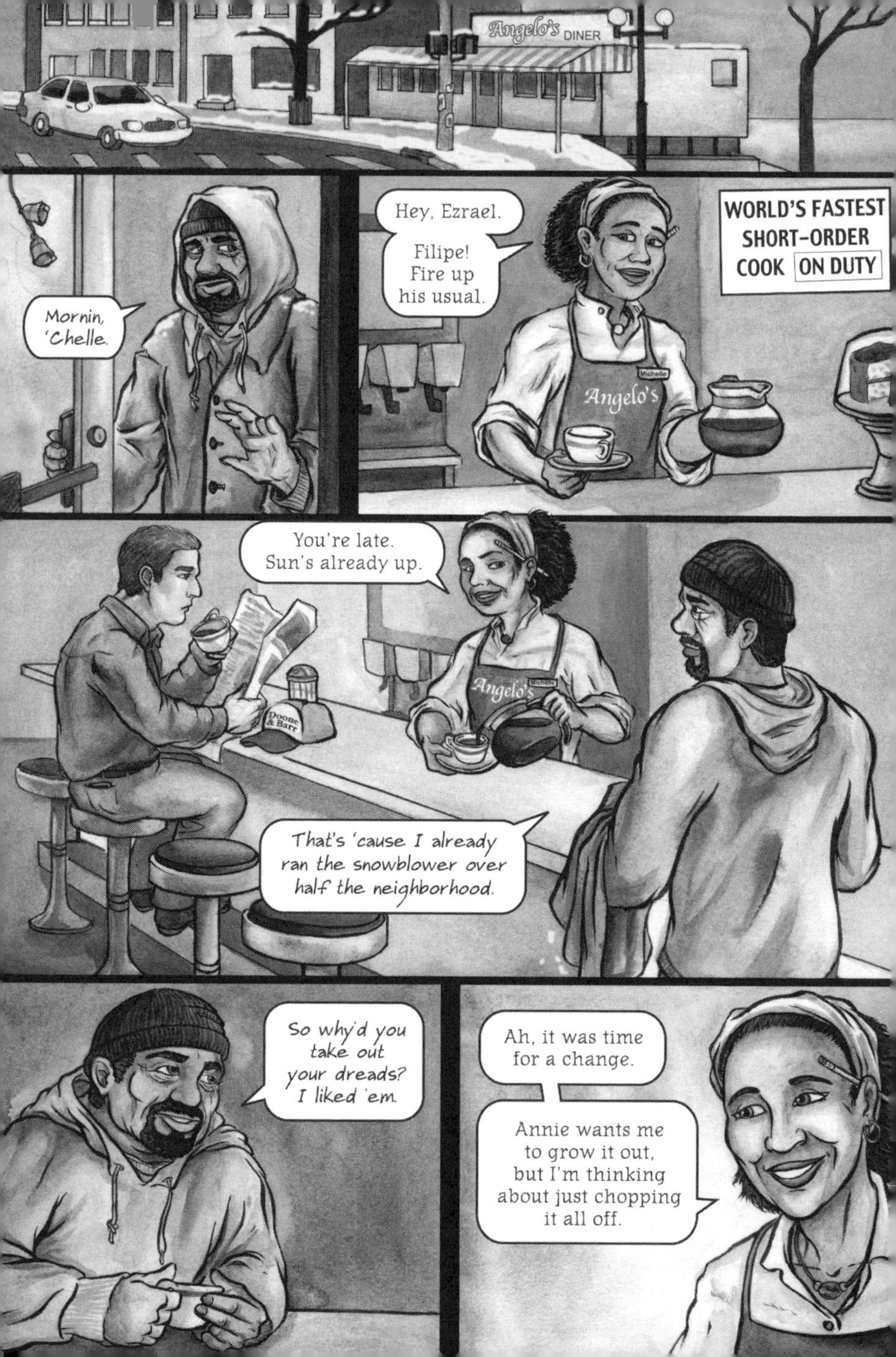
Angelo's DINER
Mornin, 'Chelle.
Hey, Ezrael.
Filipe! Fire up his usual.
WORLD'S FASTEST SHORT-ORDER COOK ON DUTY
Angelo's
You're late. Sun's already up.
Doone & Barr
Angelo's
That's 'cause I already ran the snowblower over half the neighborhood.
So why'd you take out your dreads? I liked 'em.
Ah, it was time for a change.
Annie wants me to grow it out, but I'm thinking about just chopping it all off.

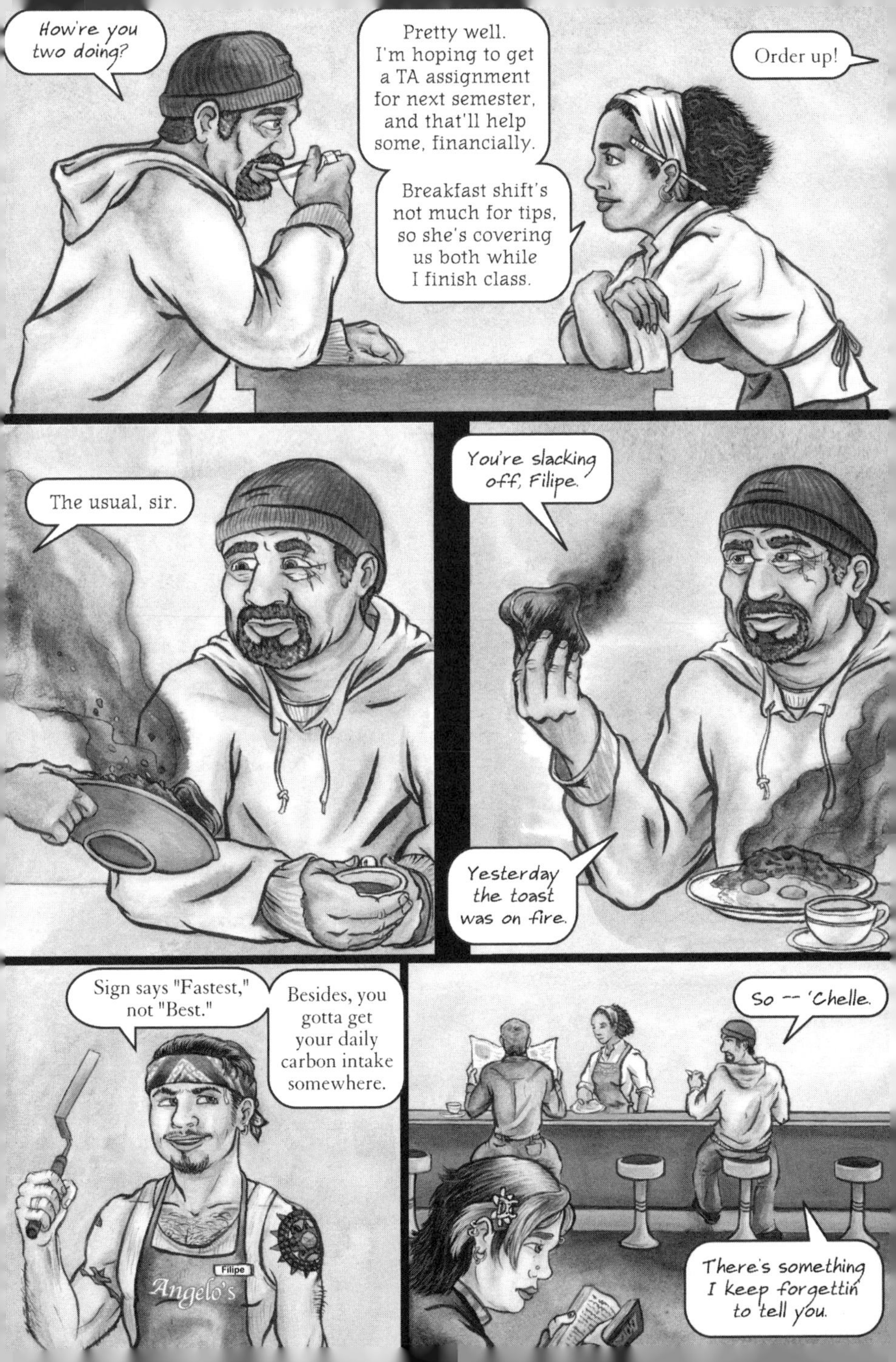
How're you two doing?
Pretty well. I'm hoping to get a TA assignment for next semester, and that'll help some, financially.
Breakfast shift's not much for tips, so she's covering us both while I finish class.
Order up!
The usual, sir.
You're slacking off, Filipe.
Yesterday the toast was on fire.
Sign says "Fastest," not "Best."
Besides, you gotta get your daily carbon intake somewhere.
Filipe
Angelo's
So -- 'Chelle.
There's something I keep forgettin to tell you.

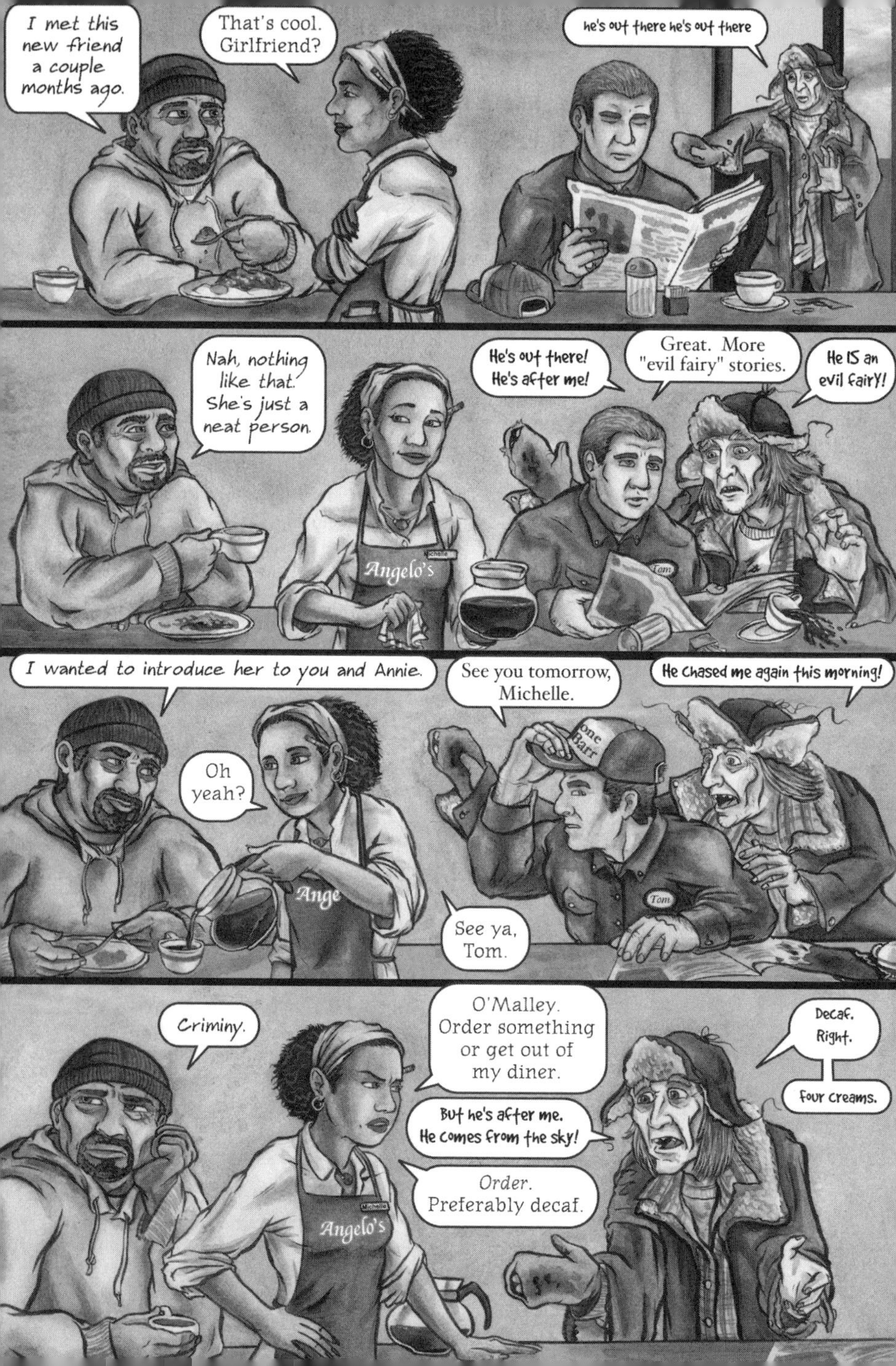

I met this new friend a couple months ago.
That's cool. Girlfriend?
he's out there he's out there
Nah, nothing like that. She's just a neat person.
He's out there! He's after me!
Great. More "evil fairy" stories.
He IS an evil fairy!
I wanted to introduce her to you and Annie.
Oh yeah?
See you tomorrow, Michelle.
He chased me again this morning!
See ya, Tom.
Criminy.
O'Malley. Order something or get out of my diner.
But he's after me. He comes from the sky!
Order. Preferably decaf.
Decaf. Right.
Four creams.

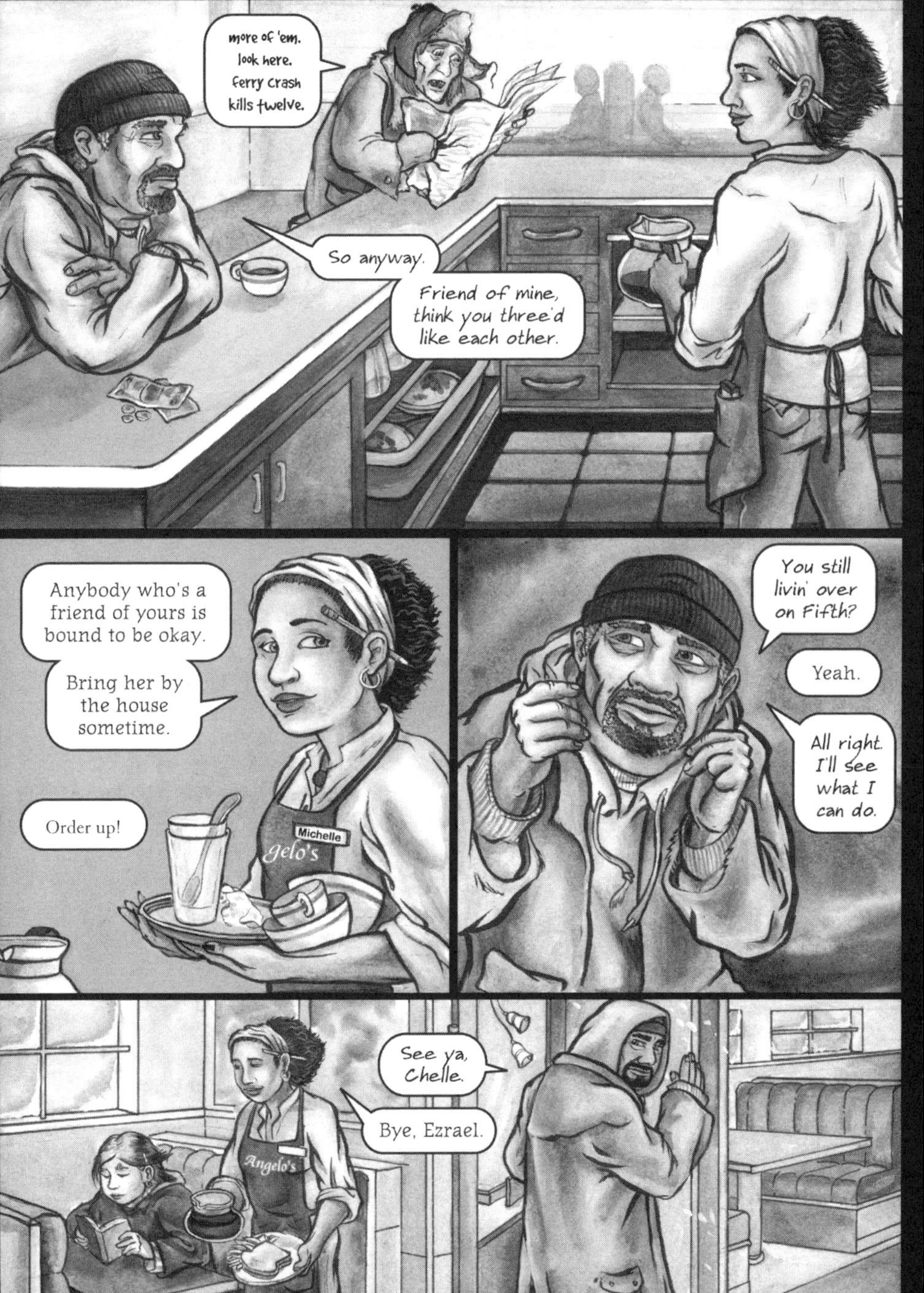
more of 'em. look here. ferry crash kills twelve.
So anyway.
Friend of mine, think you three'd like each other.
Anybody who's a friend of yours is bound to be okay.
Bring her by the house sometime.
Order up!
Michelle
gelo's
You still livin' over on Fifth?
Yeah.
All right. I'll see what I can do.
Angelo's
See ya, Chelle.
Bye, Ezrael.

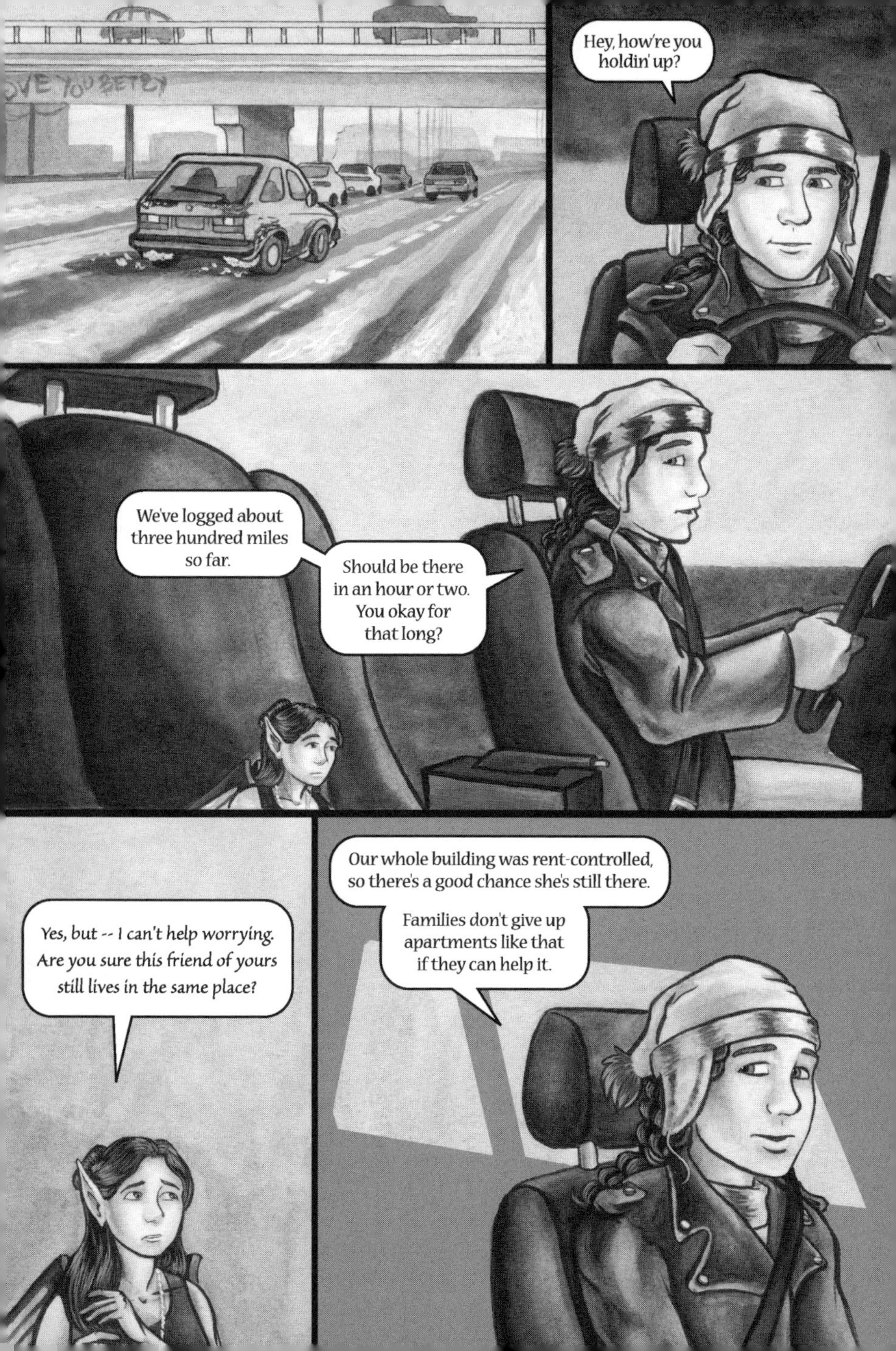
OVE YOU BETSY
Hey, how're you holdin' up?
We've logged about three hundred miles so far.
Should be there in an hour or two. You okay for that long?
Yes, but -- I can't help worrying. Are you sure this friend of yours still lives in the same place?
Our whole building was rent-controlled, so there's a good chance she's still there.
Families don't give up apartments like that if they can help it.

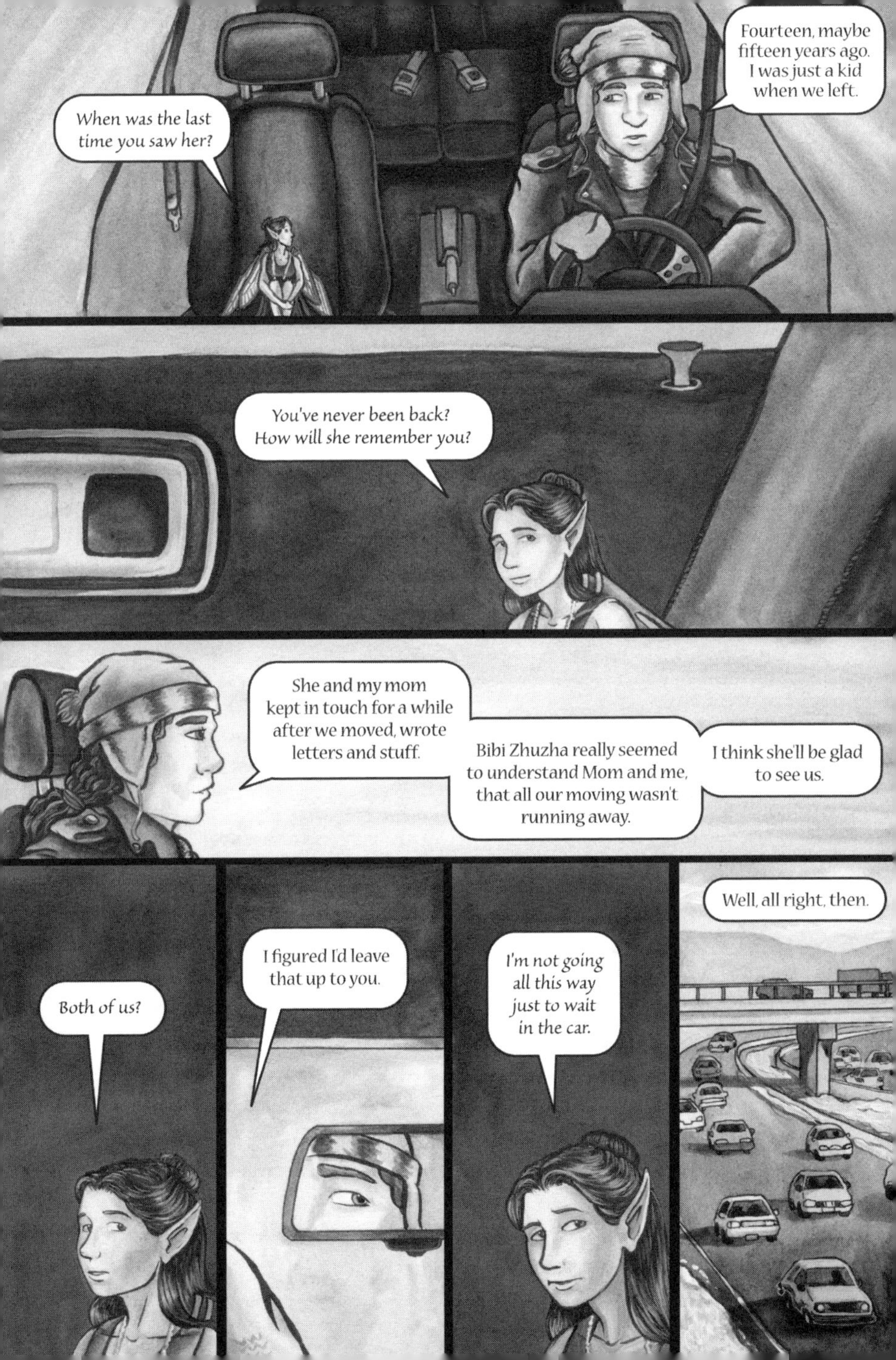
When was the last time you saw her?
Fourteen, maybe fifteen years ago. I was just a kid when we left.
You've never been back? How will she remember you?
She and my mom kept in touch for a while after we moved, wrote letters and stuff.
Bibi Zhuzha really seemed to understand Mom and me, that all our moving wasn't running away.
I think she'll be glad to see us.
Both of us?
I figured I'd leave that up to you.
I'm not going all this way just to wait in the car.
Well, all right, then.

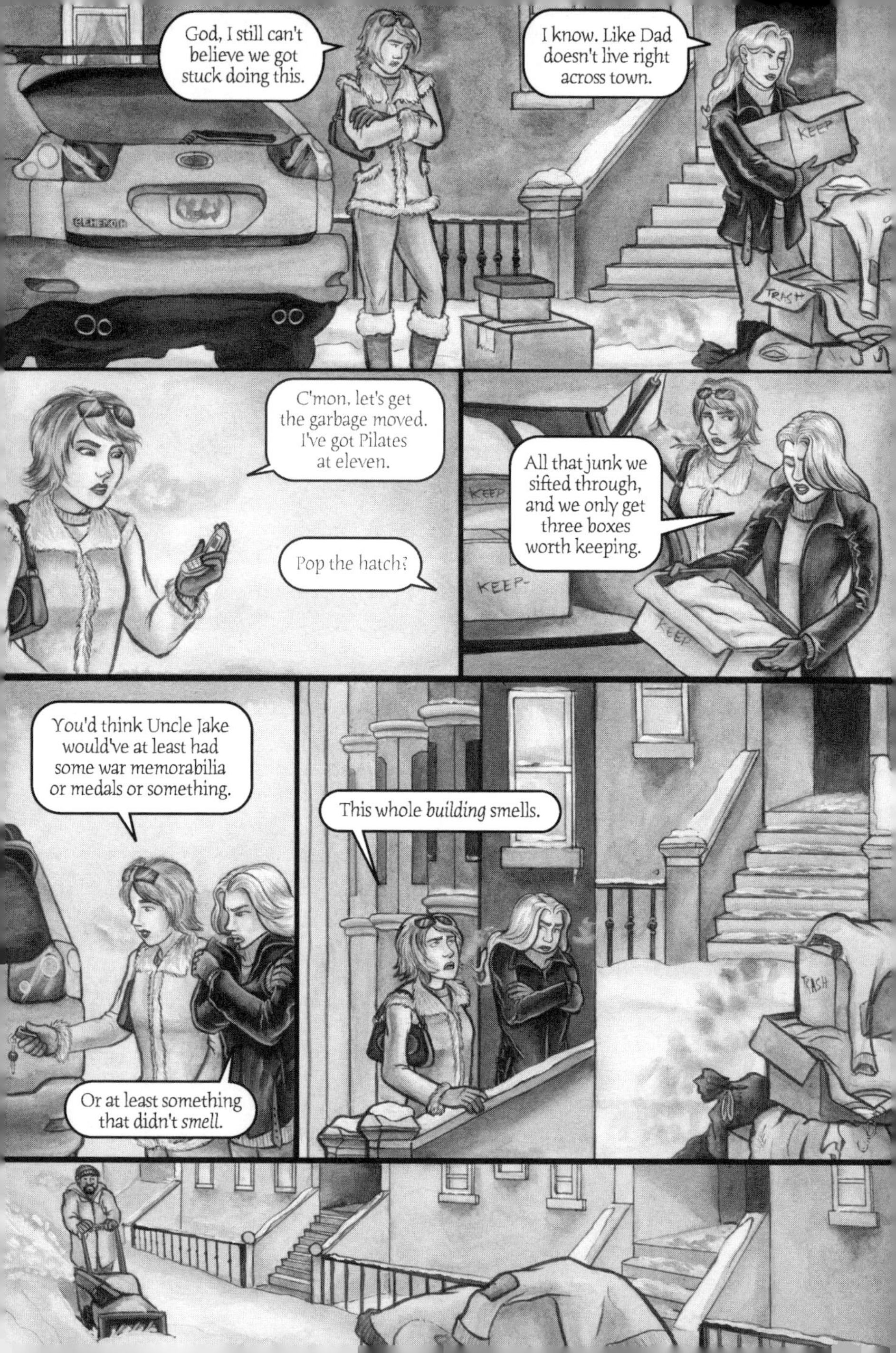
God, I still can't believe we got stuck doing this.
I know. Like Dad doesn't live right across town.
KEEP
TRASH
C'mon, let's get the garbage moved. I've got Pilates at eleven.
Pop the hatch?
All that junk we sifted through, and we only get three boxes worth keeping.
KEEP
KEEP
KEEP
You'd think Uncle Jake would've at least had some war memorabilia or medals or something.
Or at least something that didn't *smell*.
This whole *building* smells.
TRASH

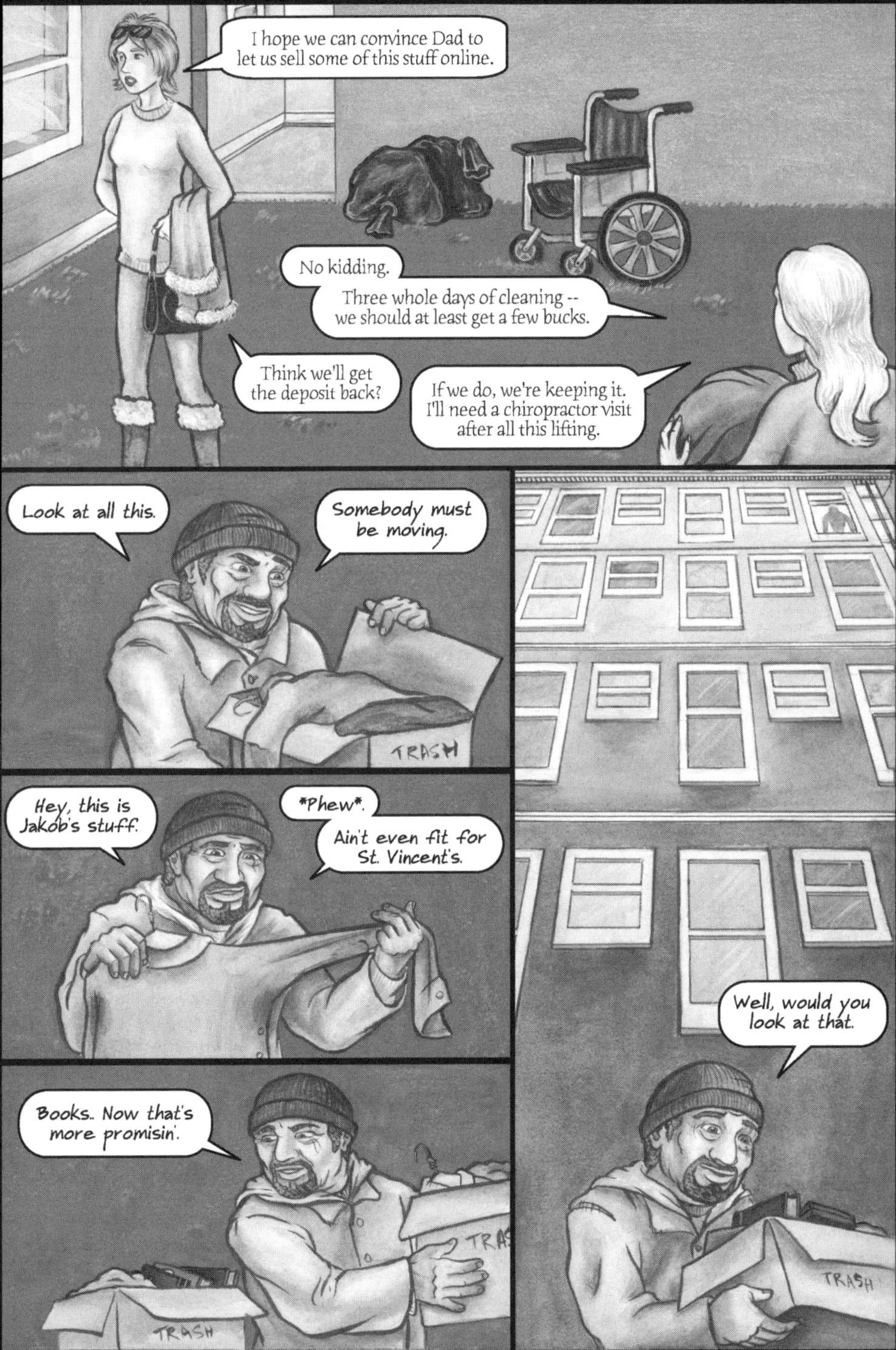
I hope we can convince Dad to let us sell some of this stuff online.
No kidding.
Three whole days of cleaning -- we should at least get a few bucks.
Think we'll get the deposit back?
If we do, we're keeping it. I'll need a chiropractor visit after all this lifting.
Look at all this.
Somebody must be moving.
TRASH
Hey, this is Jakob's stuff.
Phew.
Ain't even fit for St. Vincent's.
Books.. Now that's more promisin'.
TRASH
Well, would you look at that.
TRASH

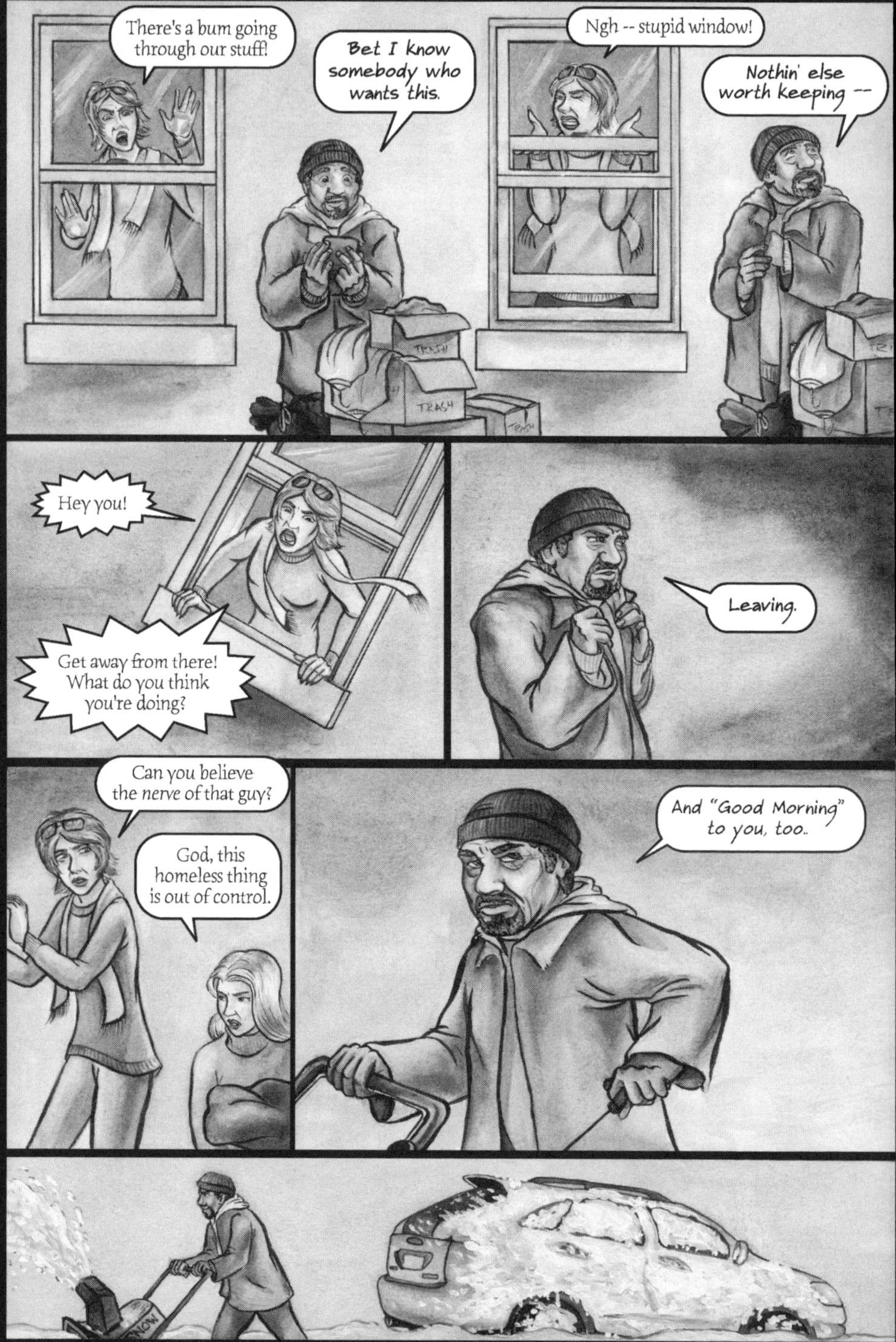
There's a bum going through our stuff!
Bet I know somebody who wants this.
Ngh -- stupid window!
Nothin' else worth keeping --
Hey you!
Get away from there! What do you think you're doing?
Leaving.
Can you believe the *nerve* of that guy?
God, this homeless thing is out of control.
And "Good Morning" to you, too..

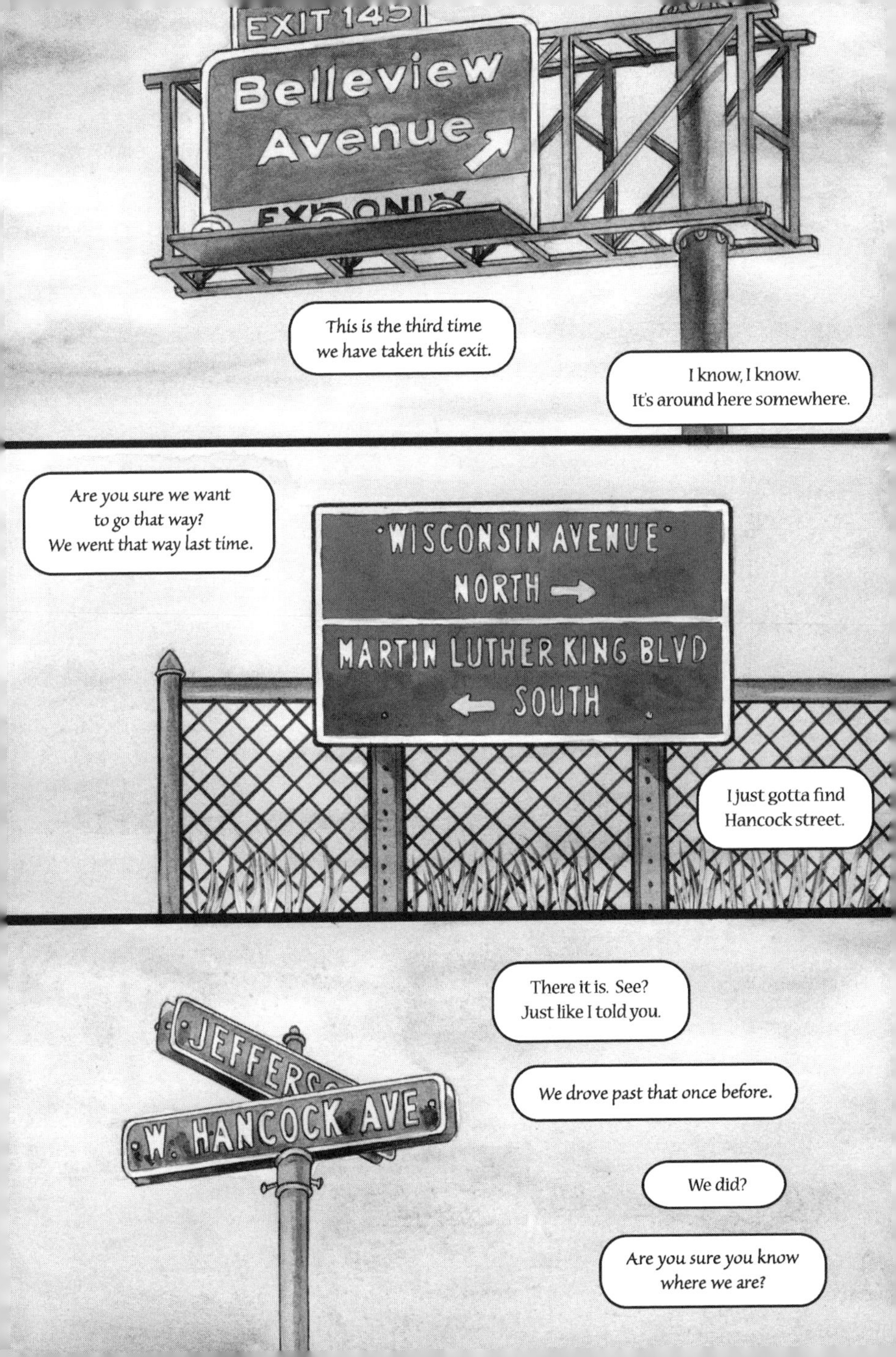
EXIT 145
Belleview Avenue
This is the third time we have taken this exit.
I know, I know. It's around here somewhere.
Are you sure we want to go that way? We went that way last time.
WISCONSIN AVENUE NORTH
MARTIN LUTHER KING BLVD SOUTH
I just gotta find Hancock street.
W. HANCOCK AVE
There it is. See? Just like I told you.
We drove past that once before.
We did?
Are you sure you know where we are?

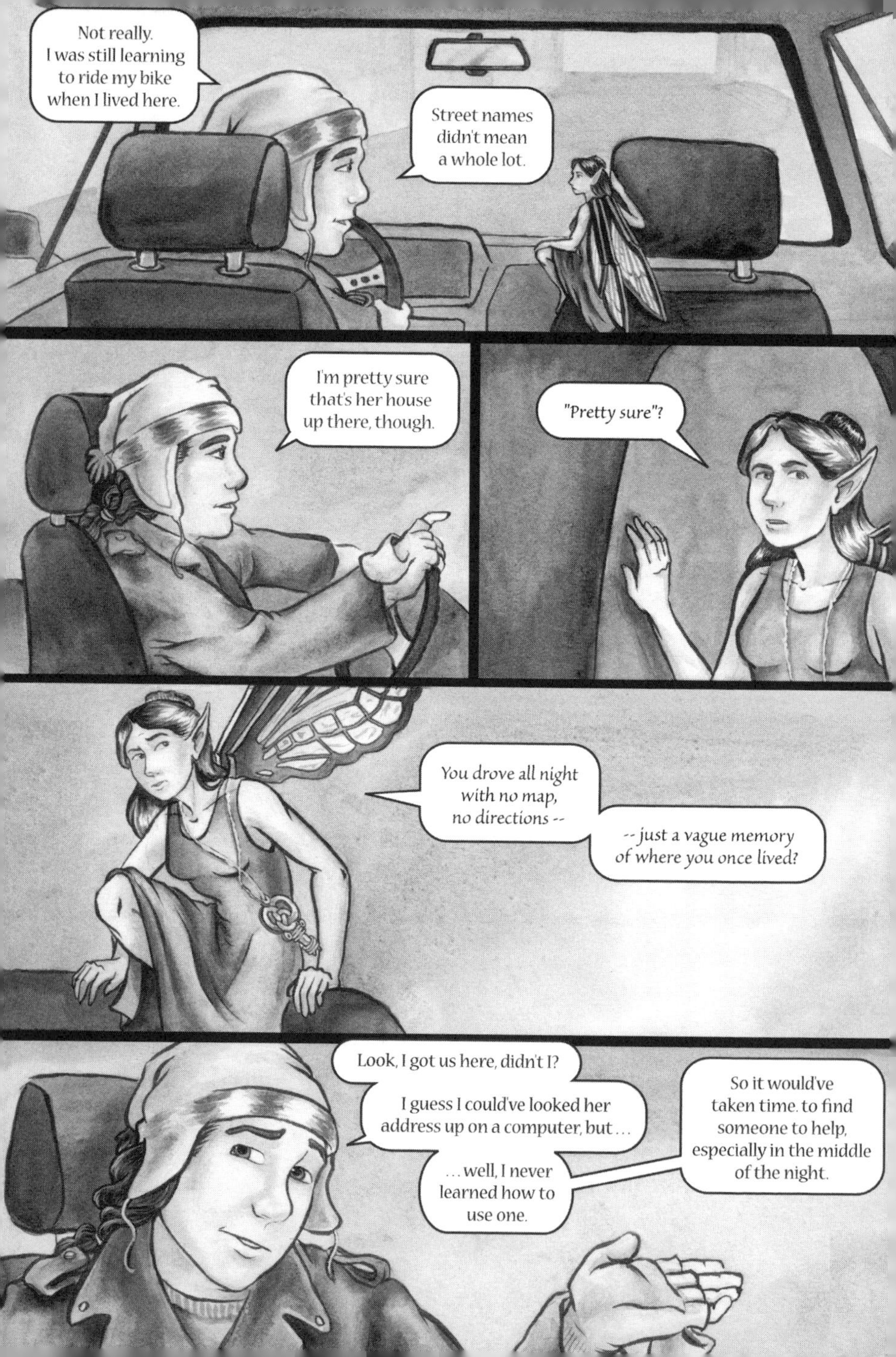

Not really. I was still learning to ride my bike when I lived here.
Street names didn't mean a whole lot.
I'm pretty sure that's her house up there, though.
"Pretty sure"?
You drove all night with no map, no directions --
-- just a vague memory of where you once lived?
Look, I got us here, didn't I?
I guess I could've looked her address up on a computer, but . . .
. . . well, I never learned how to use one.
So it would've taken time. to find someone to help, especially in the middle of the night.

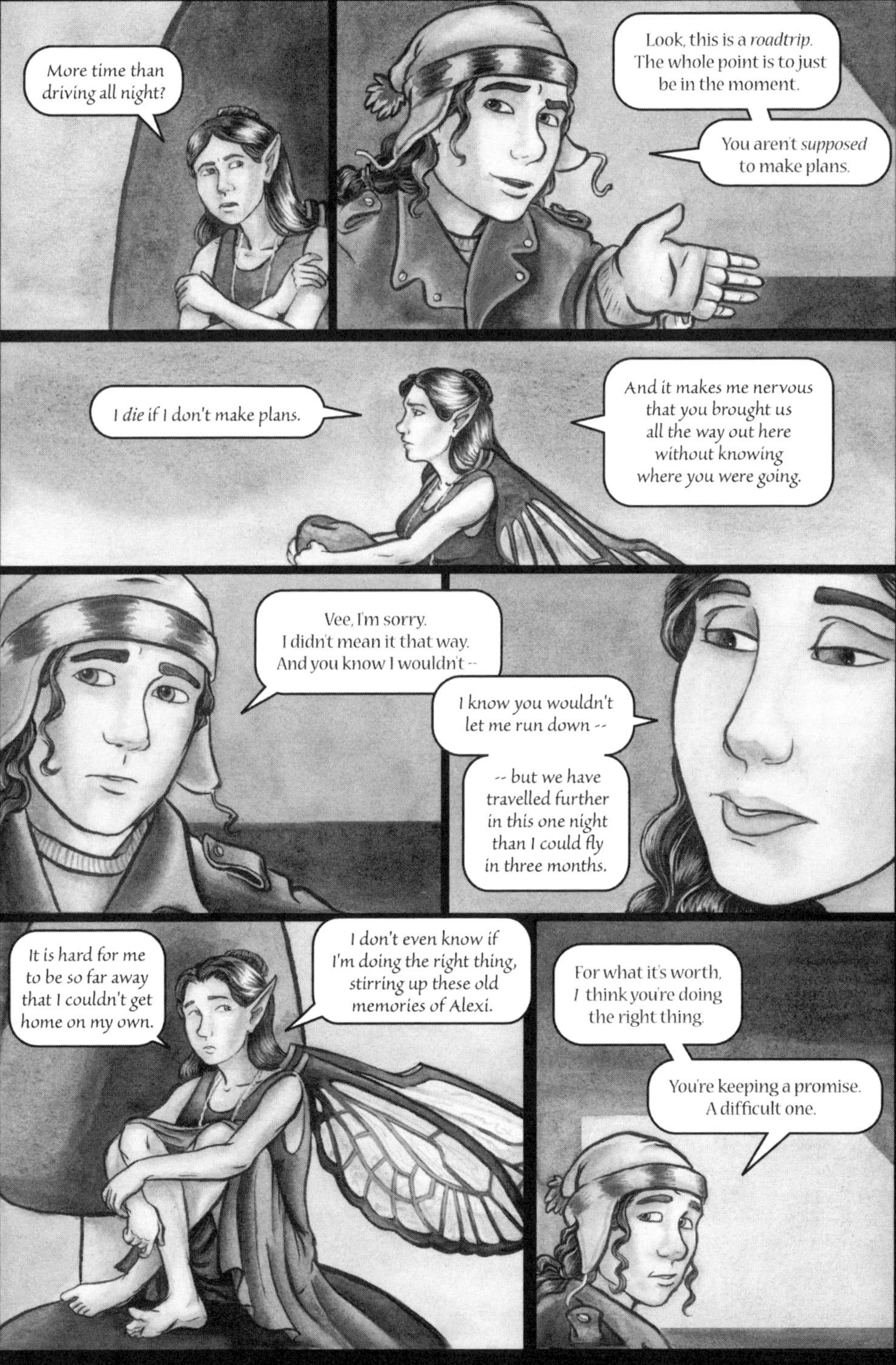
More time than driving all night?
Look, this is a *roadtrip*. The whole point is to just be in the moment.
You aren't *supposed* to make plans.
I *die* if I don't make plans.
And it makes me nervous that you brought us all the way out here without knowing where you were going.
Vee, I'm sorry. I didn't mean it that way. And you know I wouldn't --
I know you wouldn't let me run down --
-- but we have travelled further in this one night than I could fly in three months.
It is hard for me to be so far away that I couldn't get home on my own.
I don't even know if I'm doing the right thing, stirring up these old memories of Alexi.
For what it's worth, *I* think you're doing the right thing.
You're keeping a promise. A difficult one.

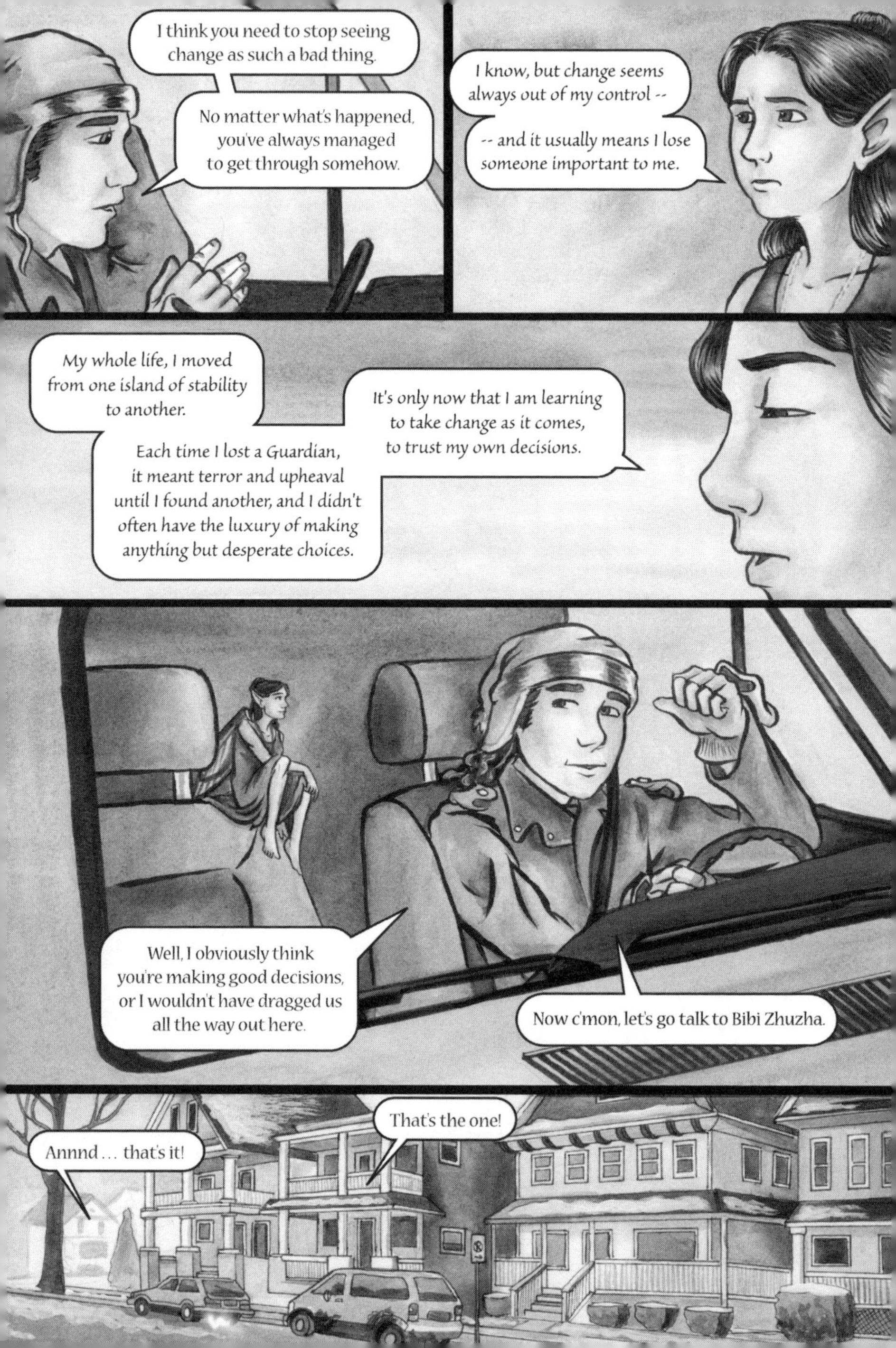
I think you need to stop seeing change as such a bad thing.
No matter what's happened, you've always managed to get through somehow.
I know, but change seems always out of my control --
-- and it usually means I lose someone important to me.
My whole life, I moved from one island of stability to another.
Each time I lost a Guardian, it meant terror and upheaval until I found another, and I didn't often have the luxury of making anything but desperate choices.
It's only now that I am learning to take change as it comes, to trust my own decisions.
Well, I obviously think you're making good decisions, or I wouldn't have dragged us all the way out here.
Now c'mon, let's go talk to Bibi Zhuzha.
Annnd ... that's it!
That's the one!

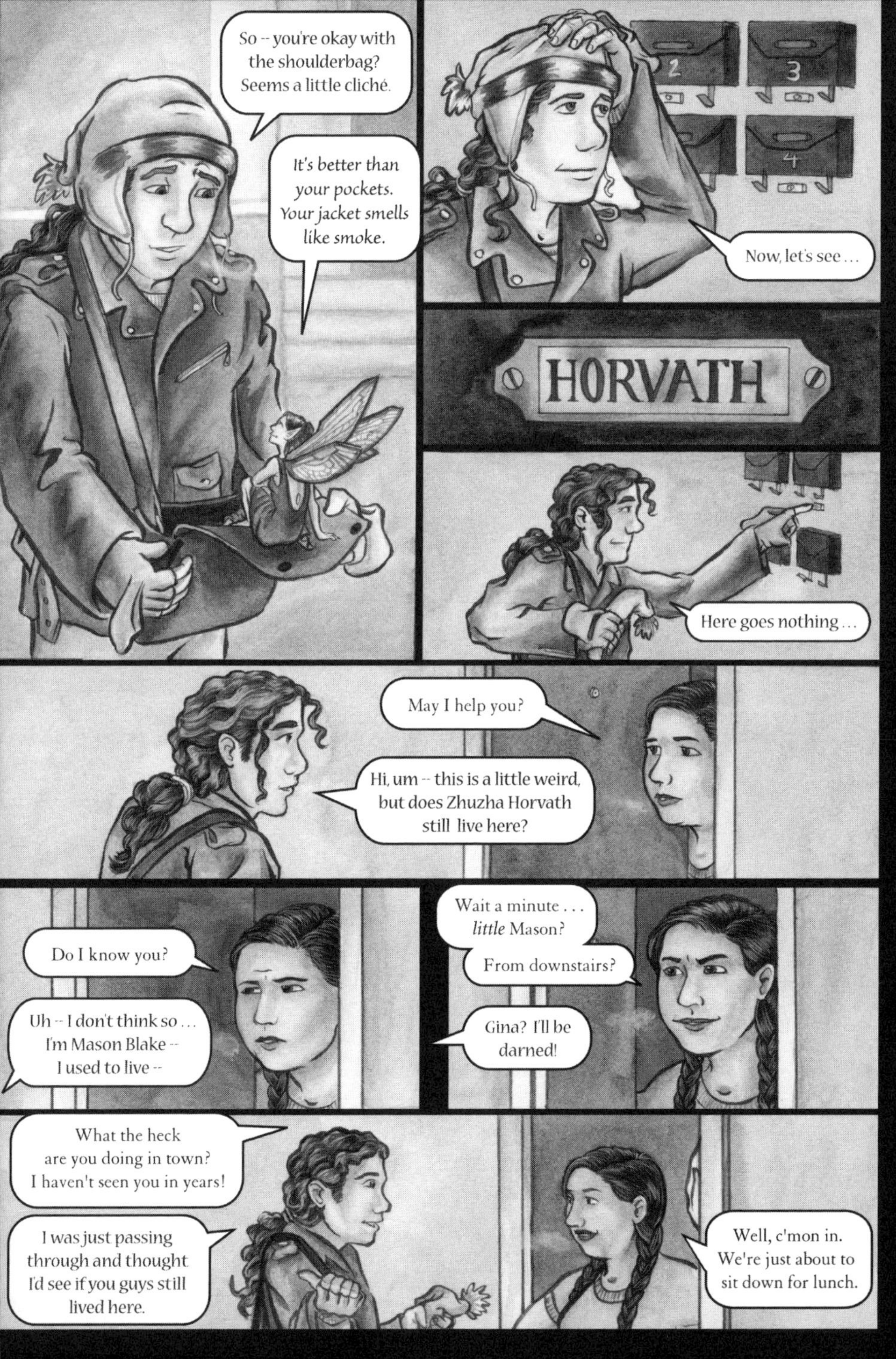
So -- you're okay with the shoulderbag? Seems a little cliché.
It's better than your pockets. Your jacket smells like smoke.
Now, let's see . . .
HORVATH
Here goes nothing . . .
May I help you?
Hi, um -- this is a little weird, but does Zhuzha Horvath still live here?
Do I know you?
Uh -- I don't think so . . . I'm Mason Blake -- I used to live --
Wait a minute . . . *little* Mason?
From downstairs?
Gina? I'll be darned!
What the heck are you doing in town? I haven't seen you in years!
I was just passing through and thought I'd see if you guys still lived here.
Well, c'mon in. We're just about to sit down for lunch.

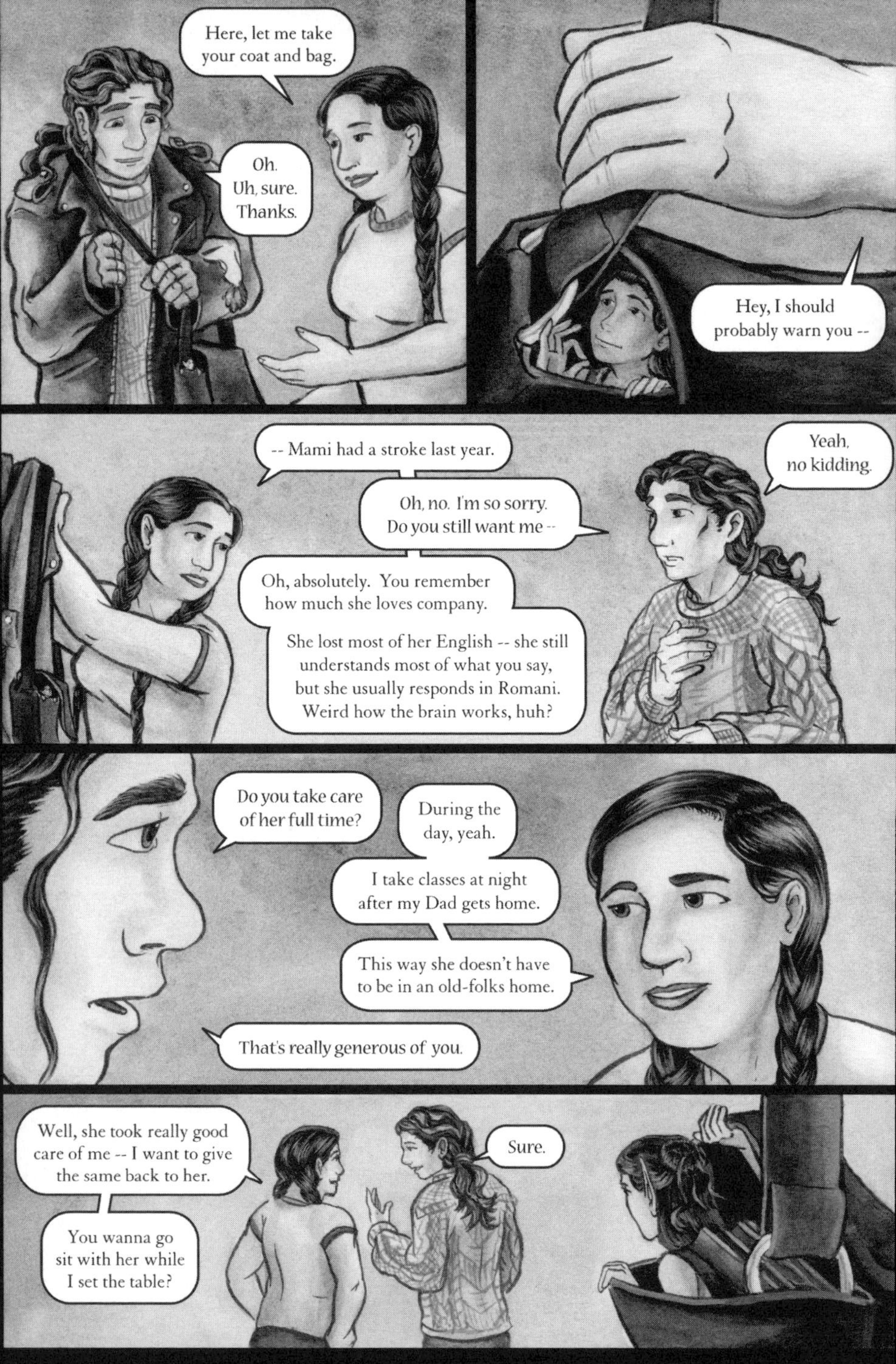
Here, let me take your coat and bag.
Oh. Uh, sure. Thanks.
Hey, I should probably warn you --
-- Mami had a stroke last year.
Yeah, no kidding.
Oh, no. I'm so sorry. Do you still want me --
Oh, absolutely. You remember how much she loves company.
She lost most of her English -- she still understands most of what you say, but she usually responds in Romani. Weird how the brain works, huh?
Do you take care of her full time?
During the day, yeah.
I take classes at night after my Dad gets home.
This way she doesn't have to be in an old-folks home.
That's really generous of you.
Well, she took really good care of me -- I want to give the same back to her.
Sure.
You wanna go sit with her while I set the table?

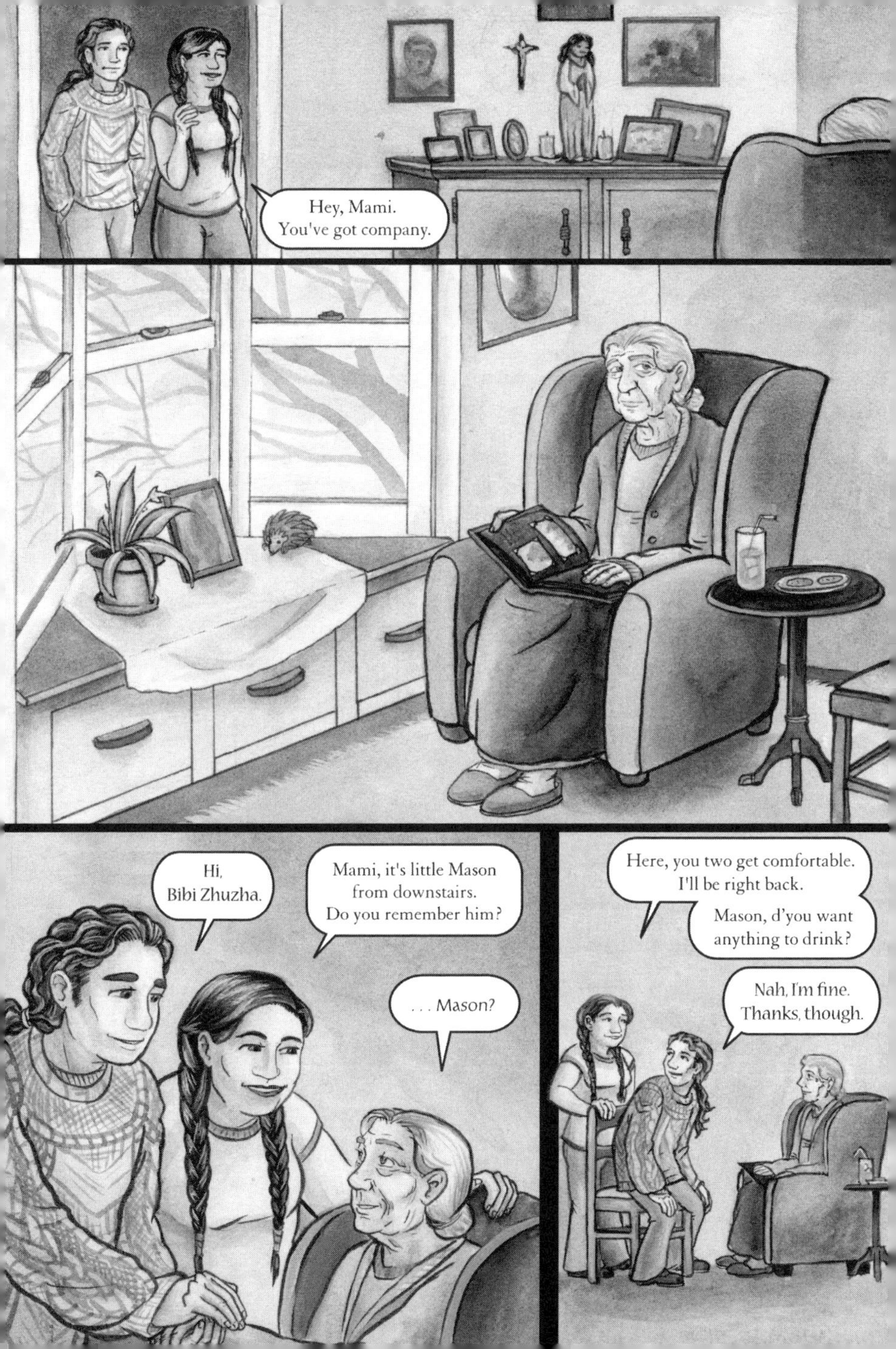
Hey, Mami.
You've got company.
Hi,
Bibi Zhuzha.
Mami, it's little Mason
from downstairs.
Do you remember him?
. . . Mason?
Here, you two get comfortable.
I'll be right back.
Mason, d'you want
anything to drink?
Nah, I'm fine.
Thanks, though.

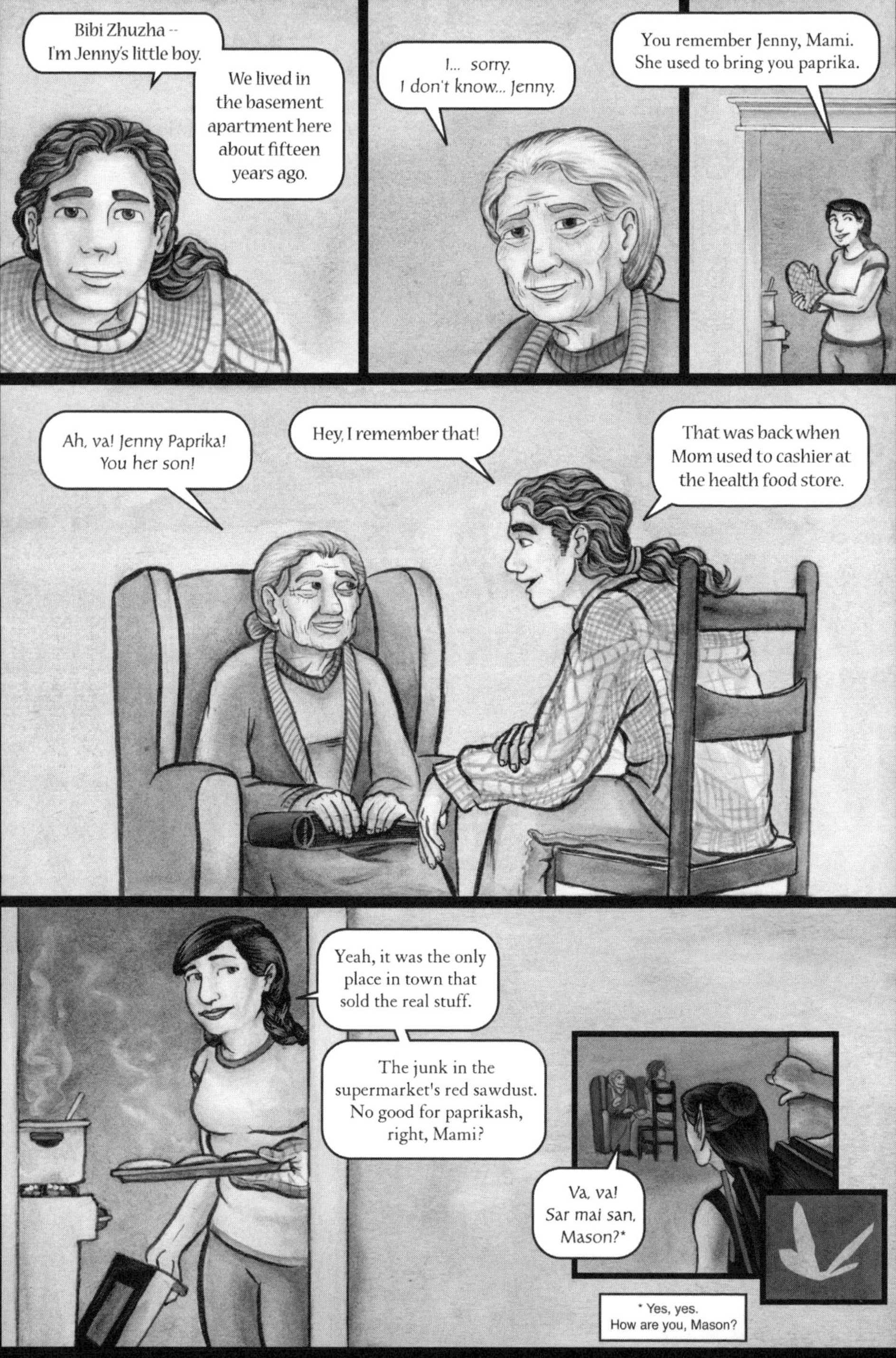
Bibi Zhuzha -- I'm Jenny's little boy.
We lived in the basement apartment here about fifteen years ago.
I... sorry. I don't know... Jenny.
You remember Jenny, Mami. She used to bring you paprika.
Ah, va! Jenny Paprika! You her son!
Hey, I remember that!
That was back when Mom used to cashier at the health food store.
Yeah, it was the only place in town that sold the real stuff.
The junk in the supermarket's red sawdust. No good for paprikash, right, Mami?
Va, va! Sar mai san, Mason?*
* Yes, yes. How are you, Mason?

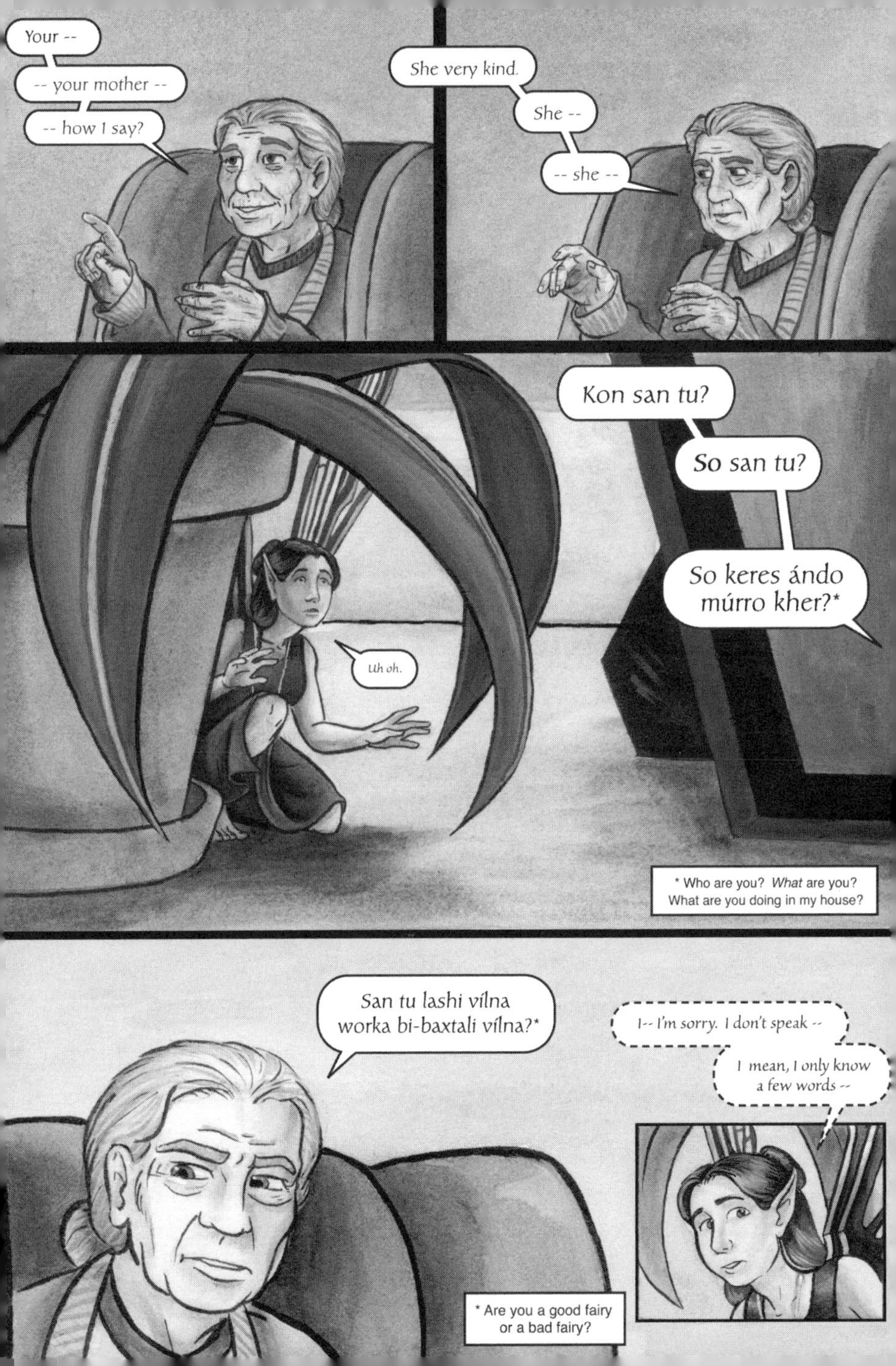
Your --
-- your mother --
-- how I say?
She very kind.
She --
-- she --
Kon san tu?
So san tu?
So keres ándo múrro kher?*
Uh oh.
* Who are you? *What* are you? What are you doing in my house?
San tu lashi vílna worka bi-baxtali vílna?*
I-- I'm sorry. I don't speak --
I mean, I only know a few words --
* Are you a good fairy or a bad fairy?

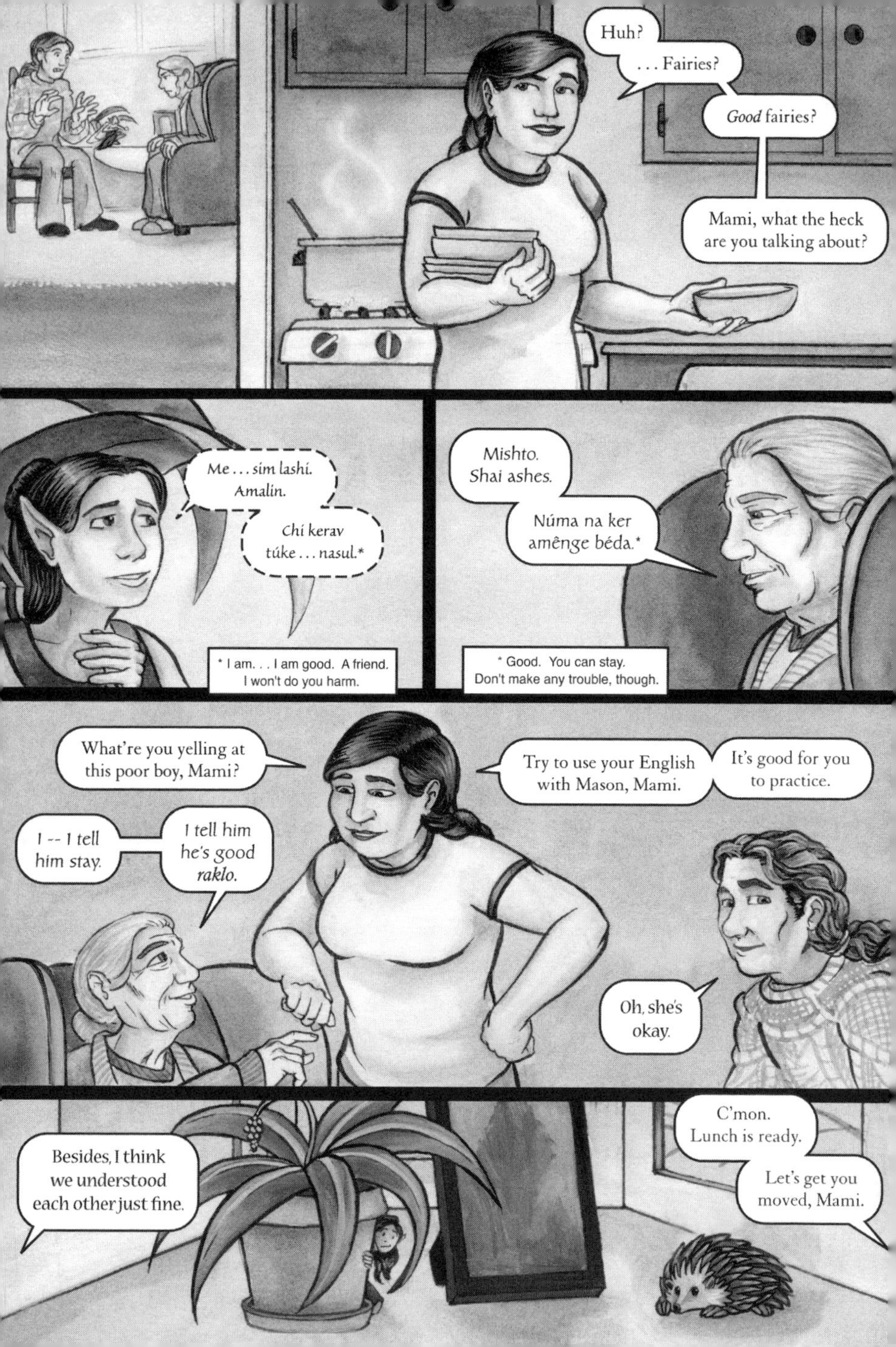

Huh?
. . . Fairies?
Good fairies?
Mami, what the heck are you talking about?
Me . . . sim lashi. Amalin.
*Chí kerav túke . . . nasul.**
* I am. . . I am good. A friend. I won't do you harm.
Mishto. Shai ashes.
*Núma na ker amênge béda.**
* Good. You can stay. Don't make any trouble, though.
What're you yelling at this poor boy, Mami?
Try to use your English with Mason, Mami.
It's good for you to practice.
I -- I tell him stay.
I tell him he's good *raklo.*
Oh, she's okay.
Besides, I think we understood each other just fine.
C'mon. Lunch is ready.
Let's get you moved, Mami.

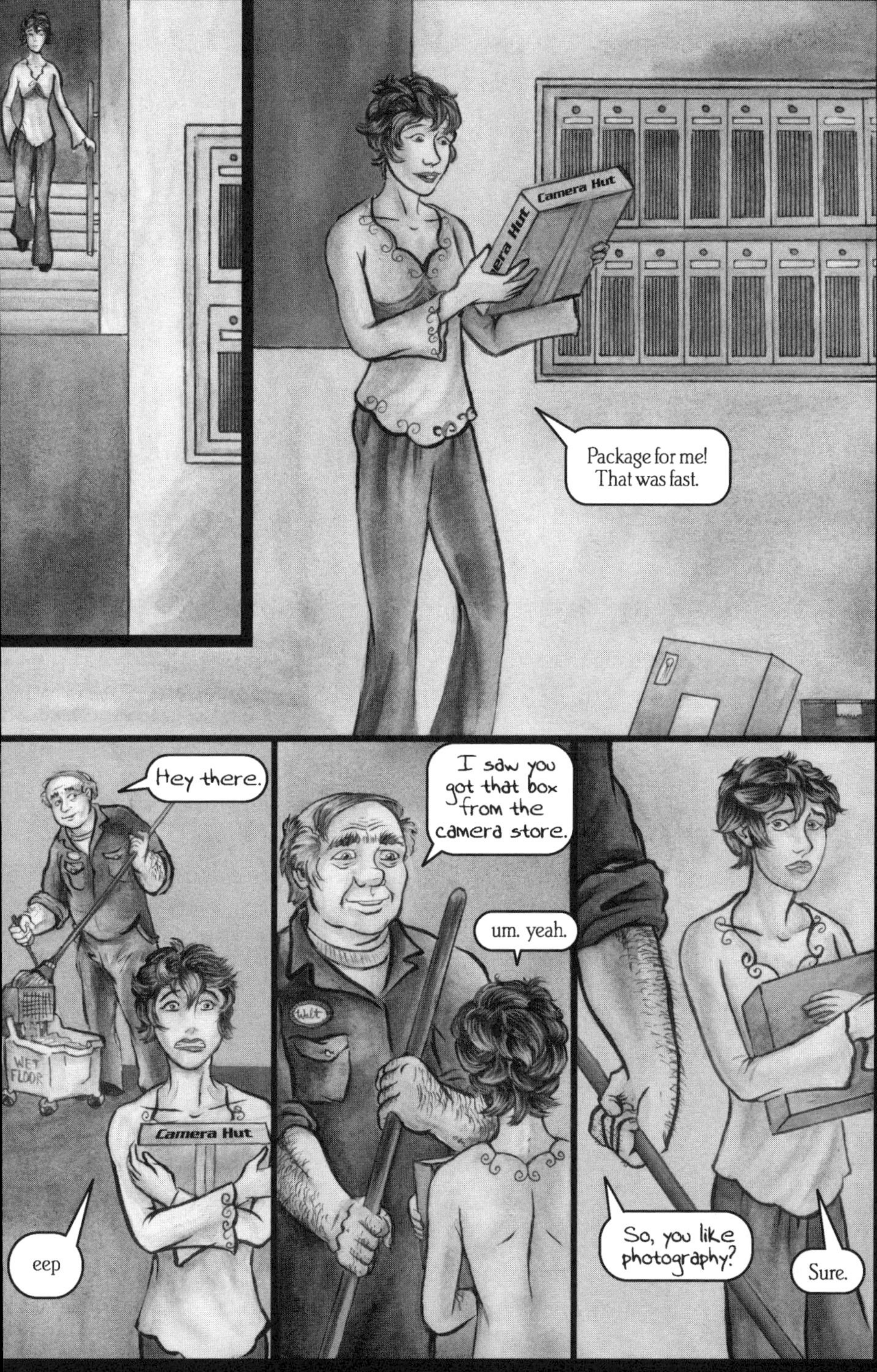
Camera Hut
Package for me! That was fast.
Hey there.
eep
Camera Hut
I saw you got that box from the camera store.
um. yeah.
So, you like photography?
Sure.

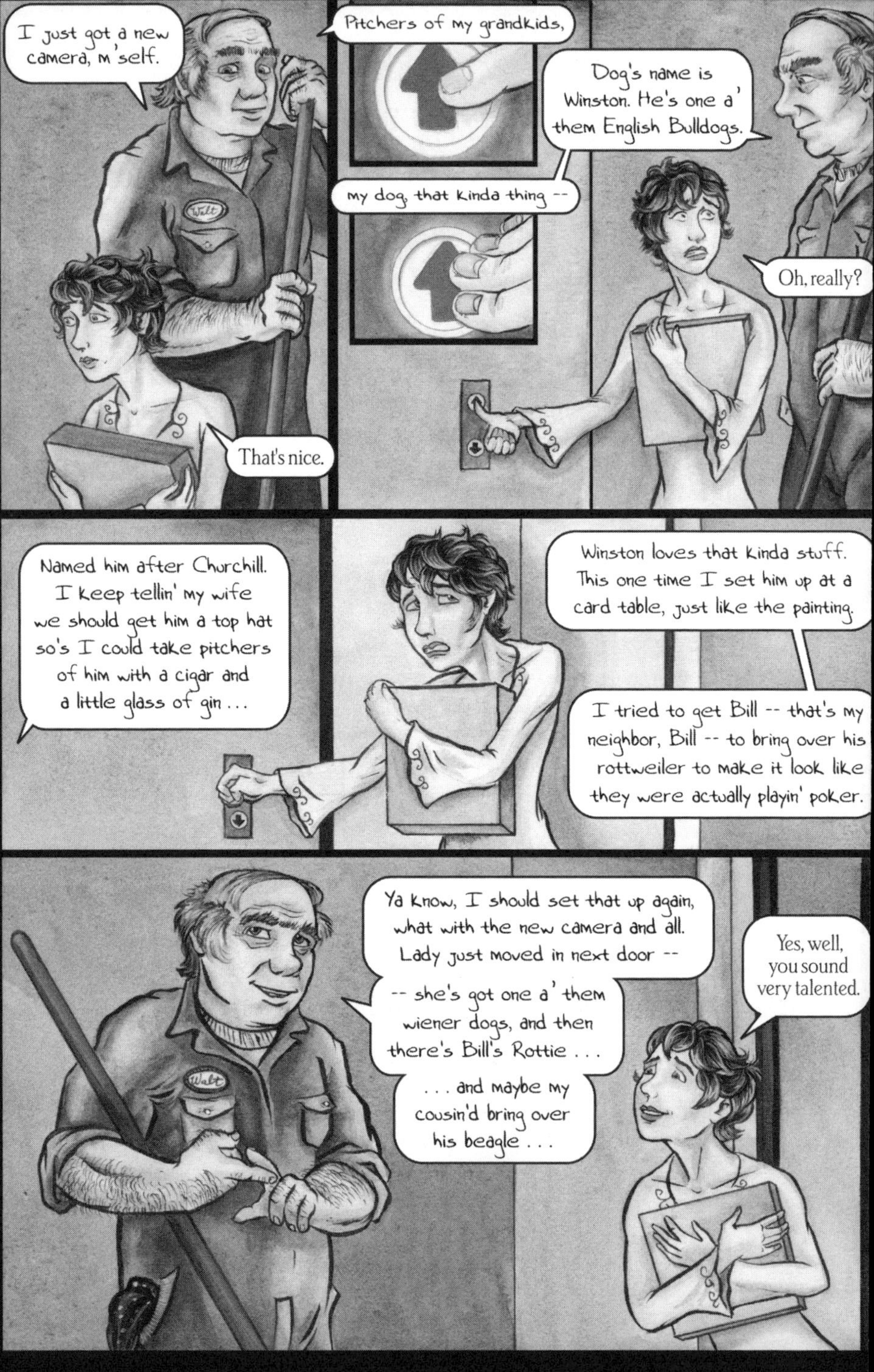
I just got a new camera, m'self.
Pitchers of my grandkids,
my dog, that kinda thing --
That's nice.
Dog's name is Winston. He's one a' them English Bulldogs.
Oh, really?
Named him after Churchill. I keep tellin' my wife we should get him a top hat so's I could take pitchers of him with a cigar and a little glass of gin . . .
Winston loves that kinda stuff. This one time I set him up at a card table, just like the painting.
I tried to get Bill -- that's my neighbor, Bill -- to bring over his rottweiler to make it look like they were actually playin' poker.
Ya know, I should set that up again, what with the new camera and all. Lady just moved in next door --
-- she's got one a' them wiener dogs, and then there's Bill's Rottie . . .
. . . and maybe my cousin'd bring over his beagle . . .
Yes, well, you sound very talented.

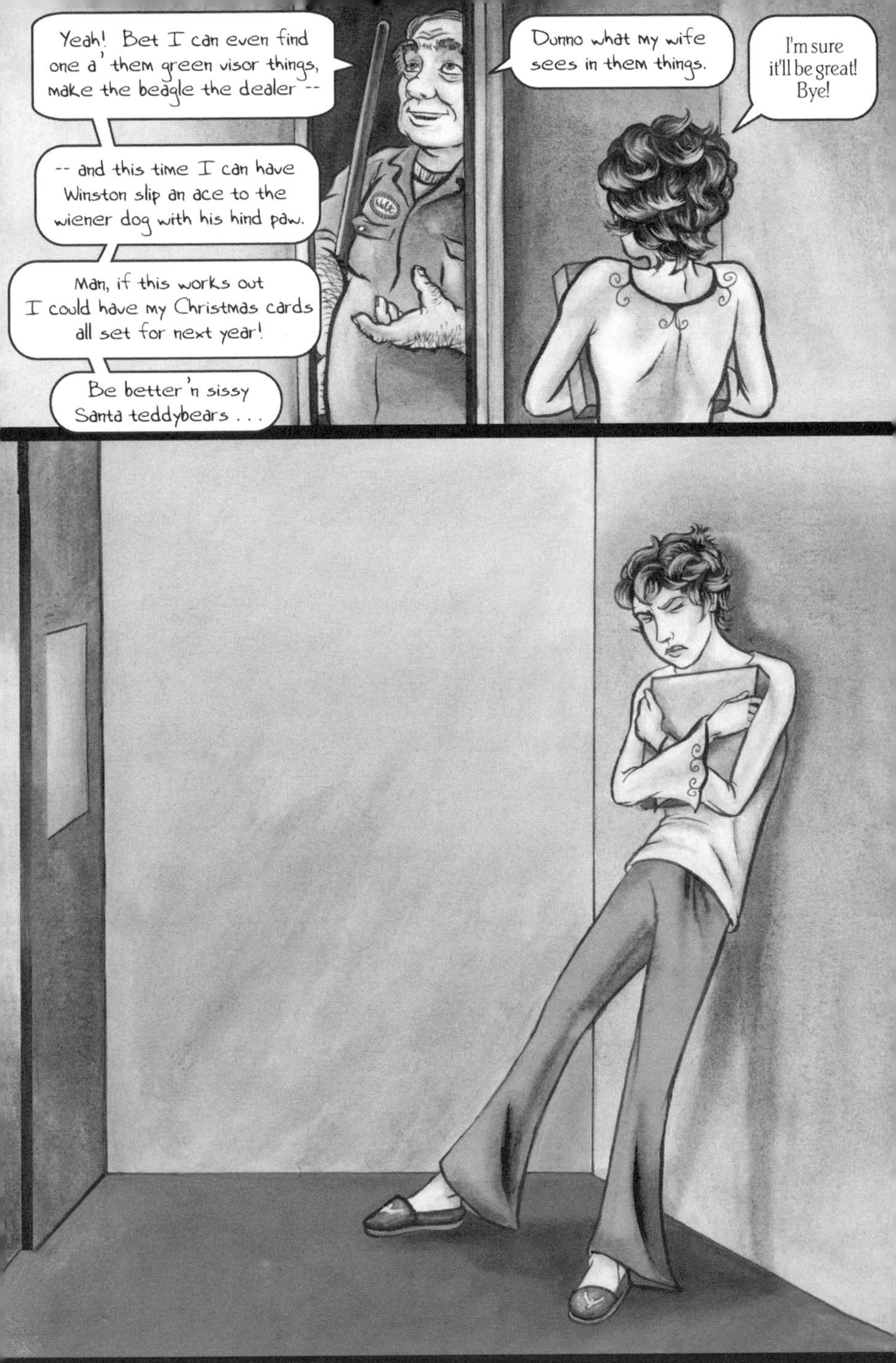
Yeah! Bet I can even find one a' them green visor things, make the beagle the dealer --
-- and this time I can have Winston slip an ace to the wiener dog with his hind paw.
Man, if this works out I could have my Christmas cards all set for next year!
Be better'n sissy Santa teddybears . . .
Dunno what my wife sees in them things.
I'm sure it'll be great! Bye!

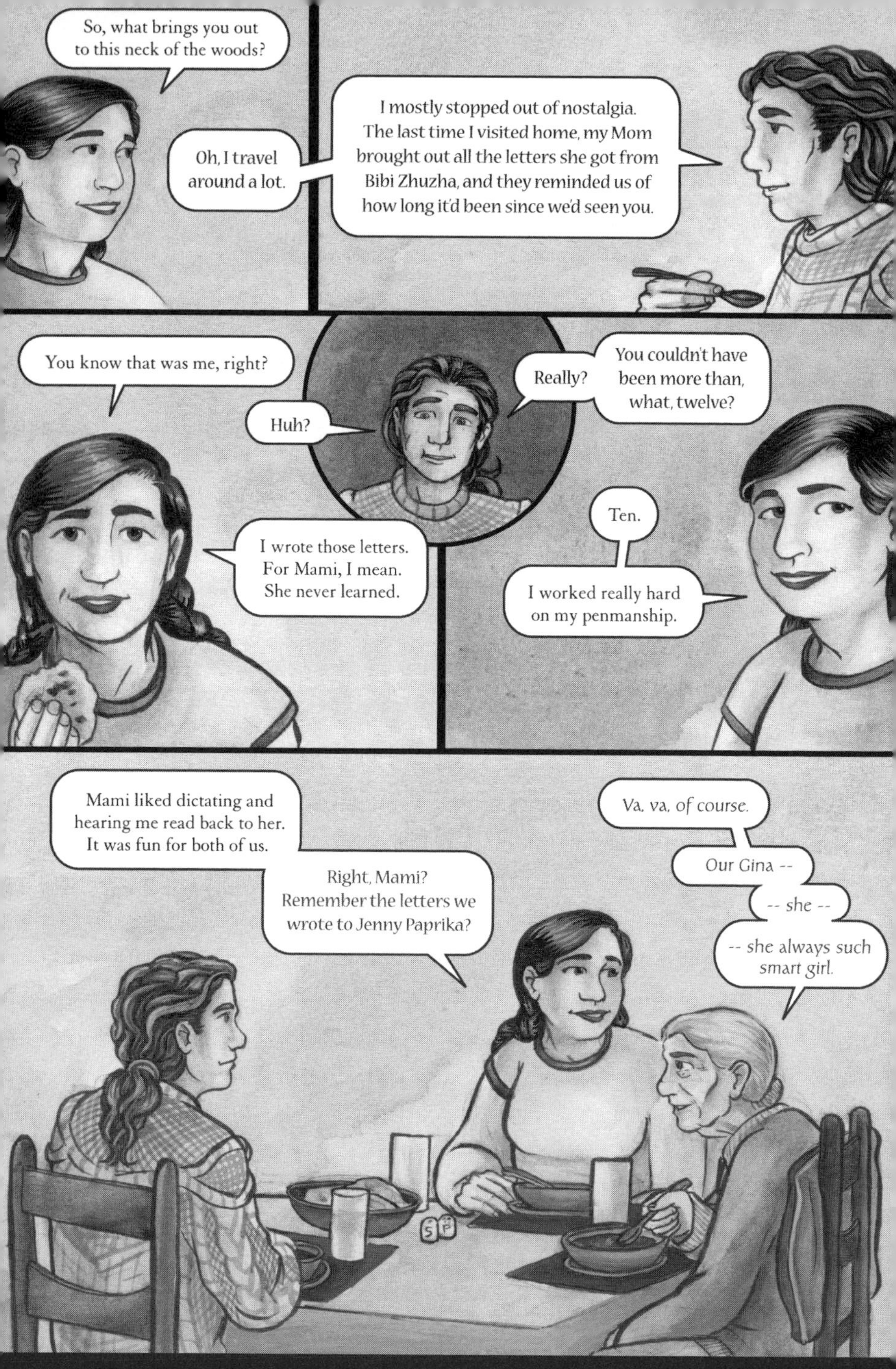
So, what brings you out to this neck of the woods?
Oh, I travel around a lot.
I mostly stopped out of nostalgia. The last time I visited home, my Mom brought out all the letters she got from Bibi Zhuzha, and they reminded us of how long it'd been since we'd seen you.
You know that was me, right?
Huh?
Really?
You couldn't have been more than, what, twelve?
I wrote those letters. For Mami, I mean. She never learned.
Ten.
I worked really hard on my penmanship.
Mami liked dictating and hearing me read back to her. It was fun for both of us.
Right, Mami? Remember the letters we wrote to Jenny Paprika?
Va, va, of course.
Our Gina --
-- she --
-- she always such smart girl.

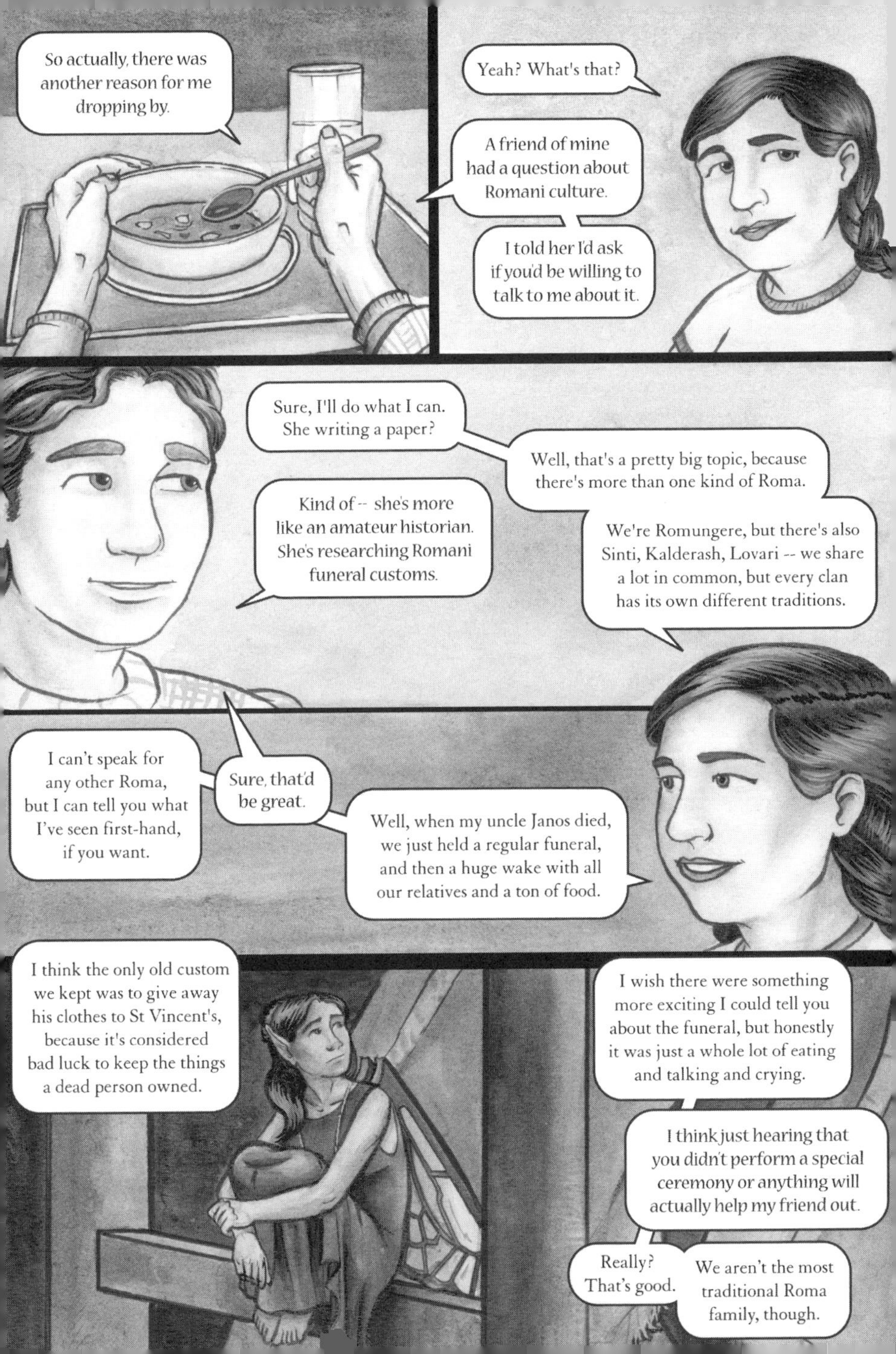

So actually, there was another reason for me dropping by.
Yeah? What's that?
A friend of mine had a question about Romani culture.
I told her I'd ask if you'd be willing to talk to me about it.
Sure, I'll do what I can. She writing a paper?
Kind of -- she's more like an amateur historian. She's researching Romani funeral customs.
Well, that's a pretty big topic, because there's more than one kind of Roma.
We're Romungere, but there's also Sinti, Kalderash, Lovari -- we share a lot in common, but every clan has its own different traditions.
I can't speak for any other Roma, but I can tell you what I've seen first-hand, if you want.
Sure, that'd be great.
Well, when my uncle Janos died, we just held a regular funeral, and then a huge wake with all our relatives and a ton of food.
I think the only old custom we kept was to give away his clothes to St Vincent's, because it's considered bad luck to keep the things a dead person owned.
I wish there were something more exciting I could tell you about the funeral, but honestly it was just a whole lot of eating and talking and crying.
I think just hearing that you didn't perform a special ceremony or anything will actually help my friend out.
Really? That's good.
We aren't the most traditional Roma family, though.

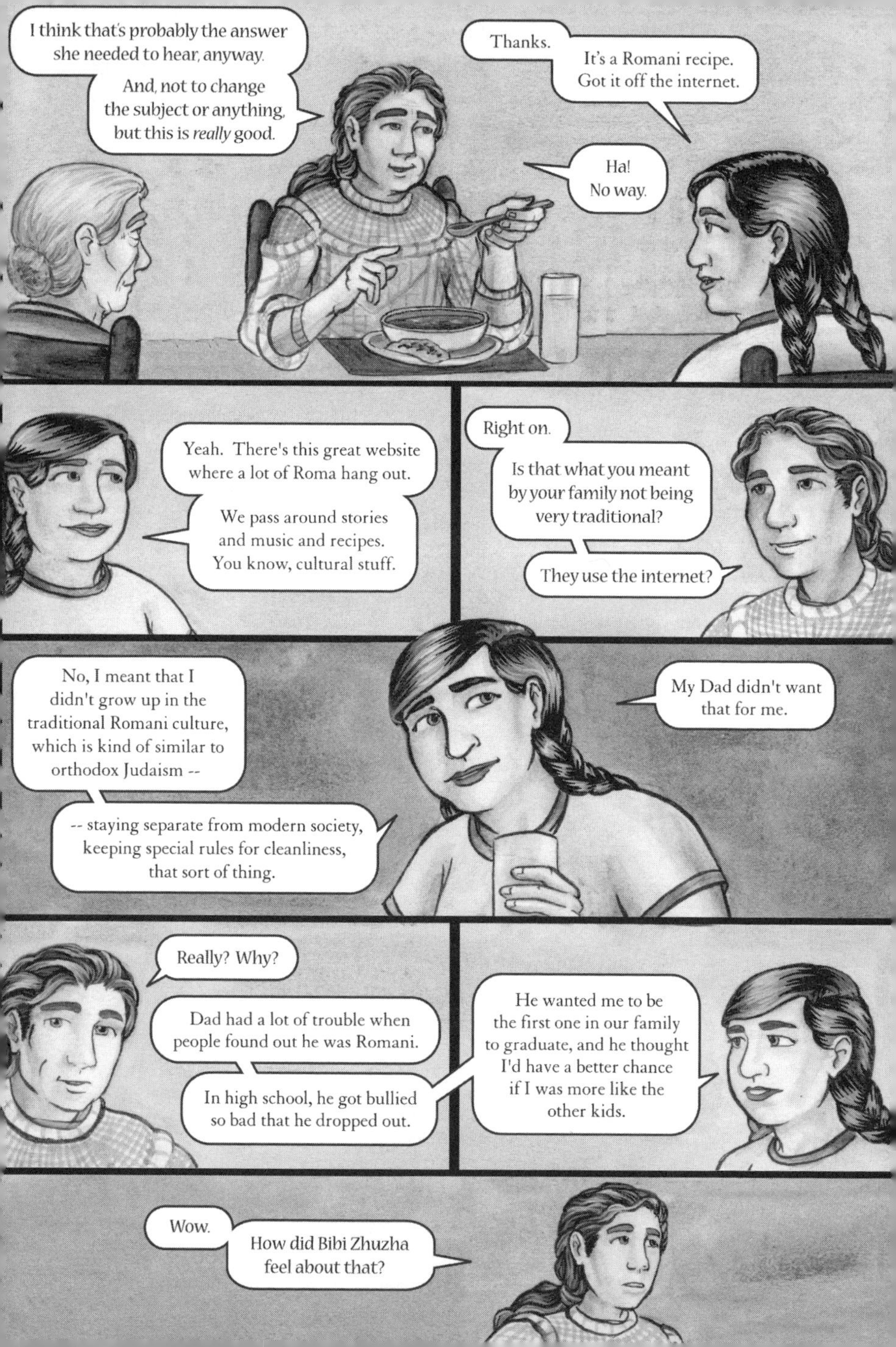
I think that's probably the answer she needed to hear, anyway.
And, not to change the subject or anything, but this is *really* good.
Thanks.
It's a Romani recipe. Got it off the internet.
Ha! No way.
Yeah. There's this great website where a lot of Roma hang out.
We pass around stories and music and recipes. You know, cultural stuff.
Right on.
Is that what you meant by your family not being very traditional?
They use the internet?
No, I meant that I didn't grow up in the traditional Romani culture, which is kind of similar to orthodox Judaism --
-- staying separate from modern society, keeping special rules for cleanliness, that sort of thing.
My Dad didn't want that for me.
Really? Why?
Dad had a lot of trouble when people found out he was Romani.
In high school, he got bullied so bad that he dropped out.
He wanted me to be the first one in our family to graduate, and he thought I'd have a better chance if I was more like the other kids.
Wow.
How did Bibi Zhuzha feel about that?

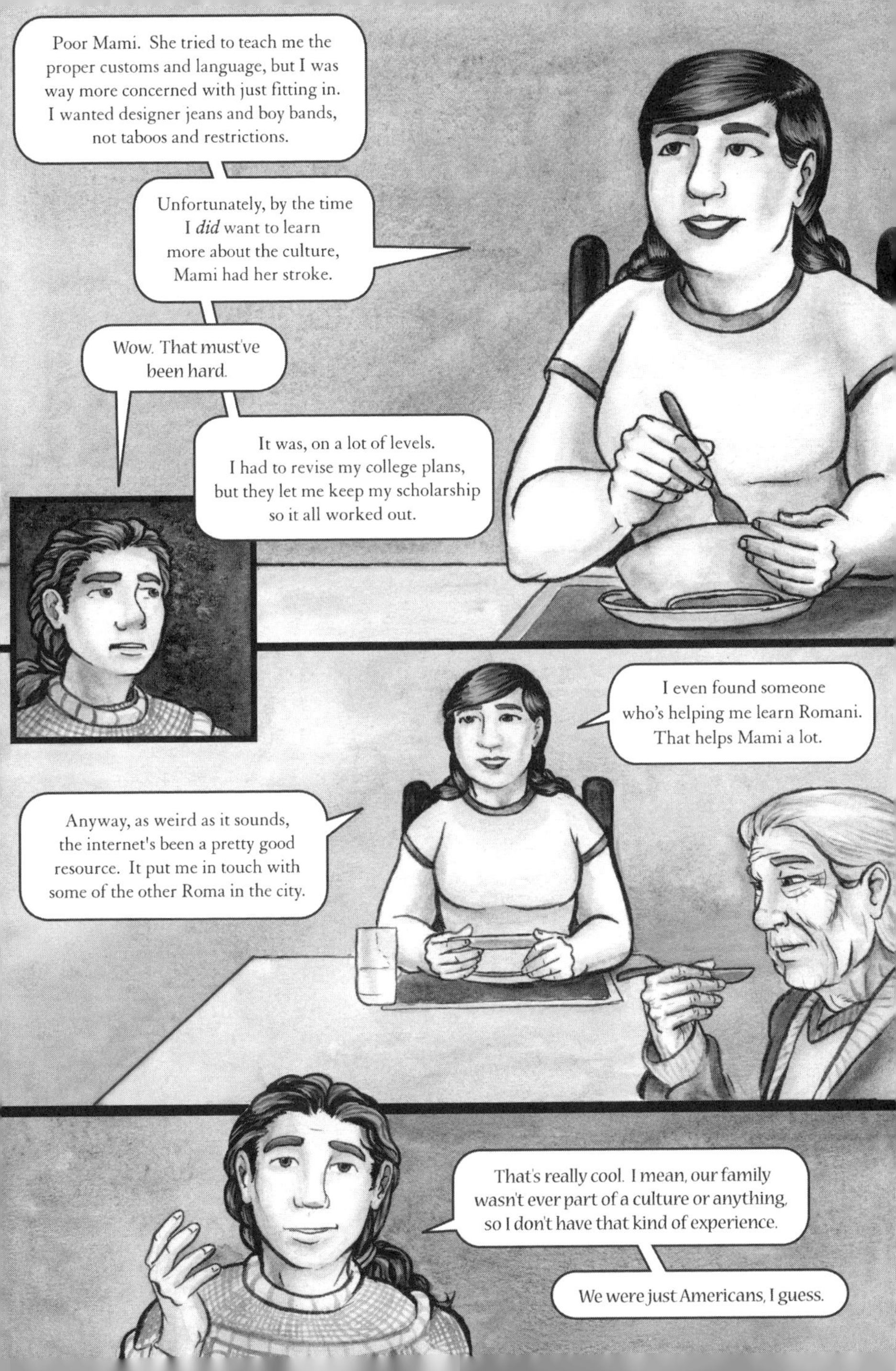
Poor Mami. She tried to teach me the proper customs and language, but I was way more concerned with just fitting in. I wanted designer jeans and boy bands, not taboos and restrictions.
Unfortunately, by the time I *did* want to learn more about the culture, Mami had her stroke.
Wow. That must've been hard.
It was, on a lot of levels. I had to revise my college plans, but they let me keep my scholarship so it all worked out.
I even found someone who's helping me learn Romani. That helps Mami a lot.
Anyway, as weird as it sounds, the internet's been a pretty good resource. It put me in touch with some of the other Roma in the city.
That's really cool. I mean, our family wasn't ever part of a culture or anything, so I don't have that kind of experience.
We were just Americans, I guess.

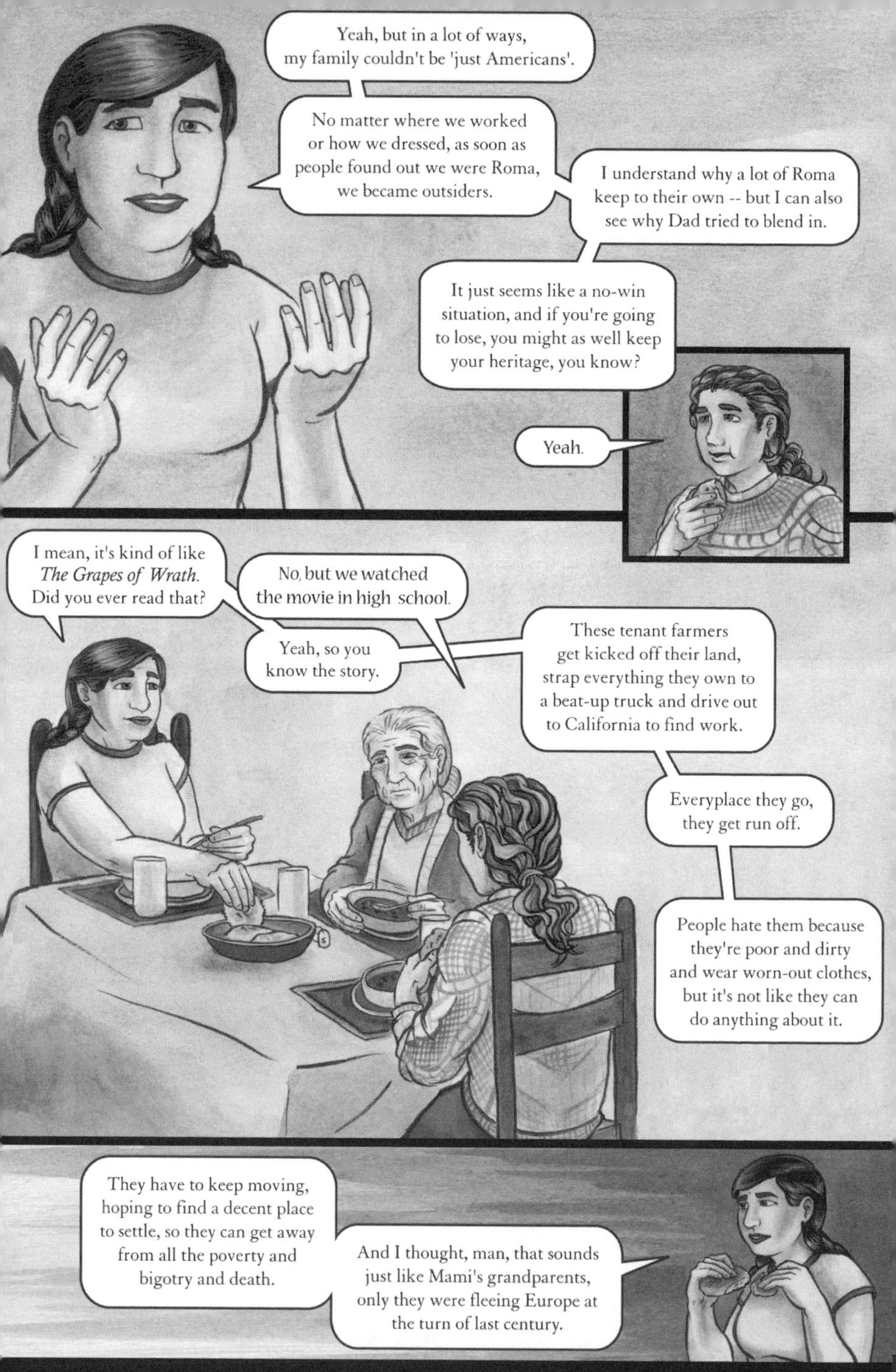
Yeah, but in a lot of ways, my family couldn't be 'just Americans'.
No matter where we worked or how we dressed, as soon as people found out we were Roma, we became outsiders.
I understand why a lot of Roma keep to their own -- but I can also see why Dad tried to blend in.
It just seems like a no-win situation, and if you're going to lose, you might as well keep your heritage, you know?
Yeah.
I mean, it's kind of like *The Grapes of Wrath*. Did you ever read that?
No, but we watched the movie in high school.
Yeah, so you know the story.
These tenant farmers get kicked off their land, strap everything they own to a beat-up truck and drive out to California to find work.
Everyplace they go, they get run off.
People hate them because they're poor and dirty and wear worn-out clothes, but it's not like they can do anything about it.
They have to keep moving, hoping to find a decent place to settle, so they can get away from all the poverty and bigotry and death.
And I thought, man, that sounds just like Mami's grandparents, only they were fleeing Europe at the turn of last century.

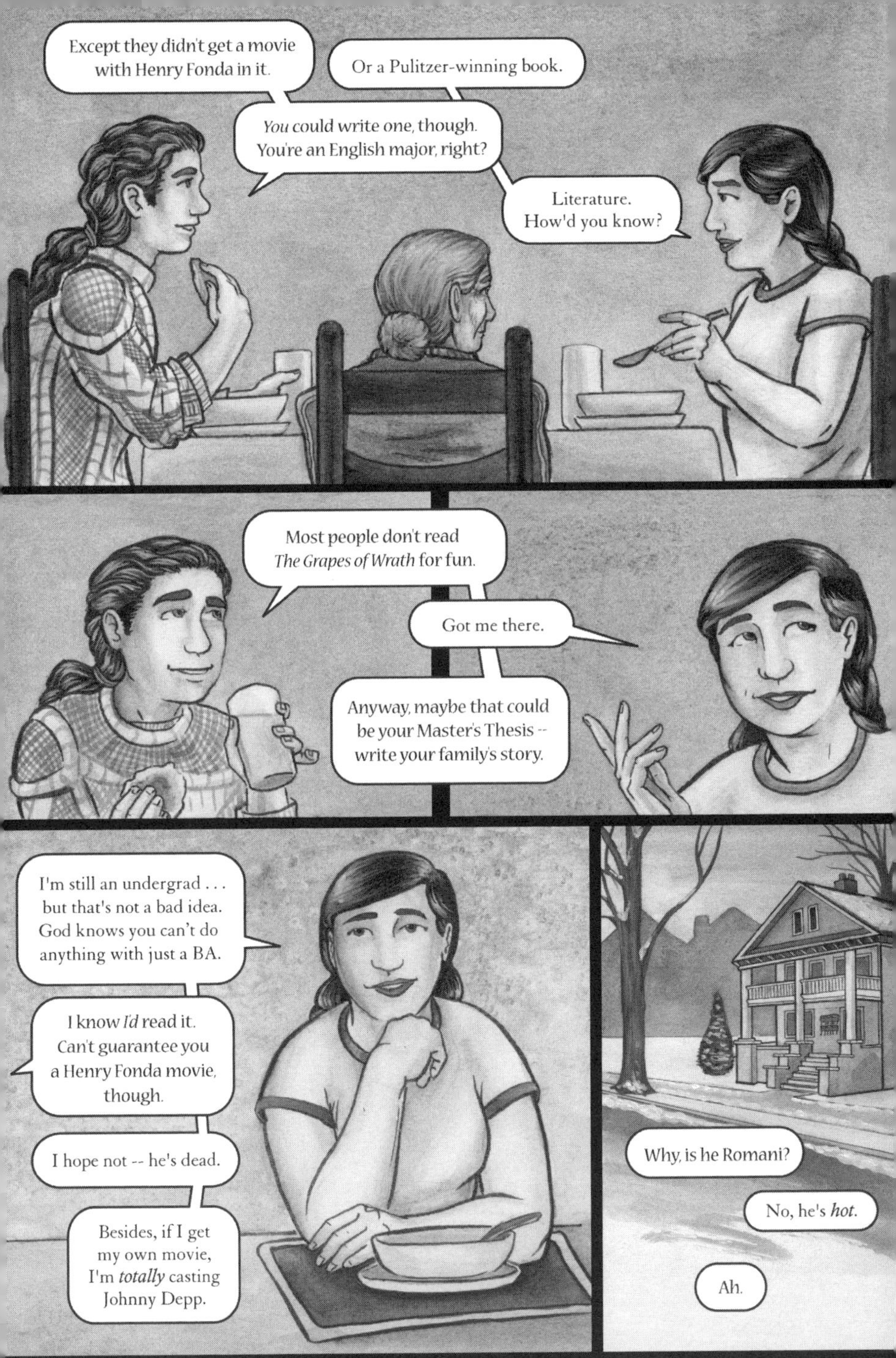
Except they didn't get a movie with Henry Fonda in it.
Or a Pulitzer-winning book.
You could write one, though. You're an English major, right?
Literature. How'd you know?
Most people don't read *The Grapes of Wrath* for fun.
Got me there.
Anyway, maybe that could be your Master's Thesis -- write your family's story.
I'm still an undergrad . . . but that's not a bad idea. God knows you can't do anything with just a BA.
I know *I'd* read it. Can't guarantee you a Henry Fonda movie, though.
I hope not -- he's dead.
Besides, if I get my own movie, I'm *totally* casting Johnny Depp.
Why, is he Romani?
No, he's *hot*.
Ah.

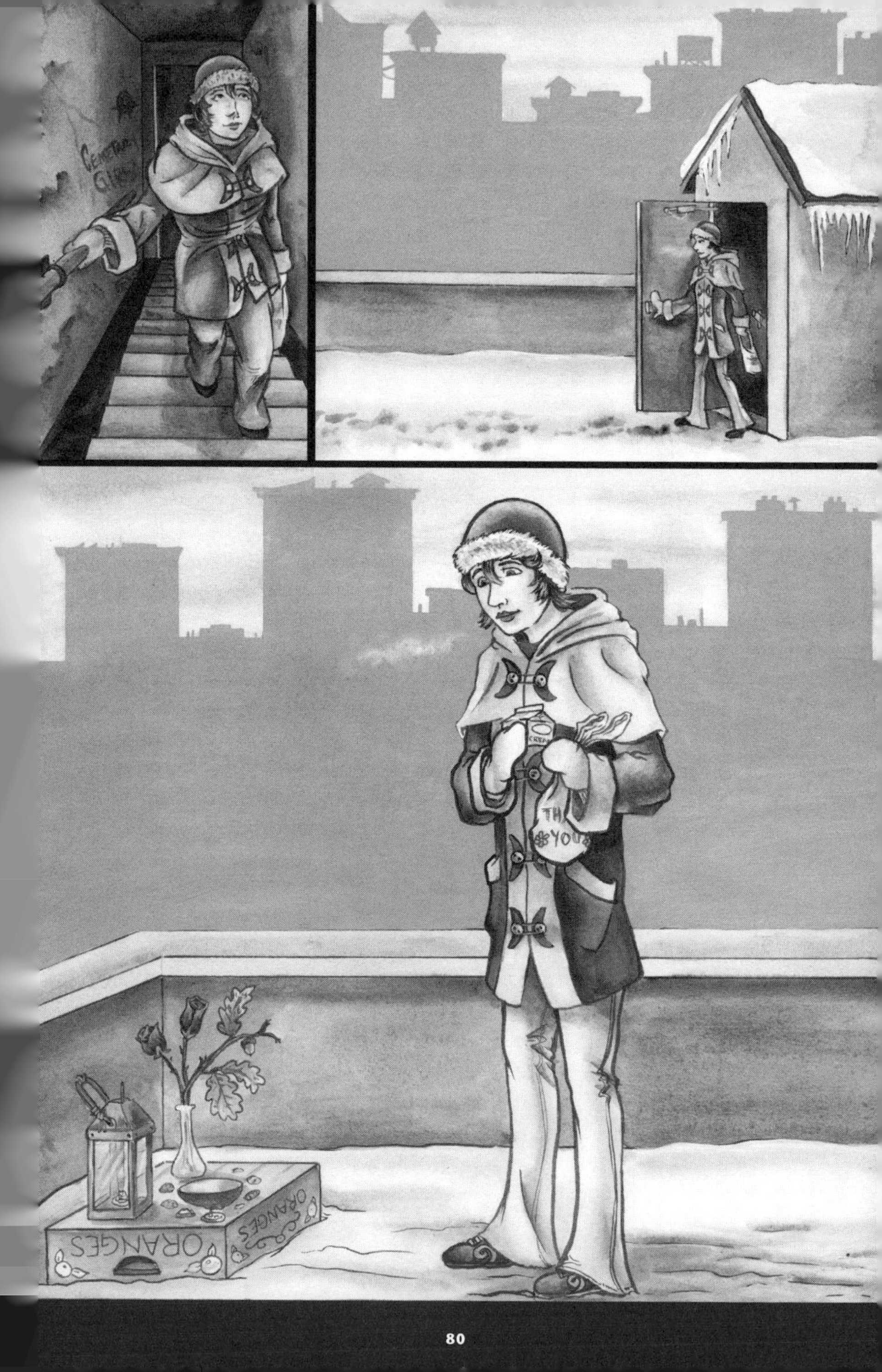
ORANGES
ORANGES

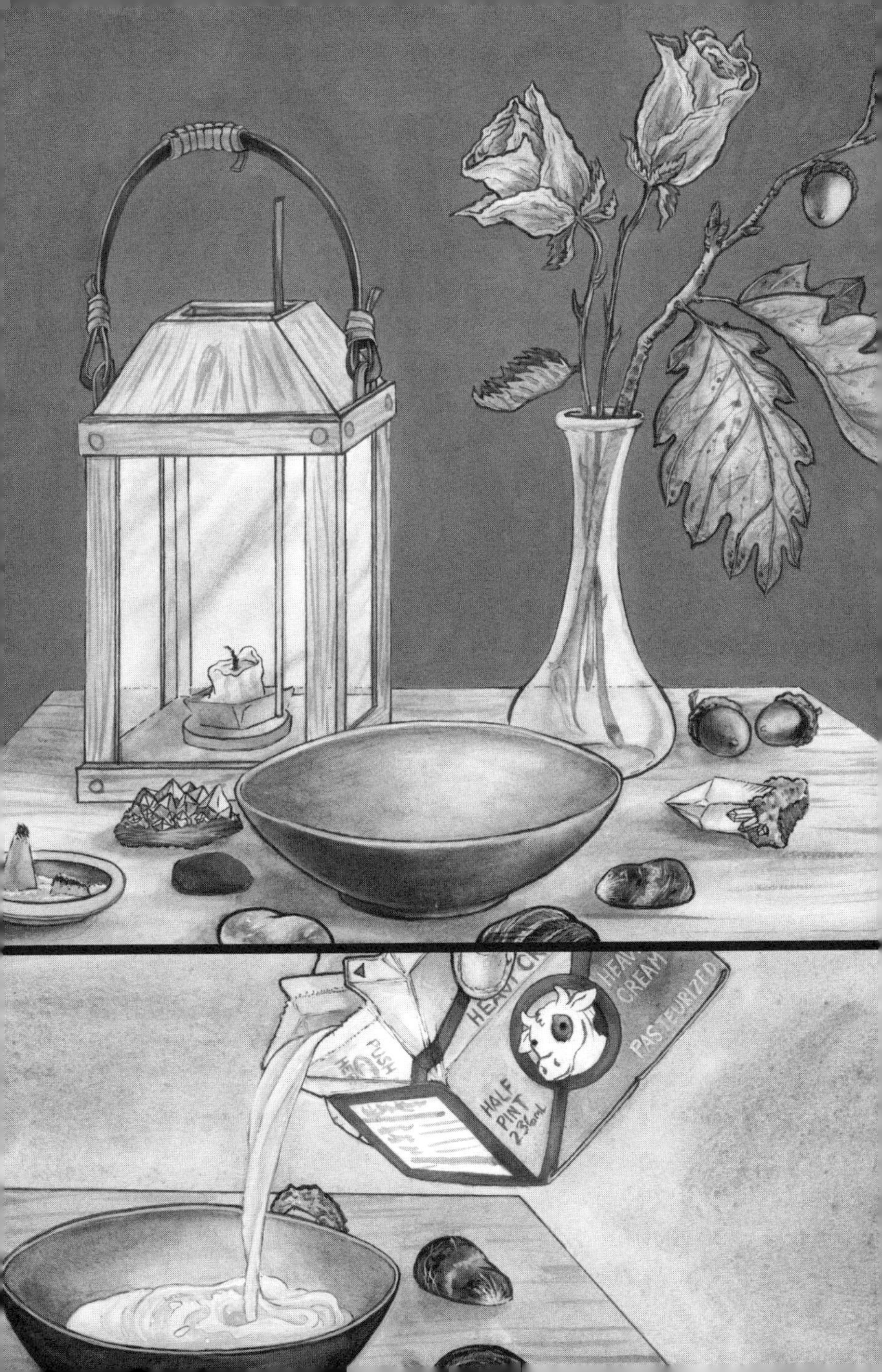

CREAM
PASTEURIZED
PUSH
HALF PINT 236mL

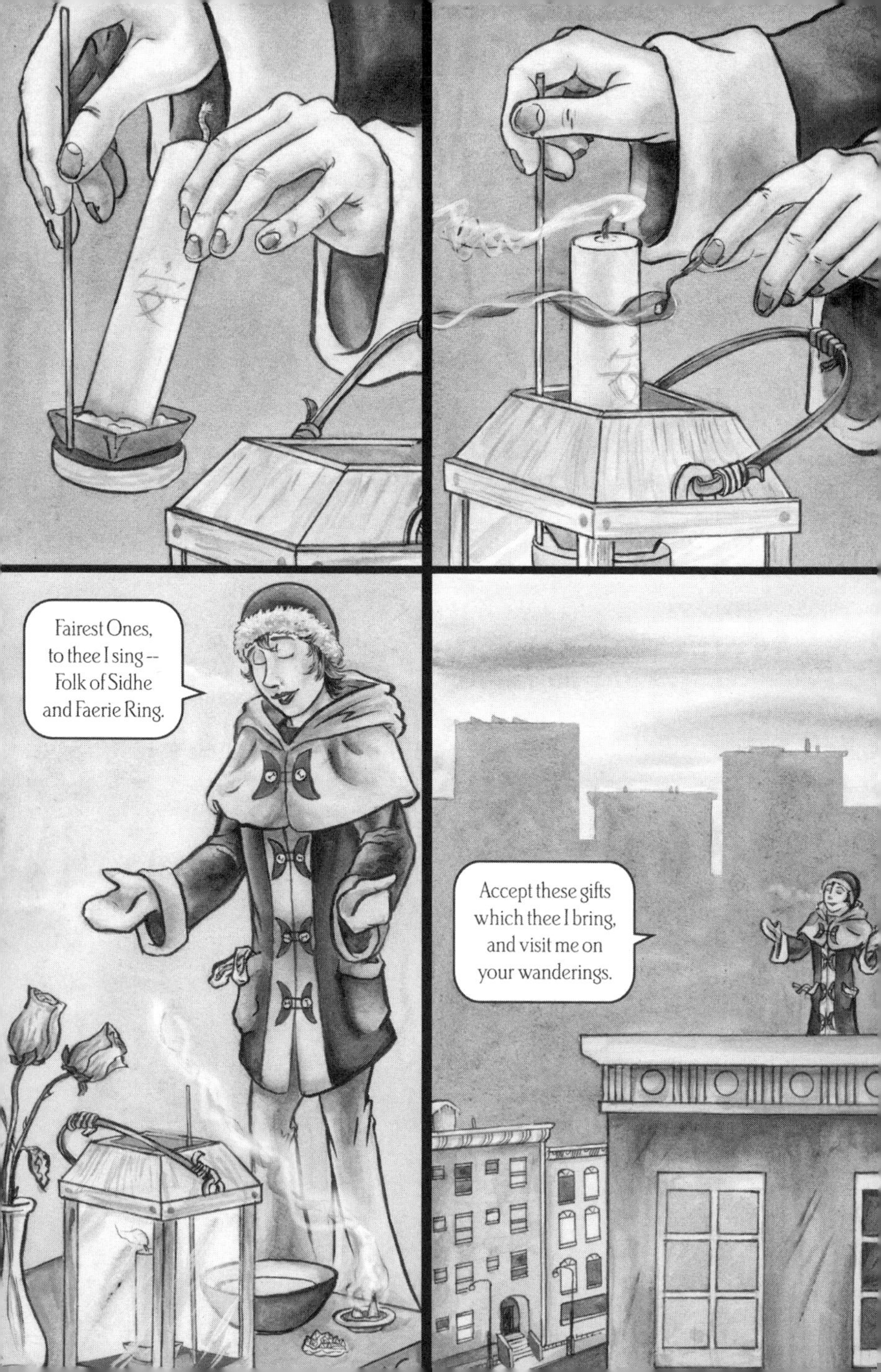
Fairest Ones, to thee I sing -- Folk of Sidhe and Faerie Ring.
Accept these gifts which thee I bring, and visit me on your wanderings.

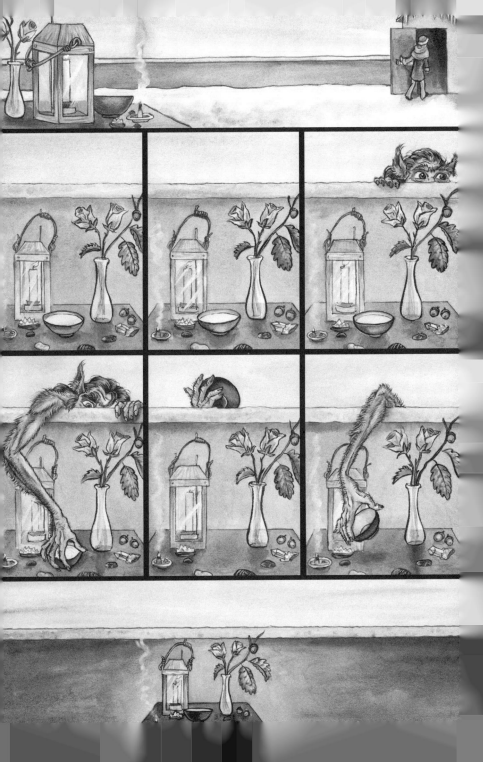

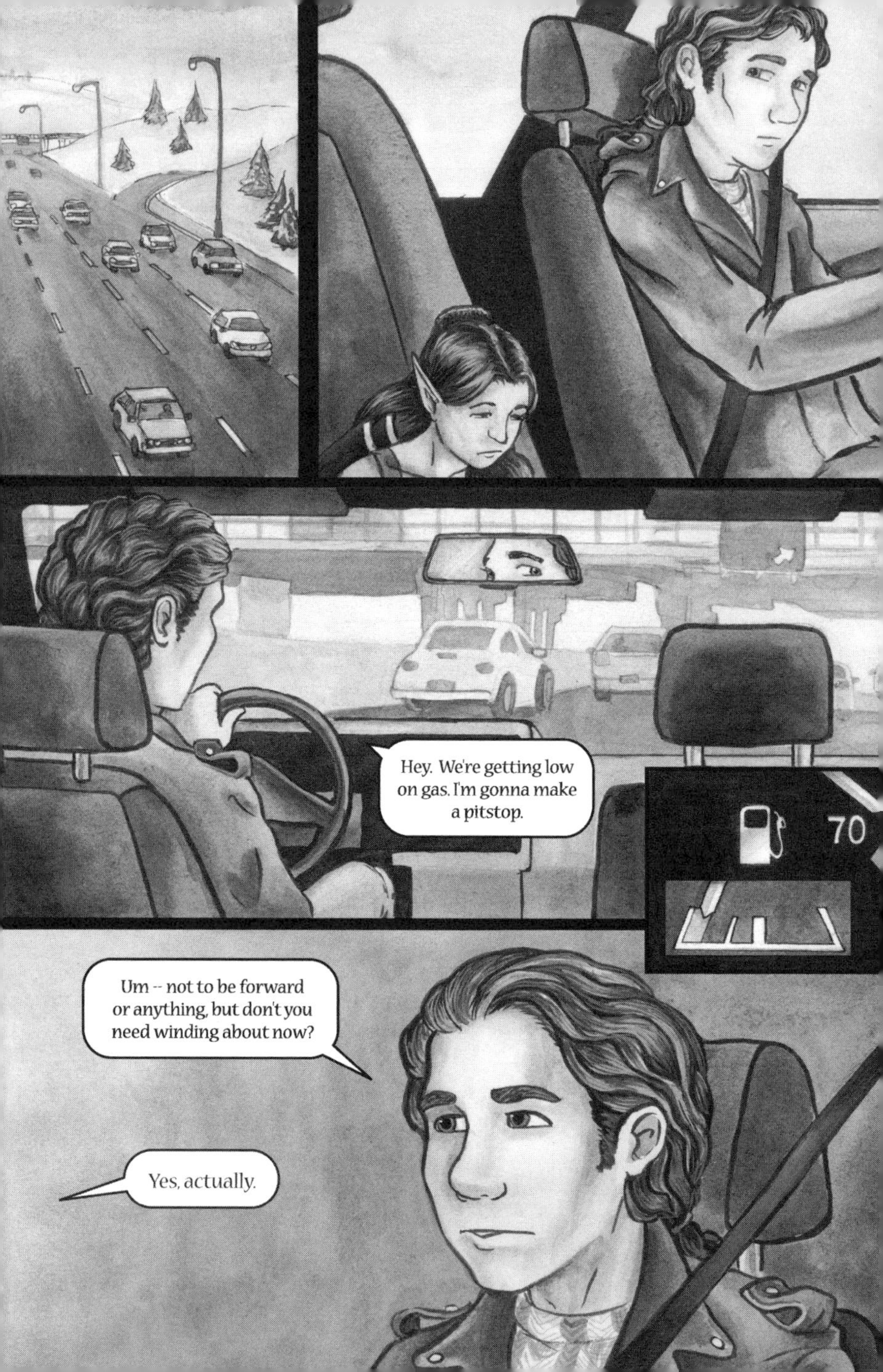
70
Hey. We're getting low on gas. I'm gonna make a pitstop.
Um -- not to be forward or anything, but don't you need winding about now?
Yes, actually.

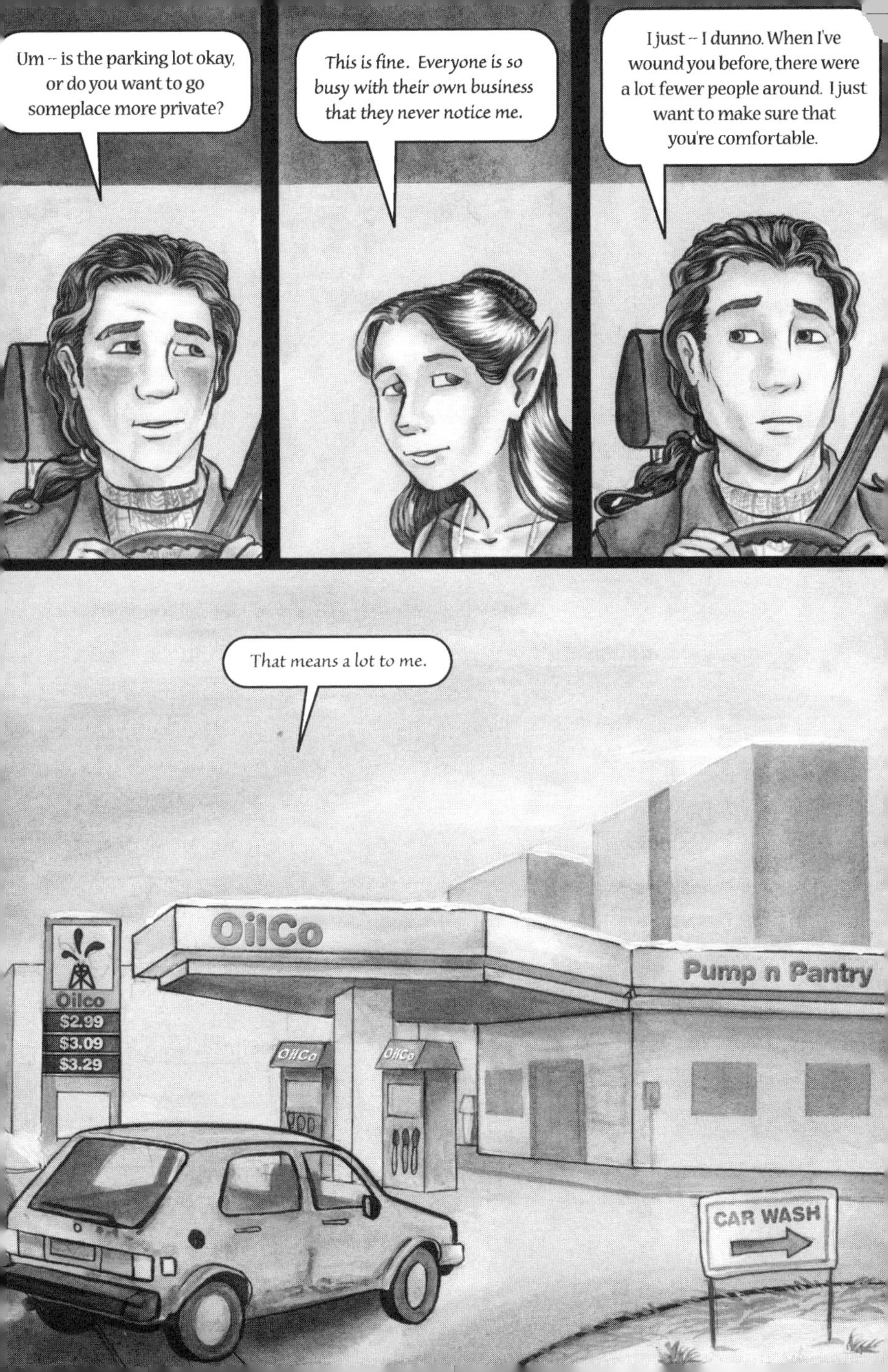
Um -- is the parking lot okay, or do you want to go someplace more private?
This is fine. Everyone is so busy with their own business that they never notice me.
I just -- I dunno. When I've wound you before, there were a lot fewer people around. I just want to make sure that you're comfortable.
That means a lot to me.
OilCo
Oilco
$2.99
$3.09
$3.29
OilCo
OilCo
Pump n Pantry
CAR WASH

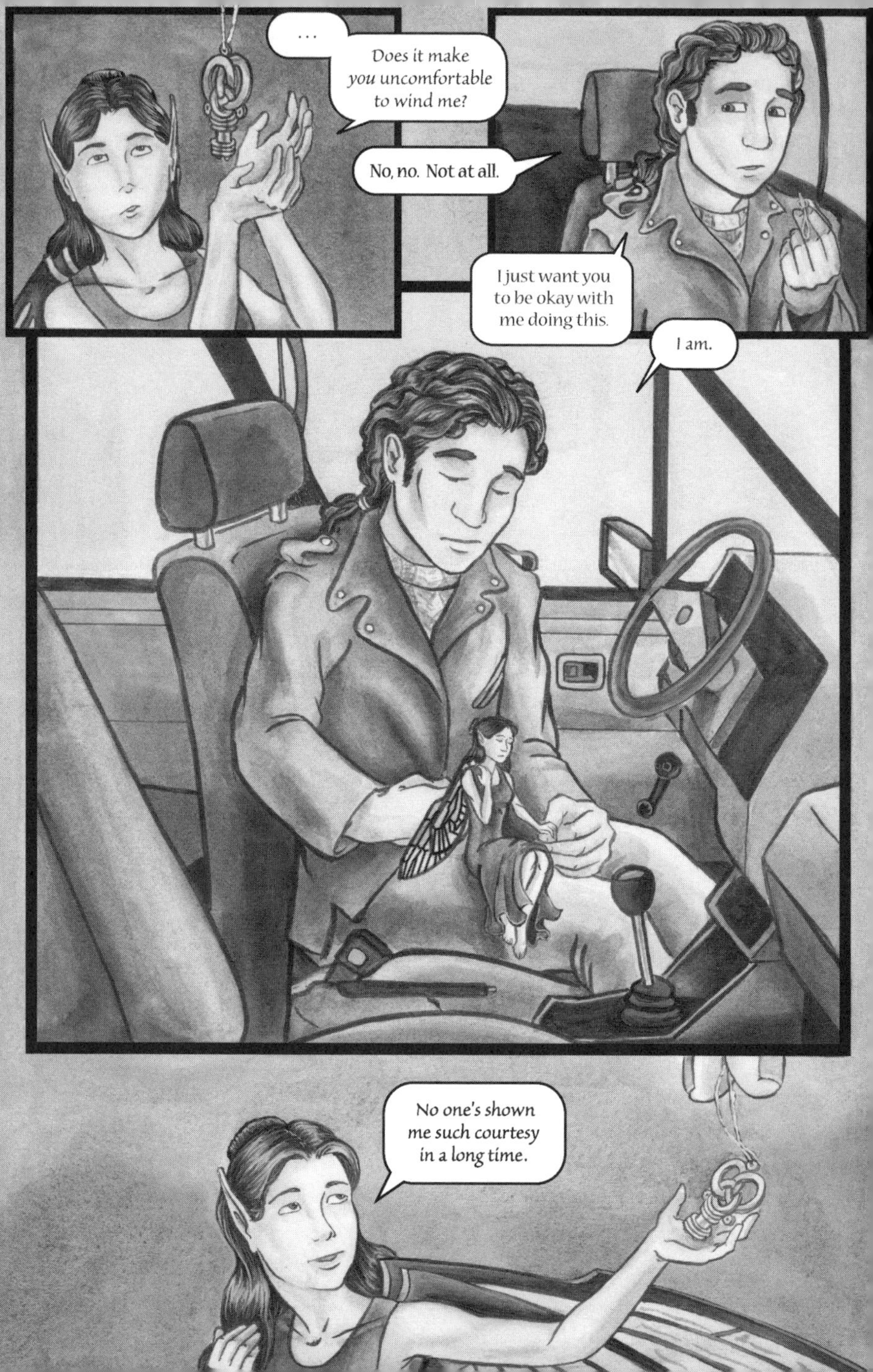
. . .
Does it make you uncomfortable to wind me?
No, no. Not at all.
I just want you to be okay with me doing this.
I am.
No one's shown me such courtesy in a long time.

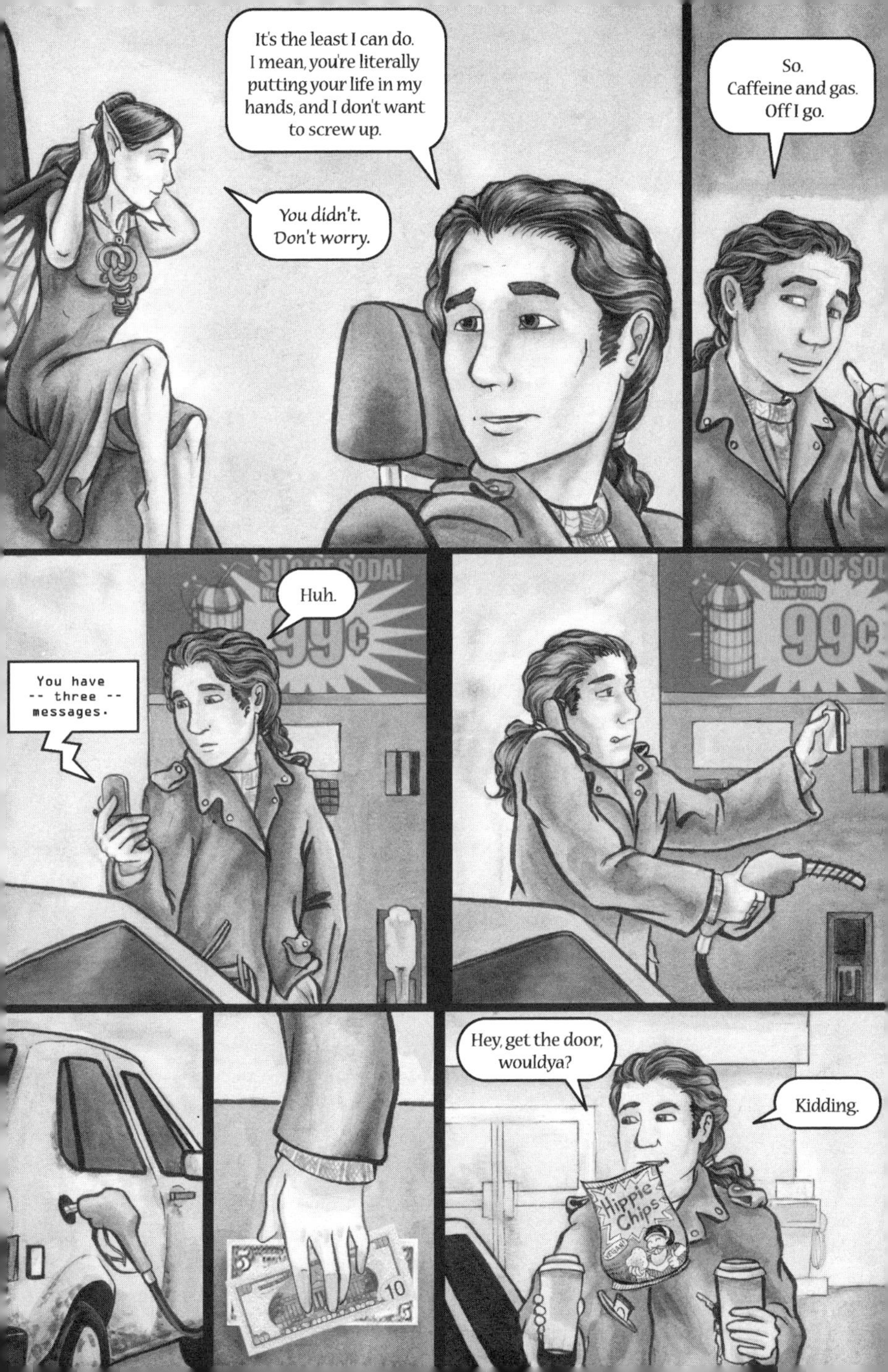
It's the least I can do. I mean, you're literally putting your life in my hands, and I don't want to screw up.
You didn't. Don't worry.
So. Caffeine and gas. Off I go.
SILO OF SODA!
99¢
You have -- three -- messages.
Huh.
SILO OF SOD
Now only
99¢
Hey, get the door, wouldya?
Hippie Chips
Kidding.

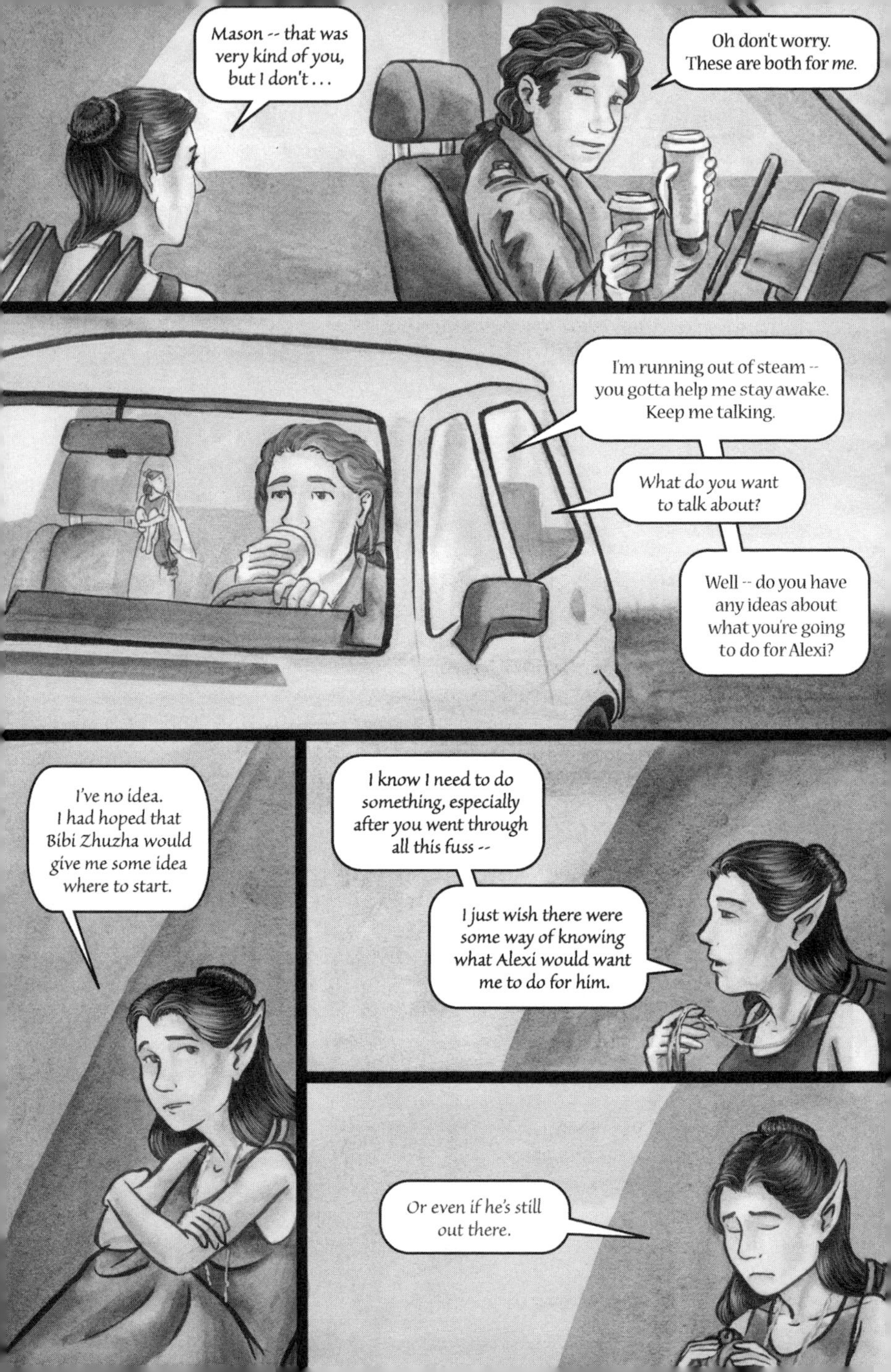
Mason -- that was very kind of you, but I don't . . .
Oh don't worry. These are both for *me*.
I'm running out of steam -- you gotta help me stay awake. Keep me talking.
What do you want to talk about?
Well -- do you have any ideas about what you're going to do for Alexi?
I've no idea. I had hoped that Bibi Zhuzha would give me some idea where to start.
I know I need to do something, especially after you went through all this fuss --
I just wish there were some way of knowing what Alexi would want me to do for him.
Or even if he's still out there.

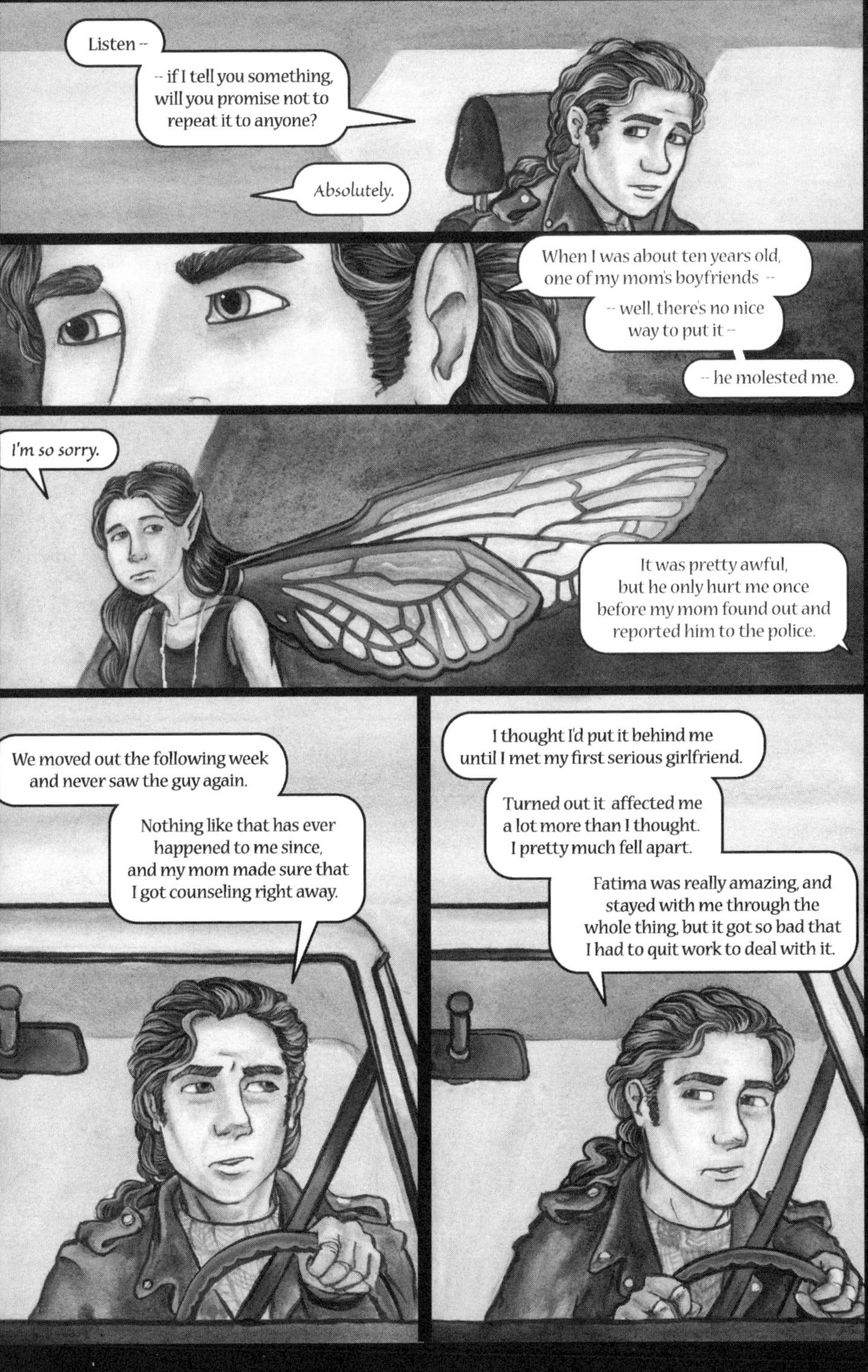
Listen --
-- if I tell you something, will you promise not to repeat it to anyone?
Absolutely.
When I was about ten years old, one of my mom's boyfriends --
-- well, there's no nice way to put it --
-- he molested me.
I'm so sorry.
It was pretty awful, but he only hurt me once before my mom found out and reported him to the police.
We moved out the following week and never saw the guy again.
Nothing like that has ever happened to me since, and my mom made sure that I got counseling right away.
I thought I'd put it behind me until I met my first serious girlfriend.
Turned out it affected me a lot more than I thought. I pretty much fell apart.
Fatima was really amazing, and stayed with me through the whole thing, but it got so bad that I had to quit work to deal with it.

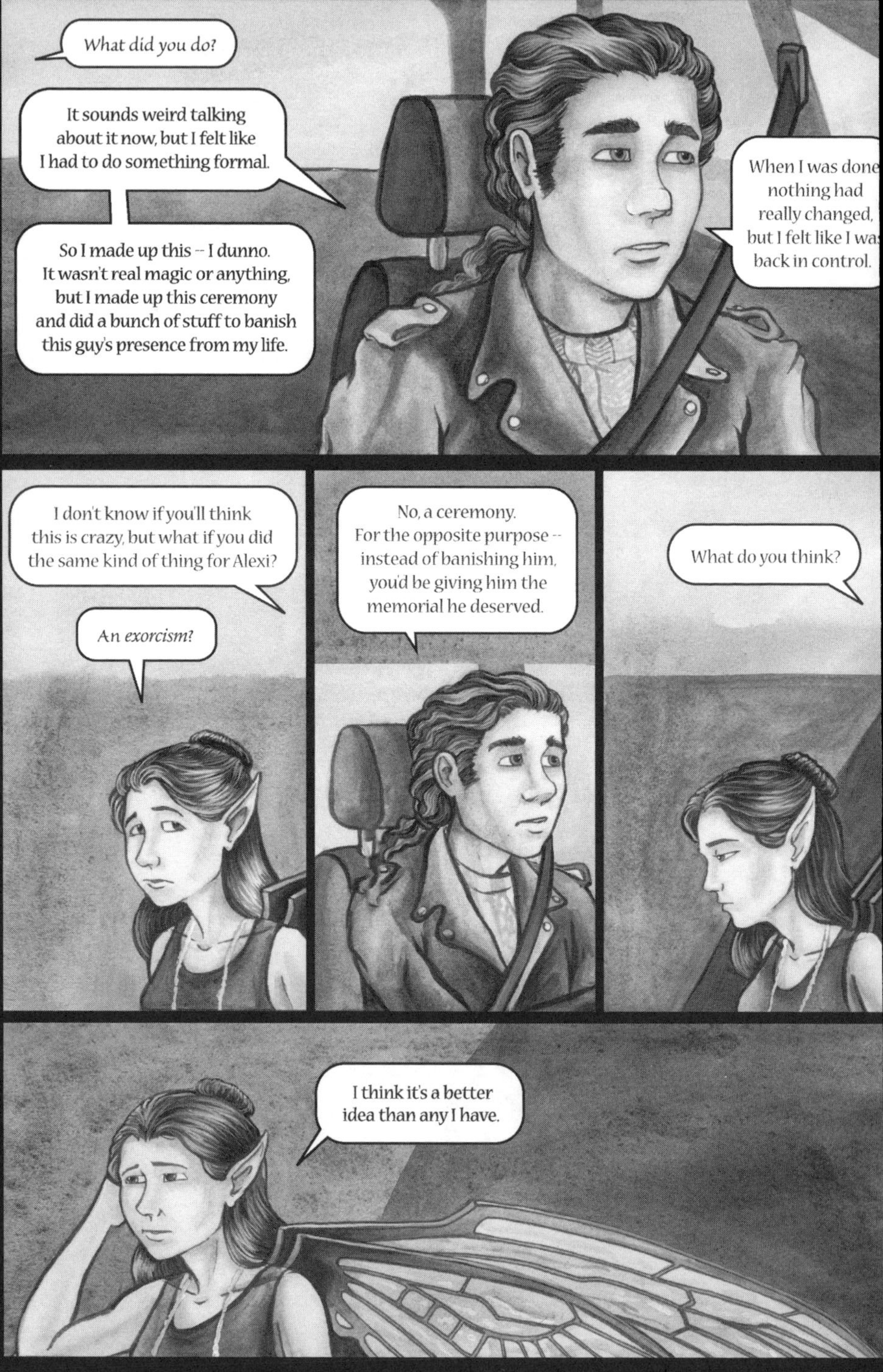
What did you do?
It sounds weird talking about it now, but I felt like I had to do something formal.
So I made up this -- I dunno. It wasn't real magic or anything, but I made up this ceremony and did a bunch of stuff to banish this guy's presence from my life.
When I was done nothing had really changed, but I felt like I wa back in control.
I don't know if you'll think this is crazy, but what if you did the same kind of thing for Alexi?
An *exorcism*?
No, a ceremony. For the opposite purpose -- instead of banishing him, you'd be giving him the memorial he deserved.
What do you think?
I think it's a better idea than any I have.

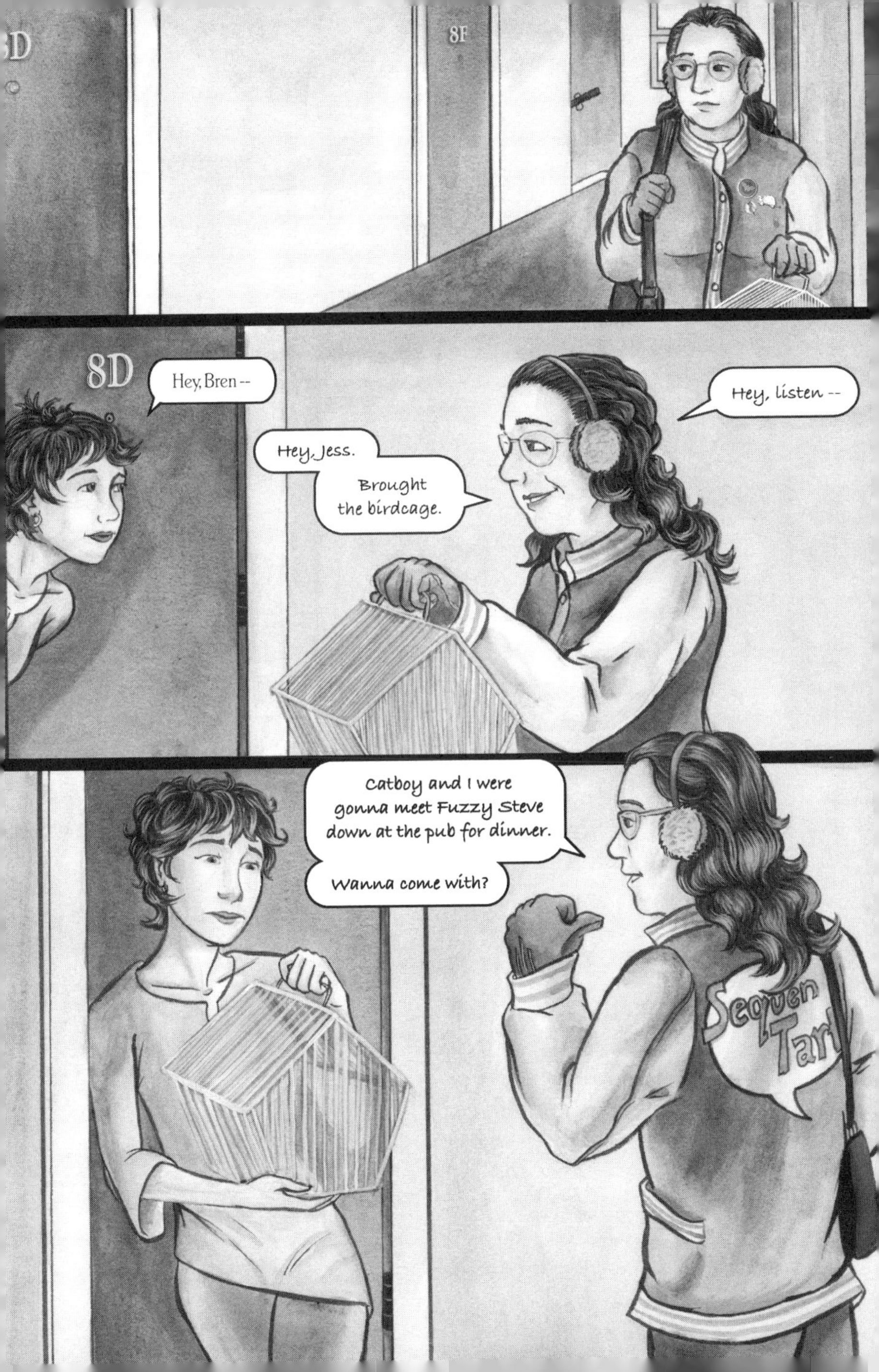
8F
8D
Hey, Bren --
Hey, Jess.
Brought the birdcage.
Hey, listen --
Catboy and I were gonna meet Fuzzy Steve down at the pub for dinner.
Wanna come with?
Sequen Tart

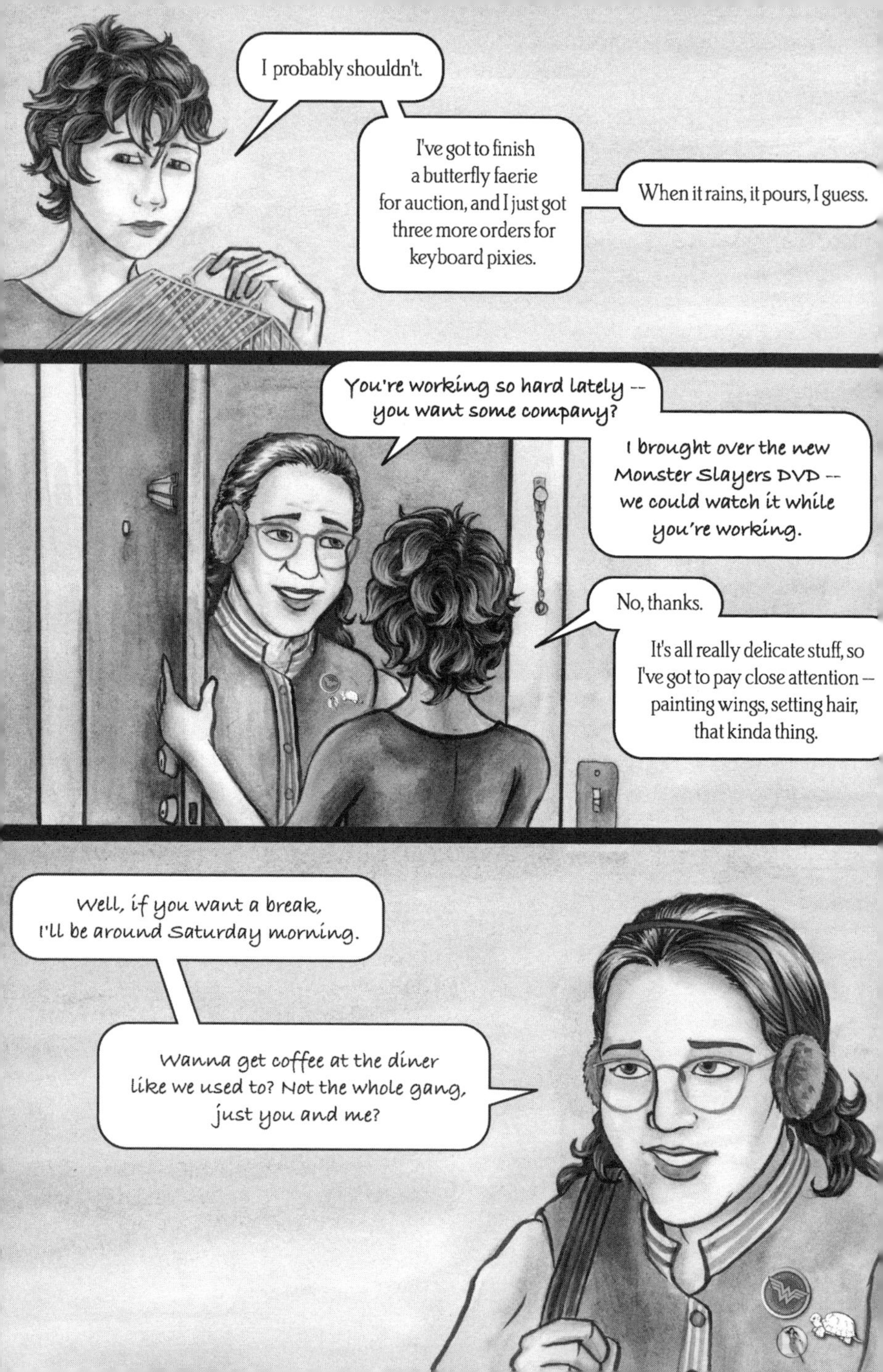
I probably shouldn't.
I've got to finish a butterfly faerie for auction, and I just got three more orders for keyboard pixies.
When it rains, it pours, I guess.
You're working so hard lately -- you want some company?
I brought over the new Monster Slayers DVD -- we could watch it while you're working.
No, thanks.
It's all really delicate stuff, so I've got to pay close attention -- painting wings, setting hair, that kinda thing.
Well, if you want a break, I'll be around Saturday morning.
Wanna get coffee at the diner like we used to? Not the whole gang, just you and me?

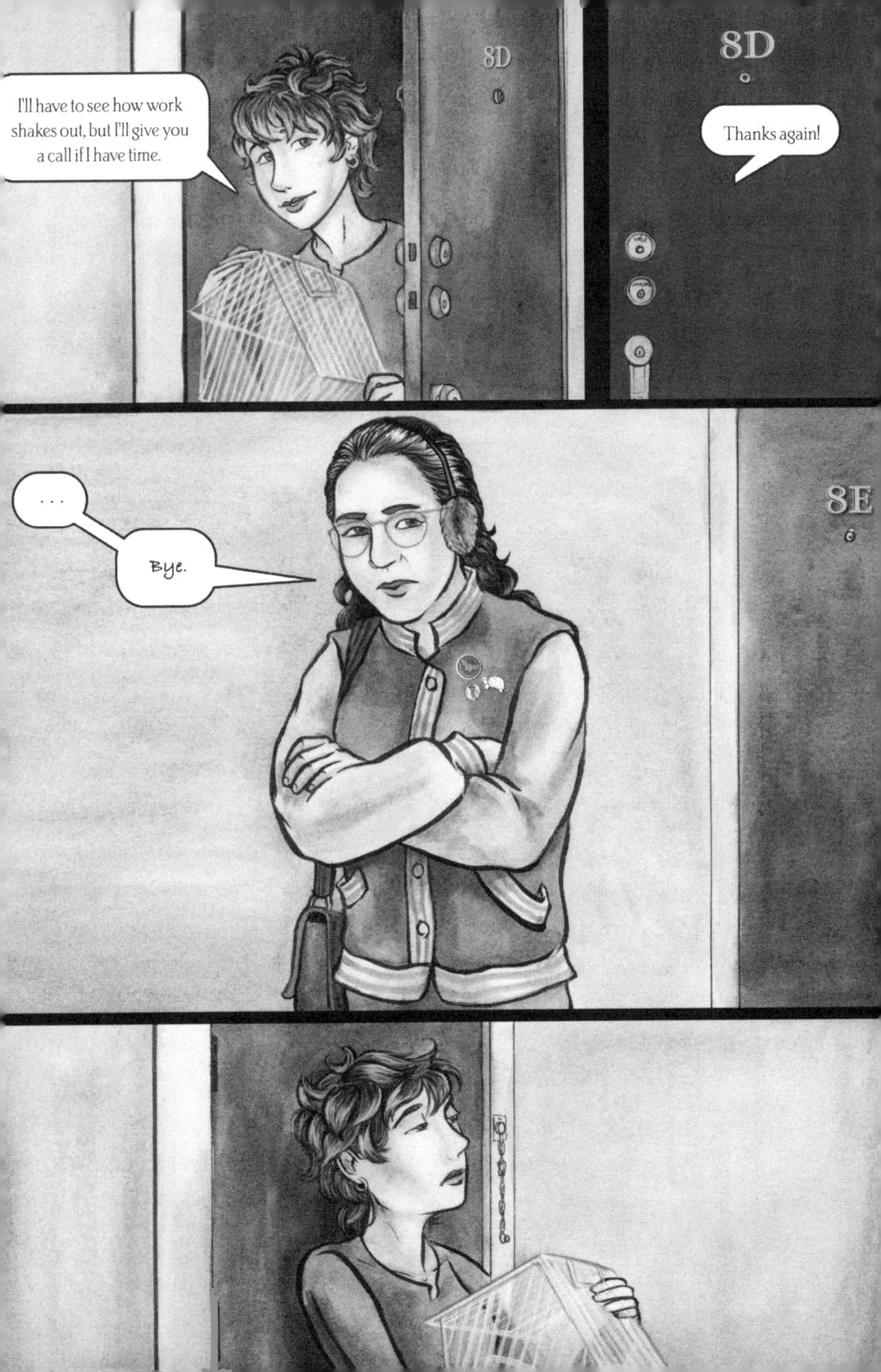
8D
I'll have to see how work shakes out, but I'll give you a call if I have time.
8D
Thanks again!
...
Bye.
8E

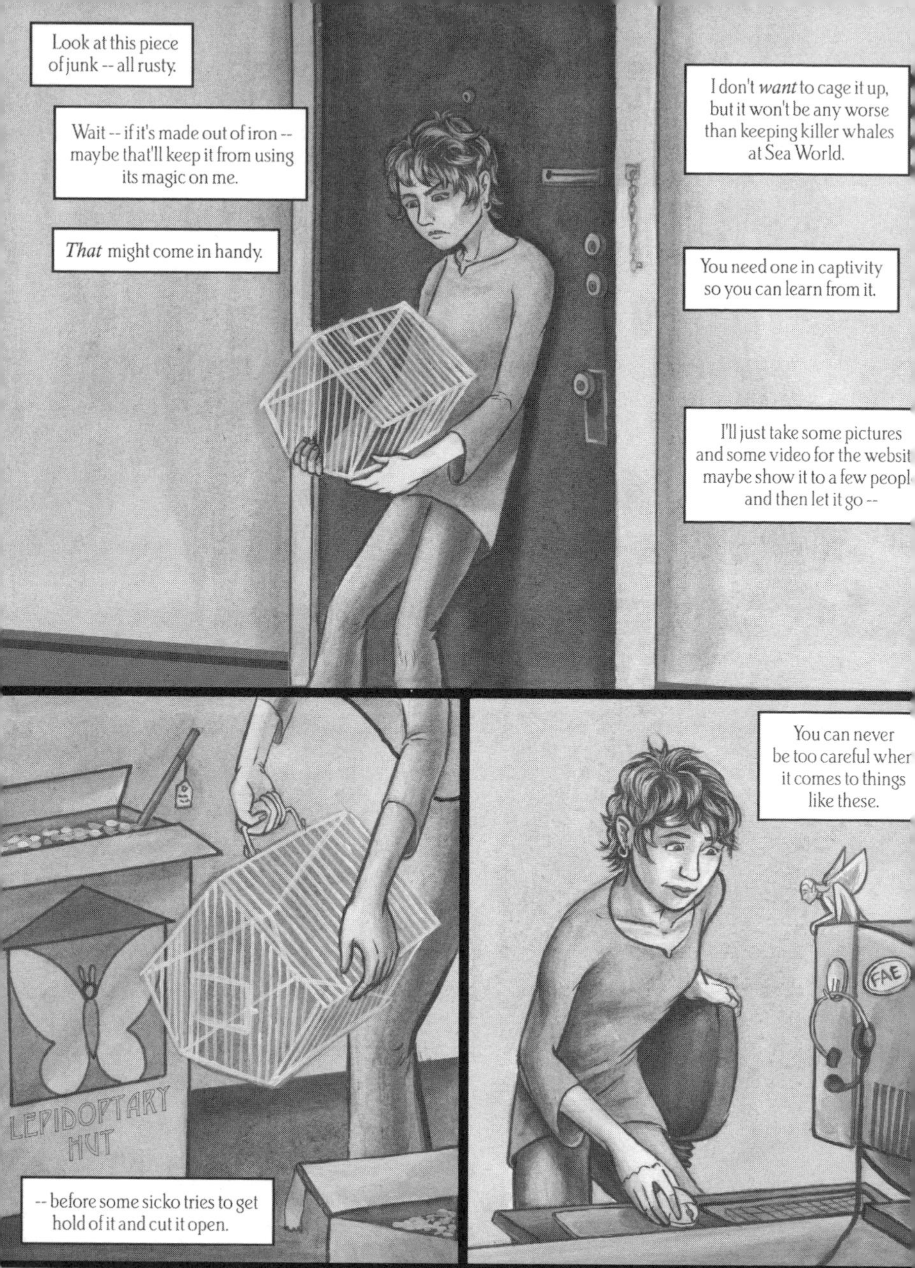
Look at this piece of junk -- all rusty.
Wait -- if it's made out of iron -- maybe that'll keep it from using its magic on me.
That might come in handy.
I don't *want* to cage it up, but it won't be any worse than keeping killer whales at Sea World.
You need one in captivity so you can learn from it.
I'll just take some pictures and some video for the websit maybe show it to a few peopl and then let it go --
LEPIDOPTARY HUT
-- before some sicko tries to get hold of it and cut it open.
You can never be too careful wher it comes to things like these.
FAE

Update your DAILYDIARY: *FaeWatch*

Subject: Almost There!

Entry: The last of my supplies arrived today! If this pans out, we can start doing away with glittery Hollywood misconceptions of the Fair Folk --

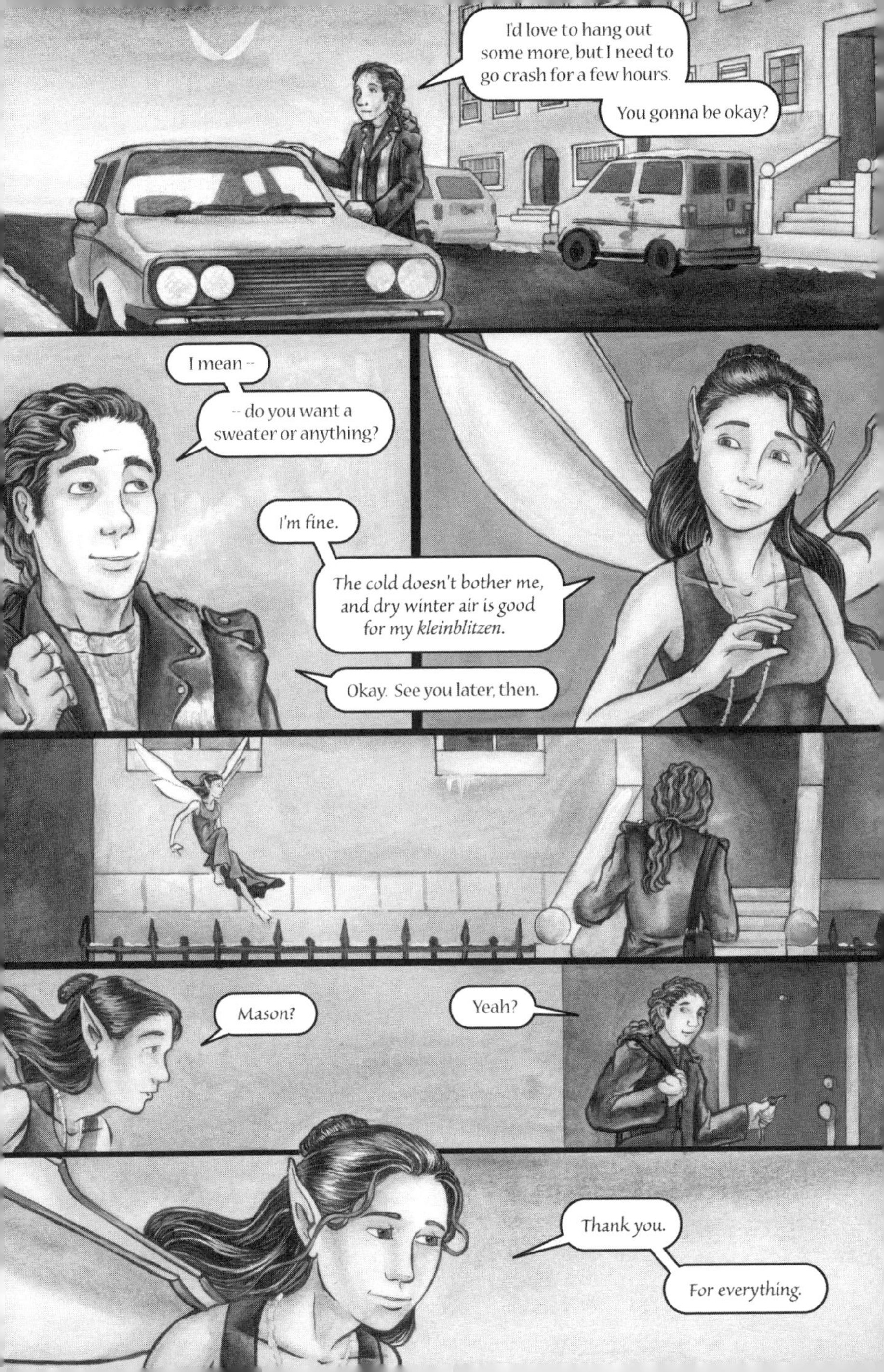
I'd love to hang out some more, but I need to go crash for a few hours.
You gonna be okay?
I mean --
-- do you want a sweater or anything?
I'm fine.
The cold doesn't bother me, and dry winter air is good for my *kleinblitzen*.
Okay. See you later, then.
Mason?
Yeah?
Thank you.
For everything.

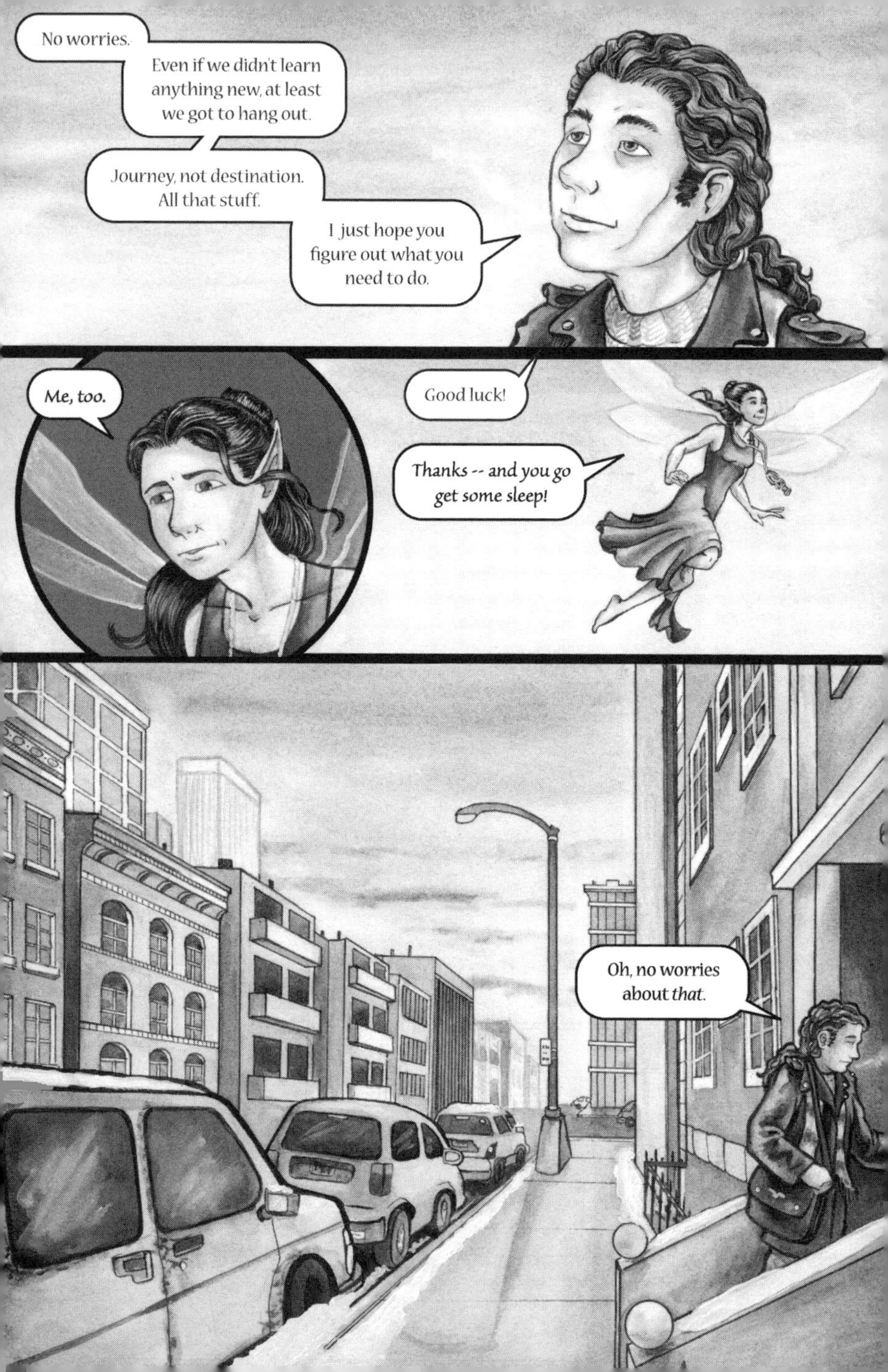
No worries.
Even if we didn't learn anything new, at least we got to hang out.
Journey, not destination. All that stuff.
I just hope you figure out what you need to do.
Me, too.
Good luck!
Thanks -- and you go get some sleep!
Oh, no worries about *that*.

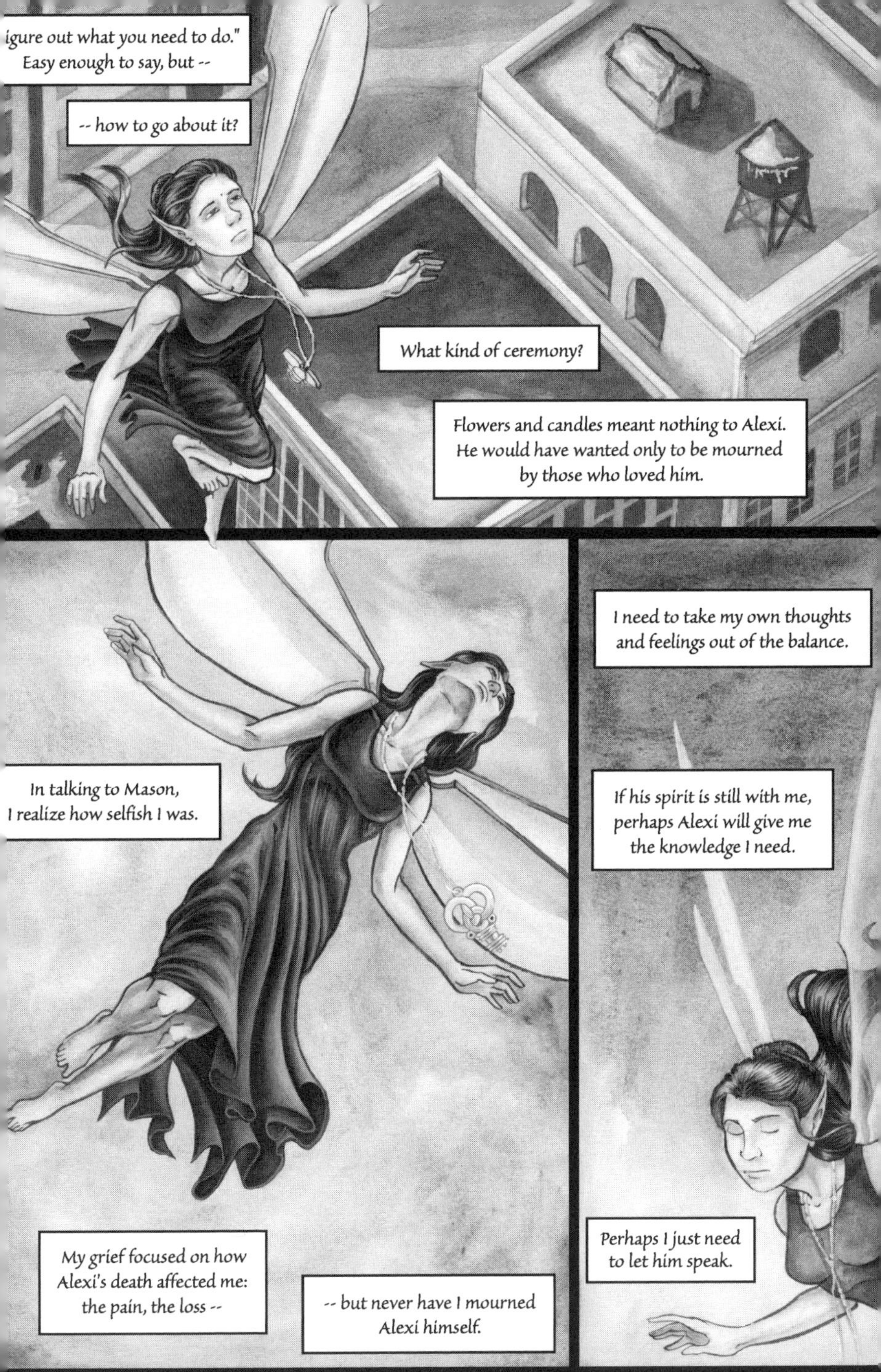
igure out what you need to do." Easy enough to say, but --
-- how to go about it?
What kind of ceremony?
Flowers and candles meant nothing to Alexi. He would have wanted only to be mourned by those who loved him.
In talking to Mason, I realize how selfish I was.
My grief focused on how Alexi's death affected me: the pain, the loss --
-- but never have I mourned Alexi himself.
I need to take my own thoughts and feelings out of the balance.
If his spirit is still with me, perhaps Alexi will give me the knowledge I need.
Perhaps I just need to let him speak.

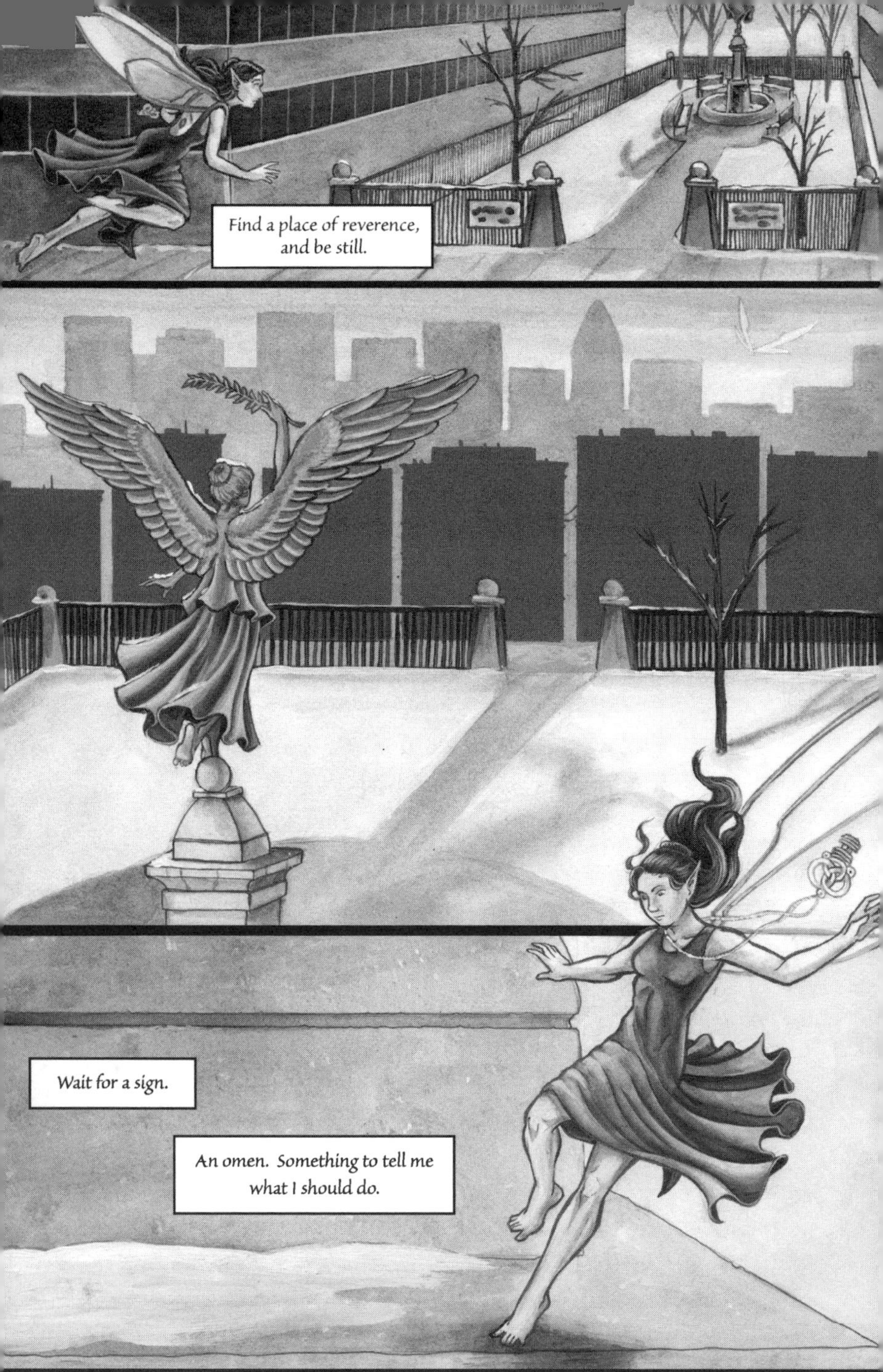
Find a place of reverence, and be still.
Wait for a sign.
An omen. Something to tell me what I should do.

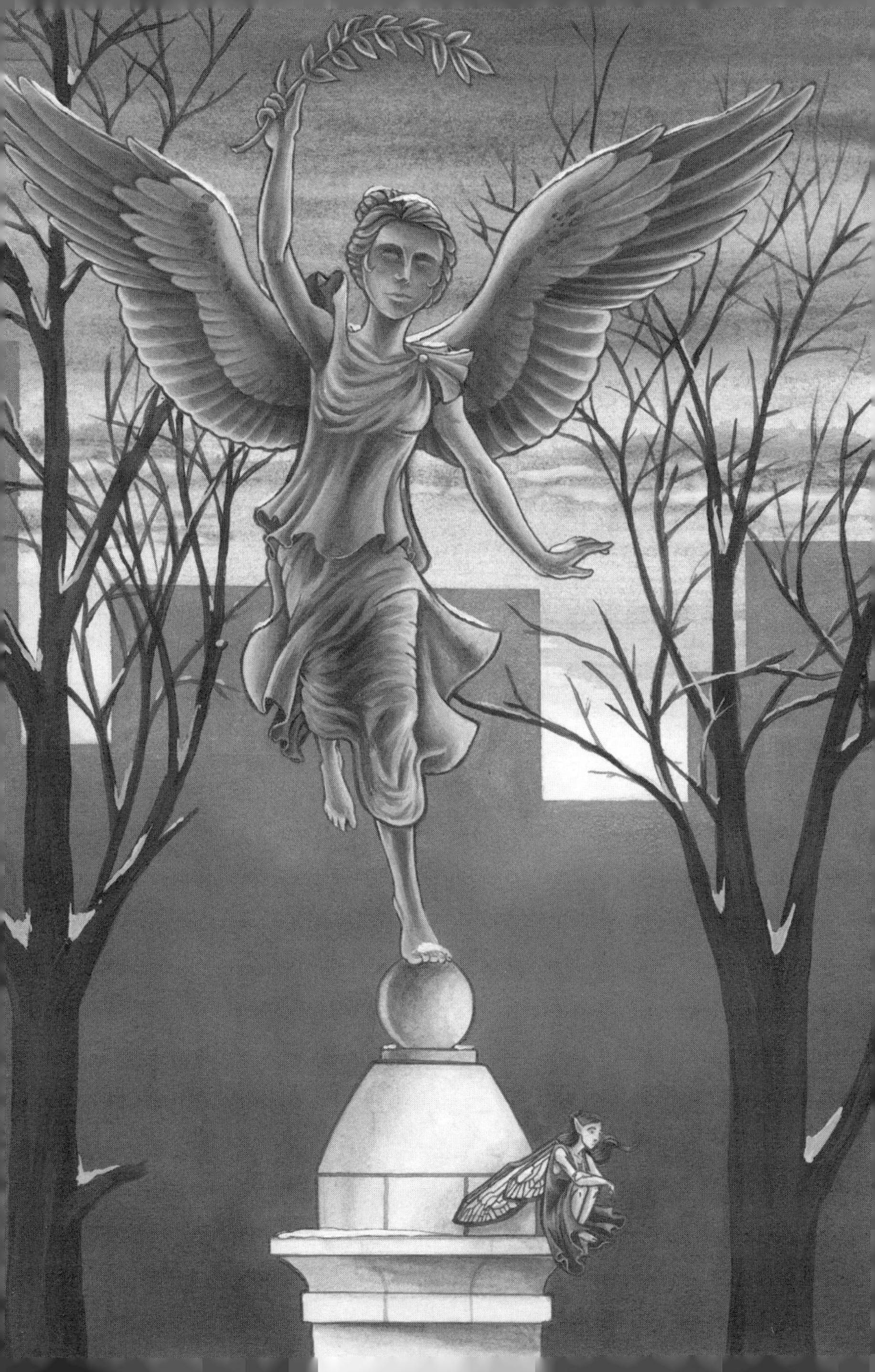

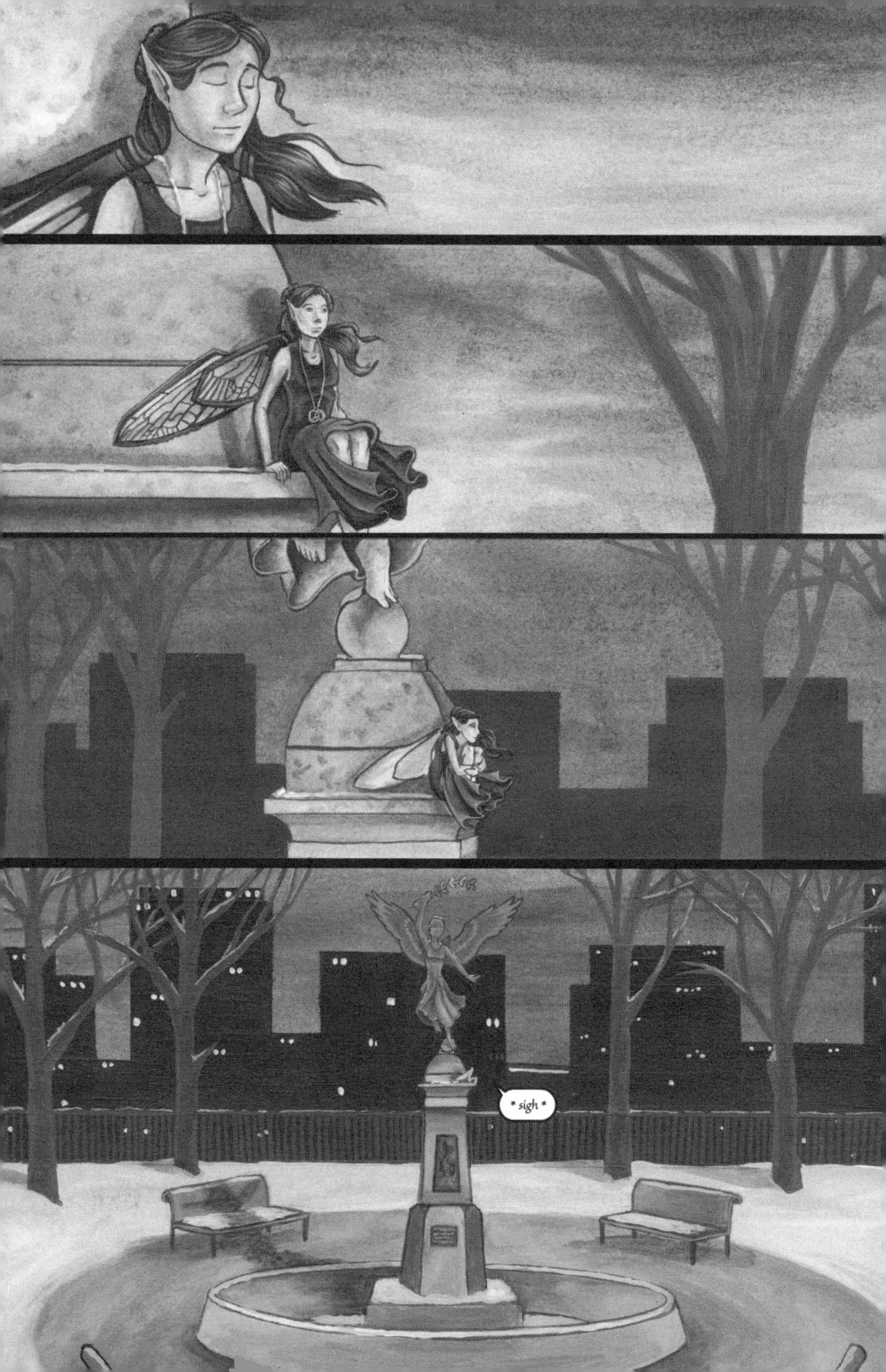
* sigh *

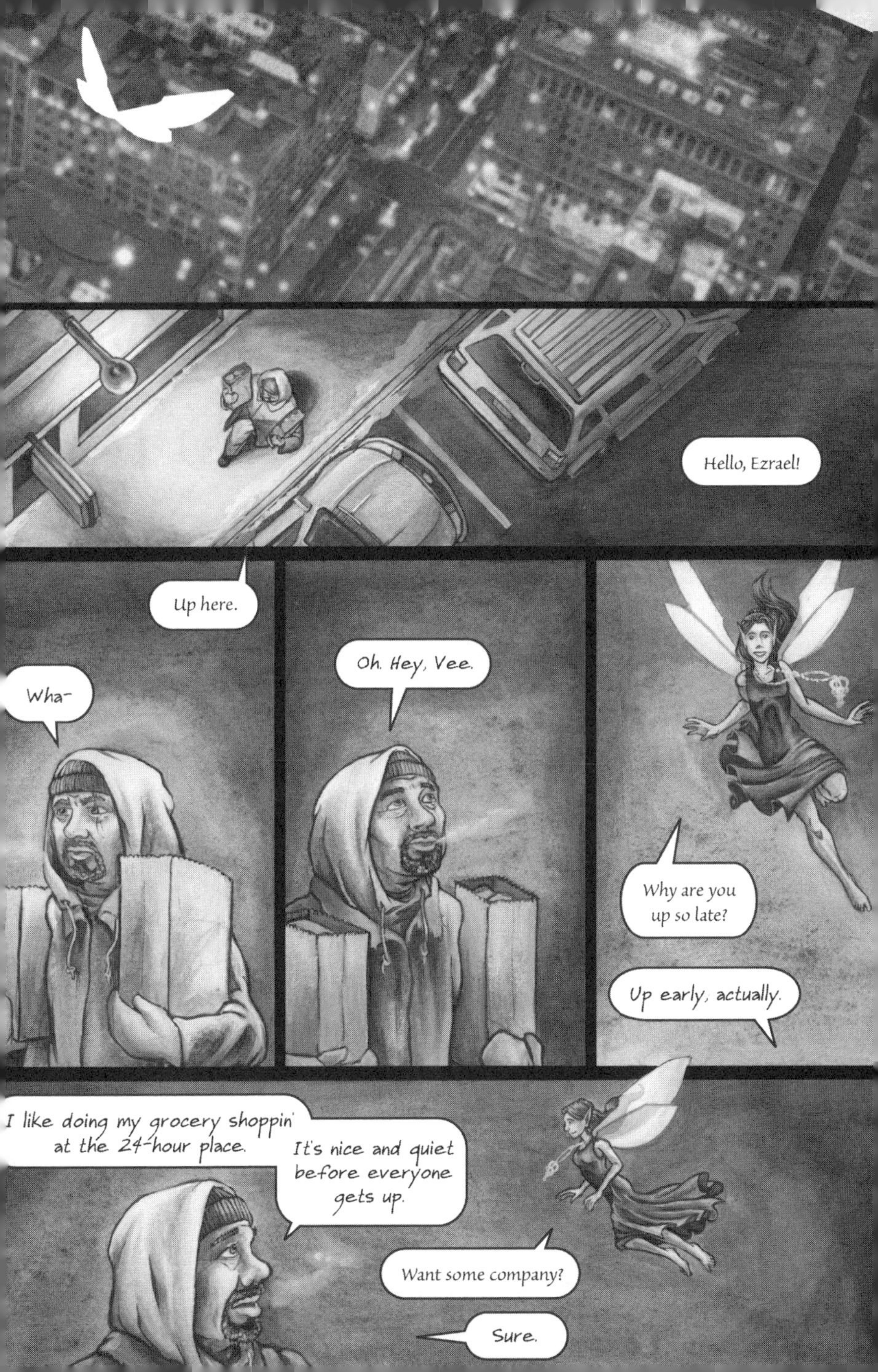
Hello, Ezrael!
Up here.
Wha-
Oh. Hey, Vee.
Why are you up so late?
Up early, actually.
I like doing my grocery shoppin' at the 24-hour place.
It's nice and quiet before everyone gets up.
Want some company?
Sure.

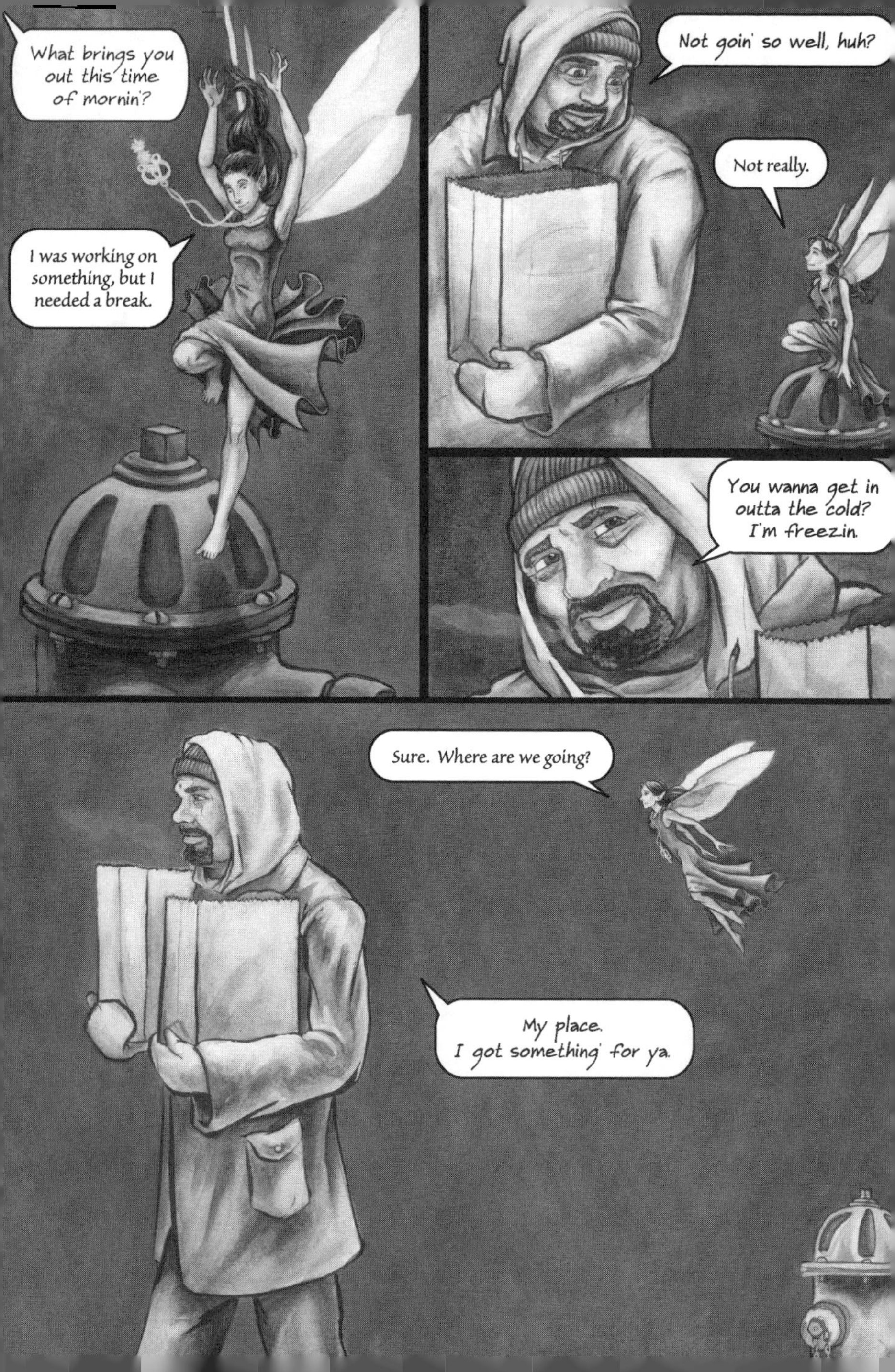
What brings you out this time of mornin'?
I was working on something, but I needed a break.
Not goin' so well, huh?
Not really.
You wanna get in outta the cold? I'm freezin.
Sure. Where are we going?
My place.
I got something for ya.

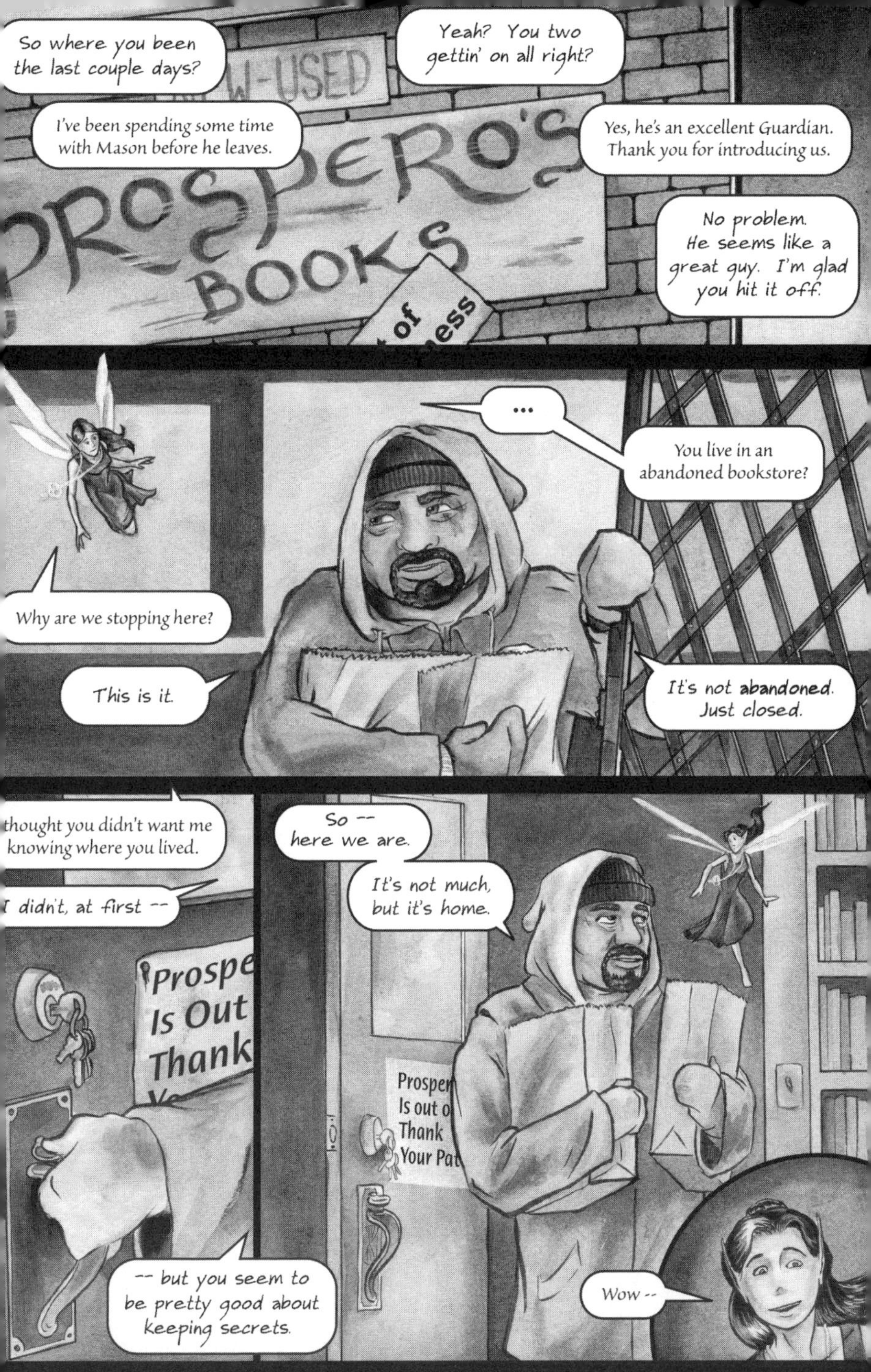
W-USED
PROSPERO'S BOOKS
So where you been the last couple days?
Yeah? You two gettin' on all right?
I've been spending some time with Mason before he leaves.
Yes, he's an excellent Guardian. Thank you for introducing us.
No problem. He seems like a great guy. I'm glad you hit it off.
...
You live in an abandoned bookstore?
Why are we stopping here?
This is it.
It's not **abandoned**. Just closed.
thought you didn't want me knowing where you lived.
I didn't, at first --
-- but you seem to be pretty good about keeping secrets.
So -- here we are.
It's not much, but it's home.
Wow --

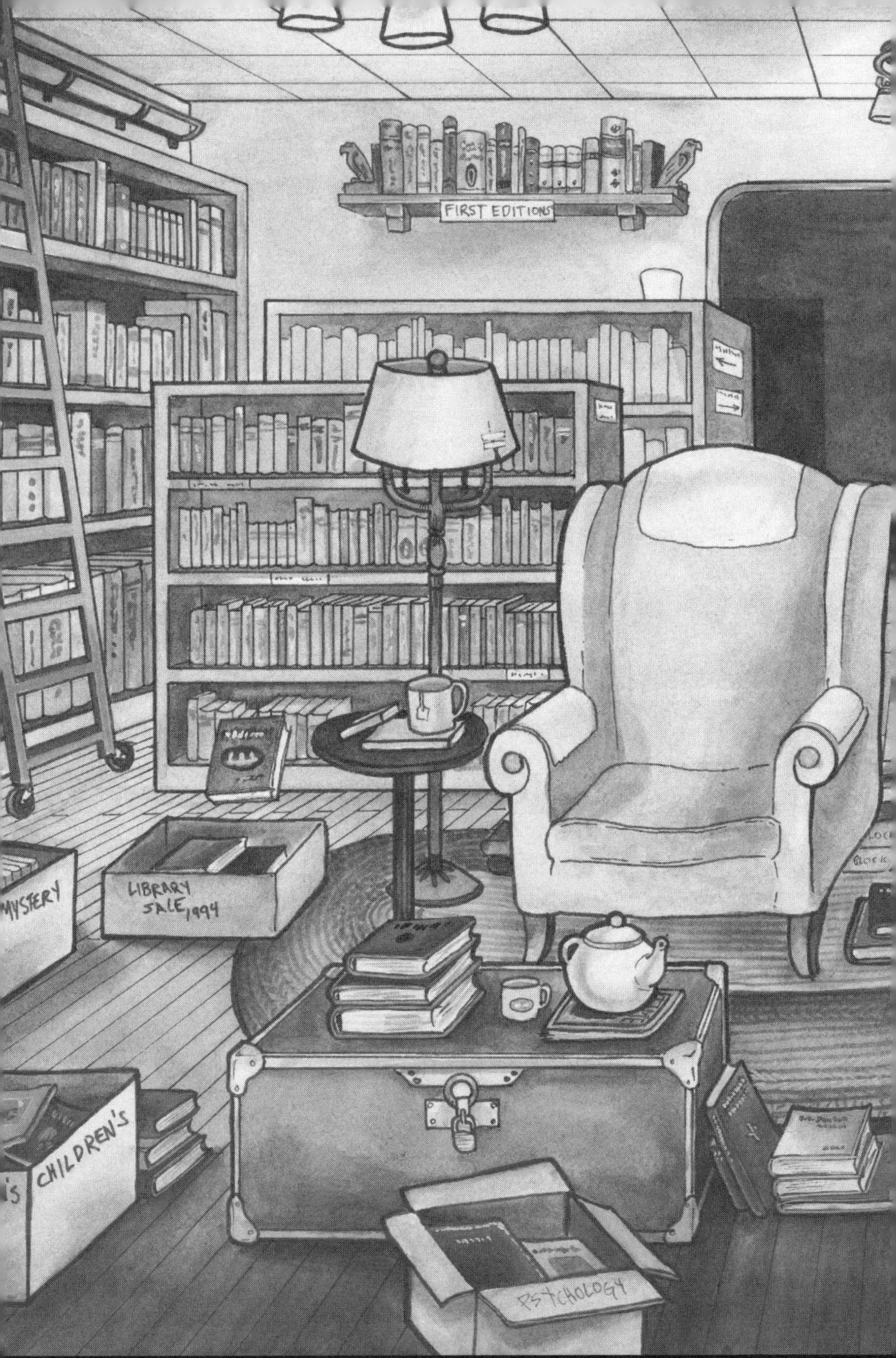
FIRST EDITIONS
MYSTERY
LIBRARY SALE 1994
CHILDREN'S
PSYCHOLOGY

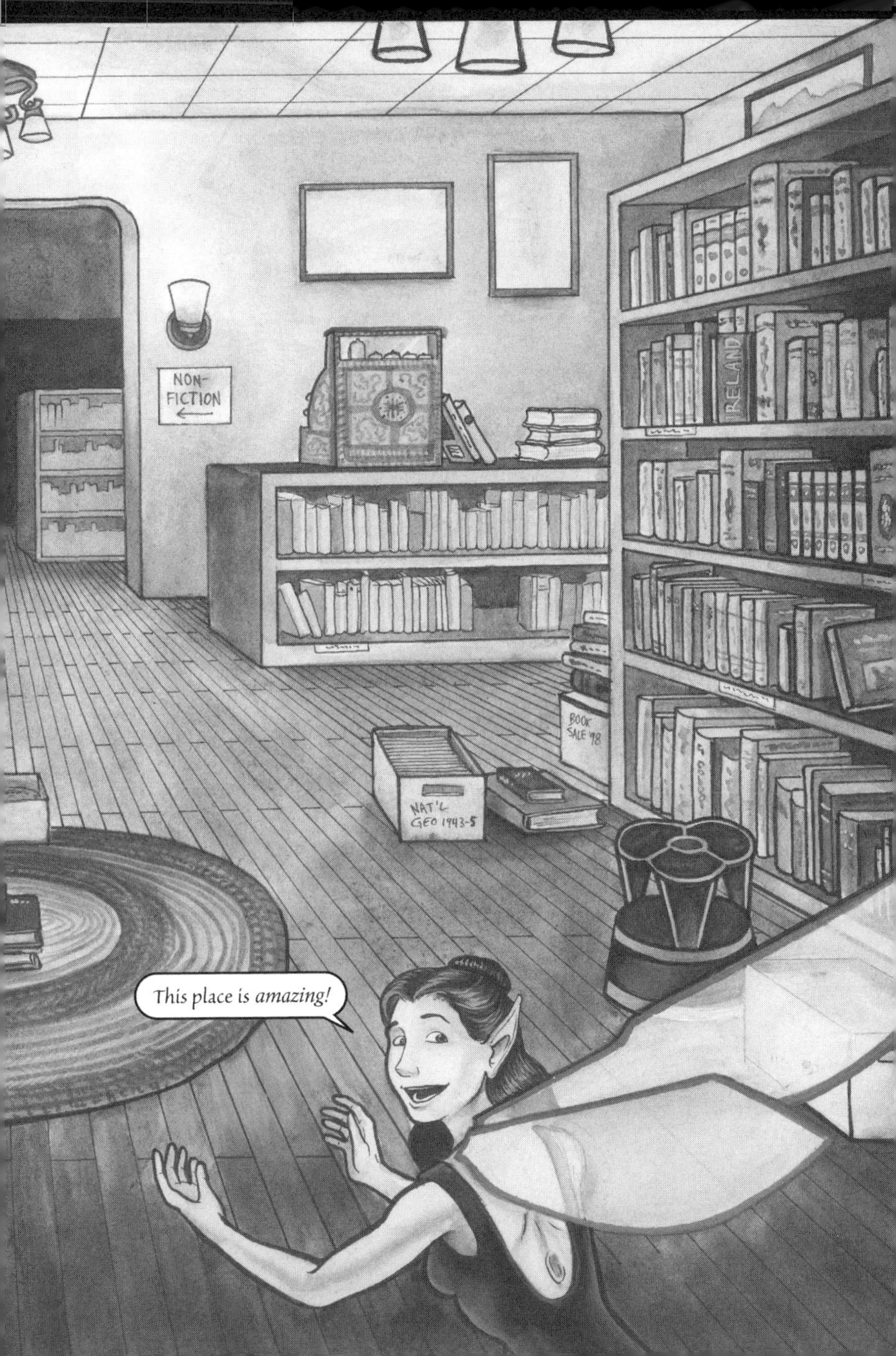
NON-FICTION
BOOK SALE '98
NAT'L GEO 1943-5
This place is *amazing!*

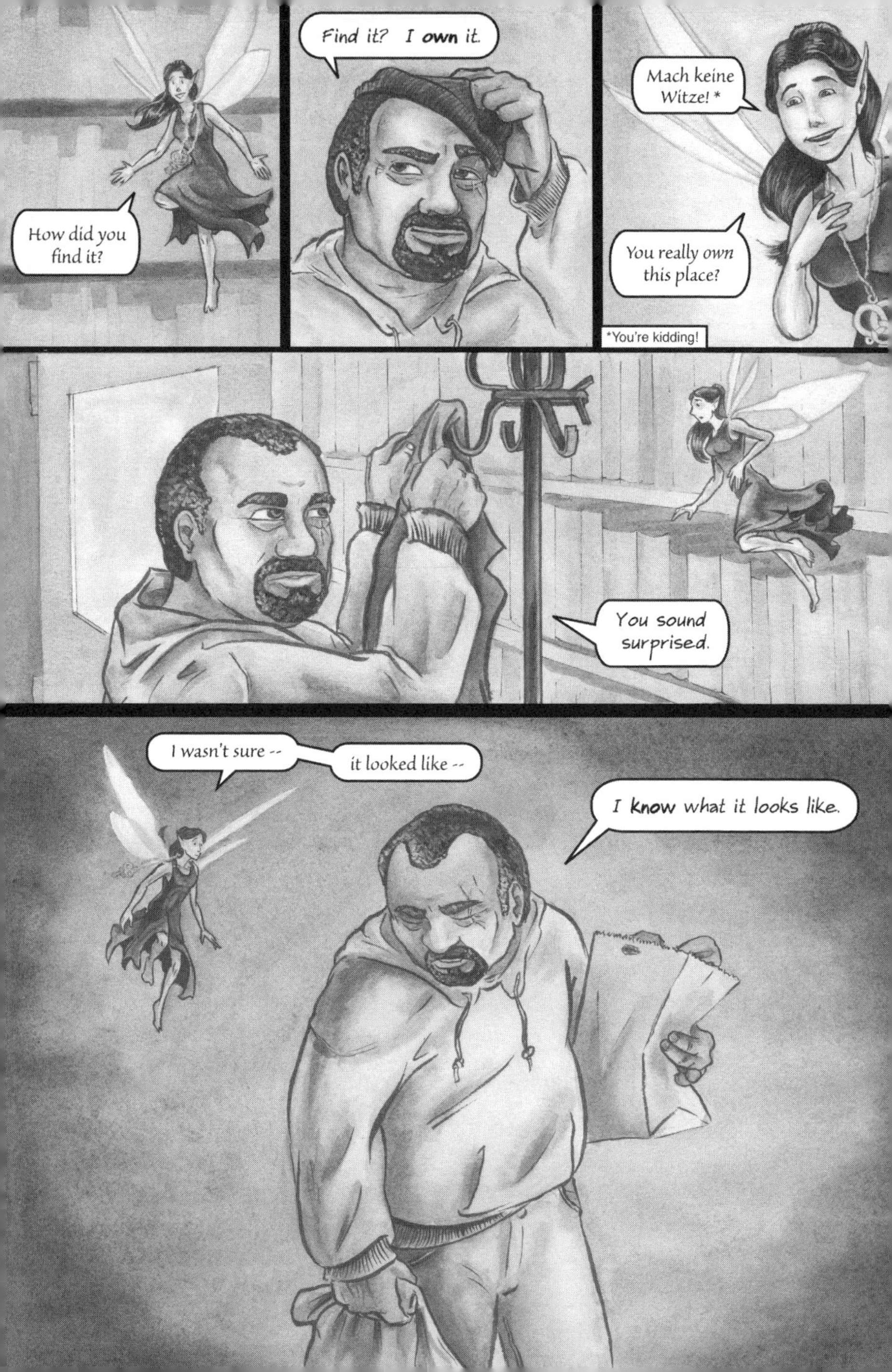
How did you find it?
Find it? I **own** it.
Mach keine Witze! *
You really *own* this place?
*You're kidding!
You sound surprised.
I wasn't sure --
it looked like --
I **know** what it looks like.

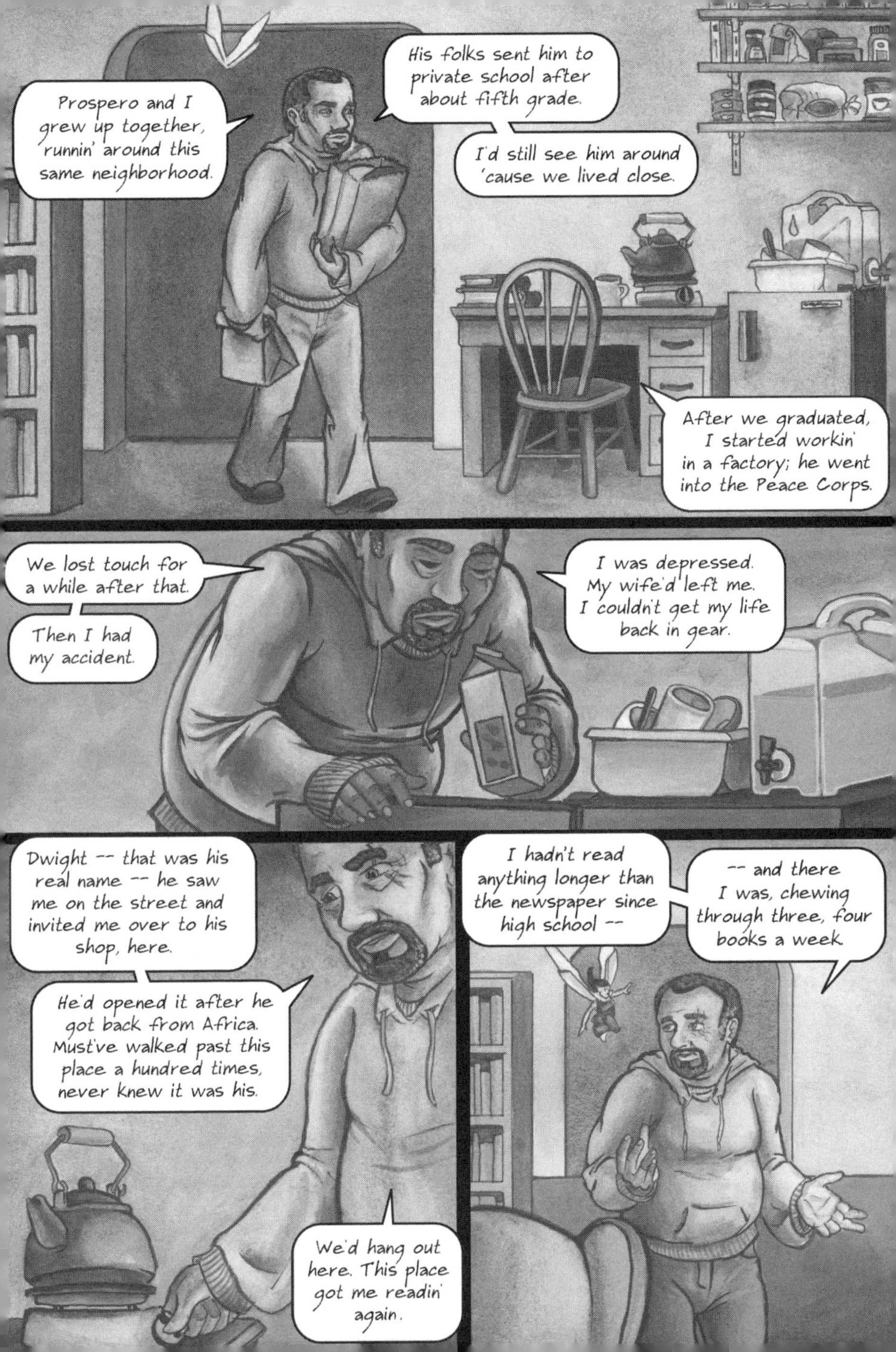

Prospero and I grew up together, runnin' around this same neighborhood.
His folks sent him to private school after about fifth grade.
I'd still see him around 'cause we lived close.
After we graduated, I started workin' in a factory; he went into the Peace Corps.
We lost touch for a while after that.
Then I had my accident.
I was depressed. My wife'd left me. I couldn't get my life back in gear.
Dwight -- that was his real name -- he saw me on the street and invited me over to his shop, here.
He'd opened it after he got back from Africa. Must've walked past this place a hundred times, never knew it was his.
We'd hang out here. This place got me readin' again.
I hadn't read anything longer than the newspaper since high school --
-- and there I was, chewing through three, four books a week.

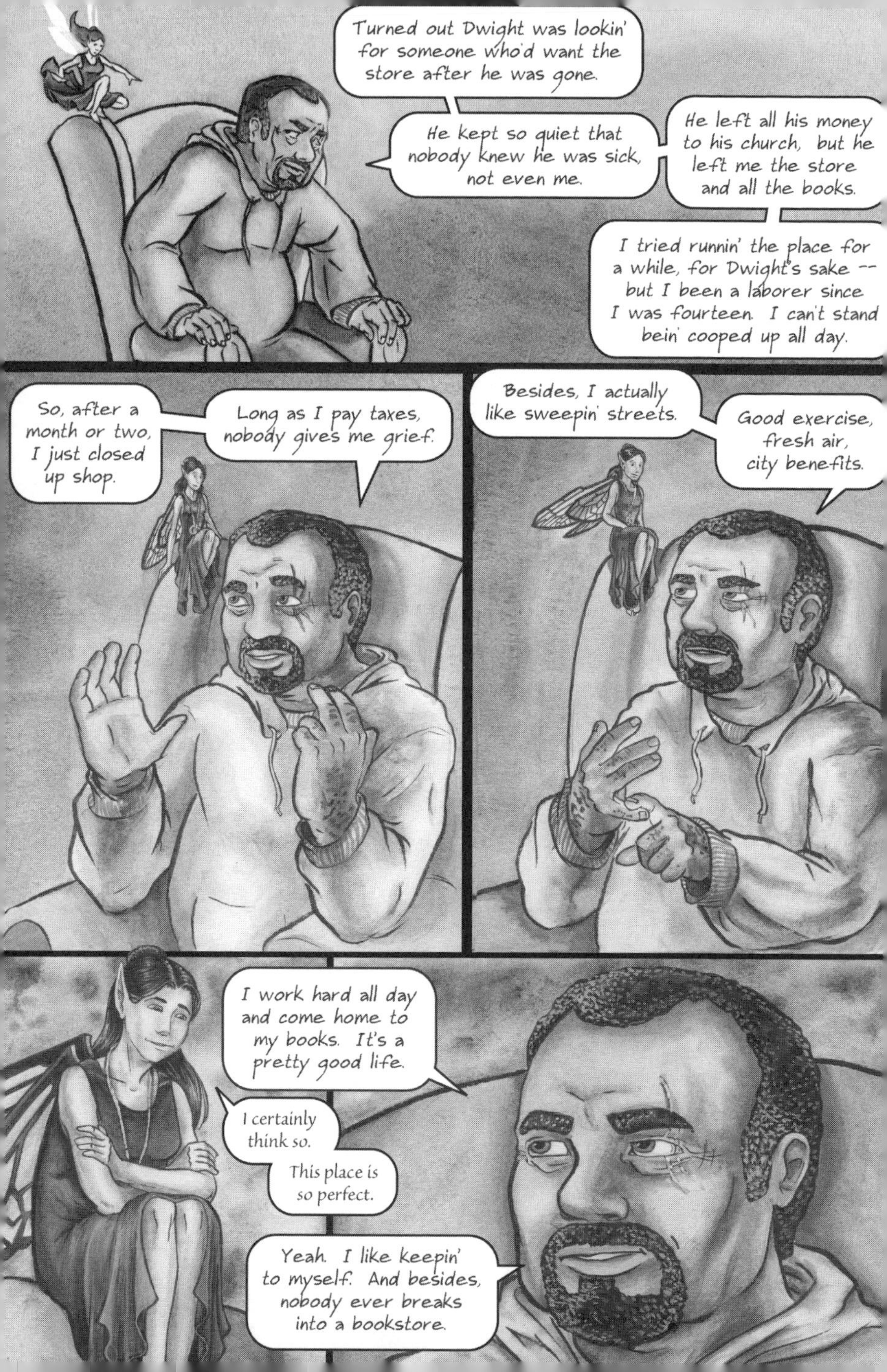

Turned out Dwight was lookin' for someone who'd want the store after he was gone.
He kept so quiet that nobody knew he was sick, not even me.
He left all his money to his church, but he left me the store and all the books.
I tried runnin' the place for a while, for Dwight's sake -- but I been a laborer since I was fourteen. I can't stand bein' cooped up all day.
So, after a month or two, I just closed up shop.
Long as I pay taxes, nobody gives me grief.
Besides, I actually like sweepin' streets.
Good exercise, fresh air, city benefits.
I work hard all day and come home to my books. It's a pretty good life.
I certainly think so.
This place is so perfect.
Yeah. I like keepin' to myself. And besides, nobody ever breaks into a bookstore.

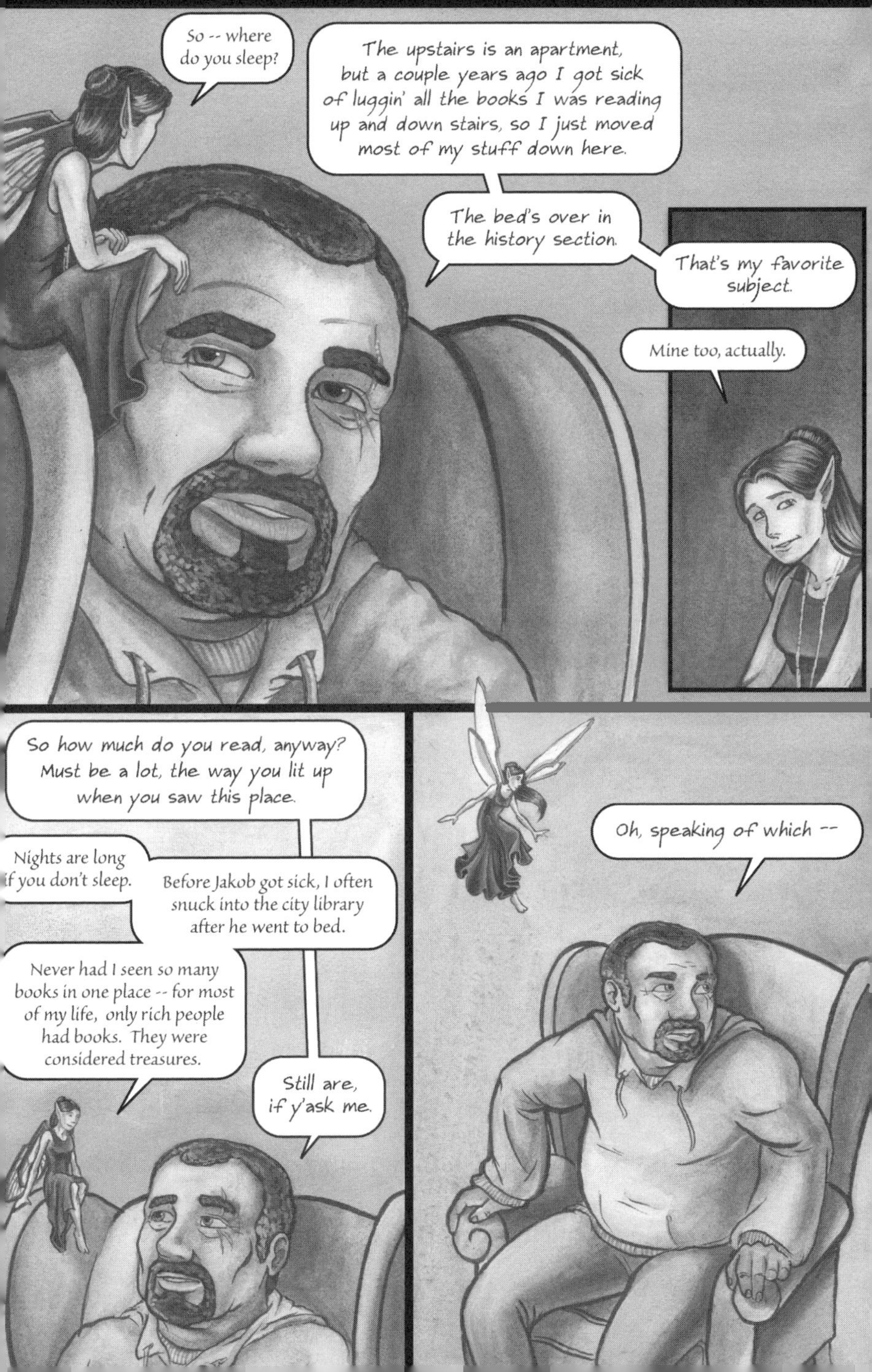

So -- where do you sleep?
The upstairs is an apartment, but a couple years ago I got sick of luggin' all the books I was reading up and down stairs, so I just moved most of my stuff down here.
The bed's over in the history section.
That's my favorite subject.
Mine too, actually.
So how much do you read, anyway? Must be a lot, the way you lit up when you saw this place.
Nights are long if you don't sleep.
Before Jakob got sick, I often snuck into the city library after he went to bed.
Never had I seen so many books in one place -- for most of my life, only rich people had books. They were considered treasures.
Still are, if y'ask me.
Oh, speaking of which --

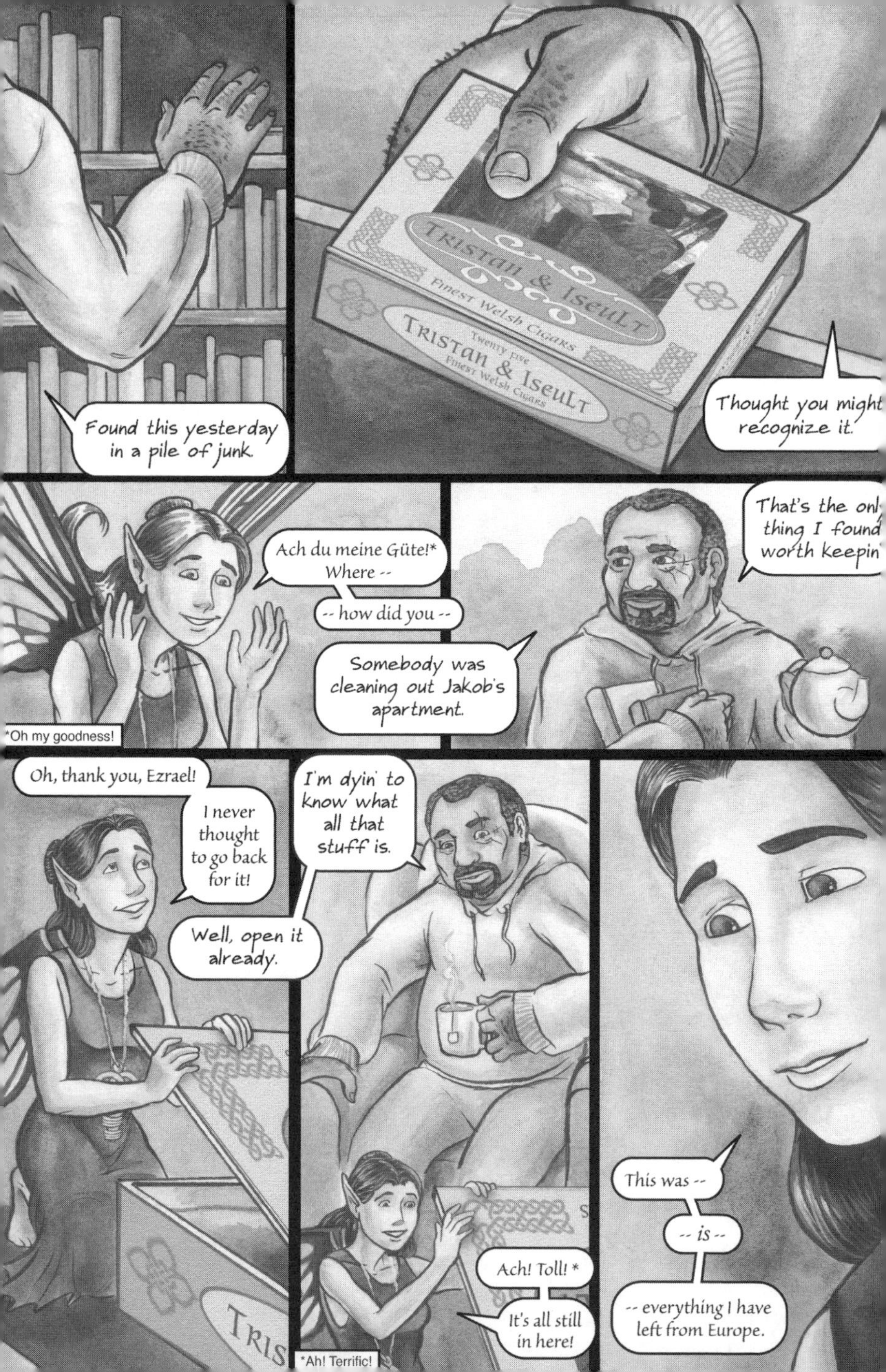
Found this yesterday in a pile of junk.
Tristan & Iseult
Finest Welsh Cigars
Twenty five
Tristan & Iseult
Finest Welsh Cigars
Thought you might recognize it.
Ach du meine Güte!* Where --
-- how did you --
Somebody was cleaning out Jakob's apartment.
*Oh my goodness!
That's the onl thing I found worth keepin'
Oh, thank you, Ezrael!
I never thought to go back for it!
Well, open it already.
I'm dyin' to know what all that stuff is.
Tris
Ach! Toll! *
It's all still in here!
*Ah! Terrific!
This was --
-- is --
-- everything I have left from Europe.

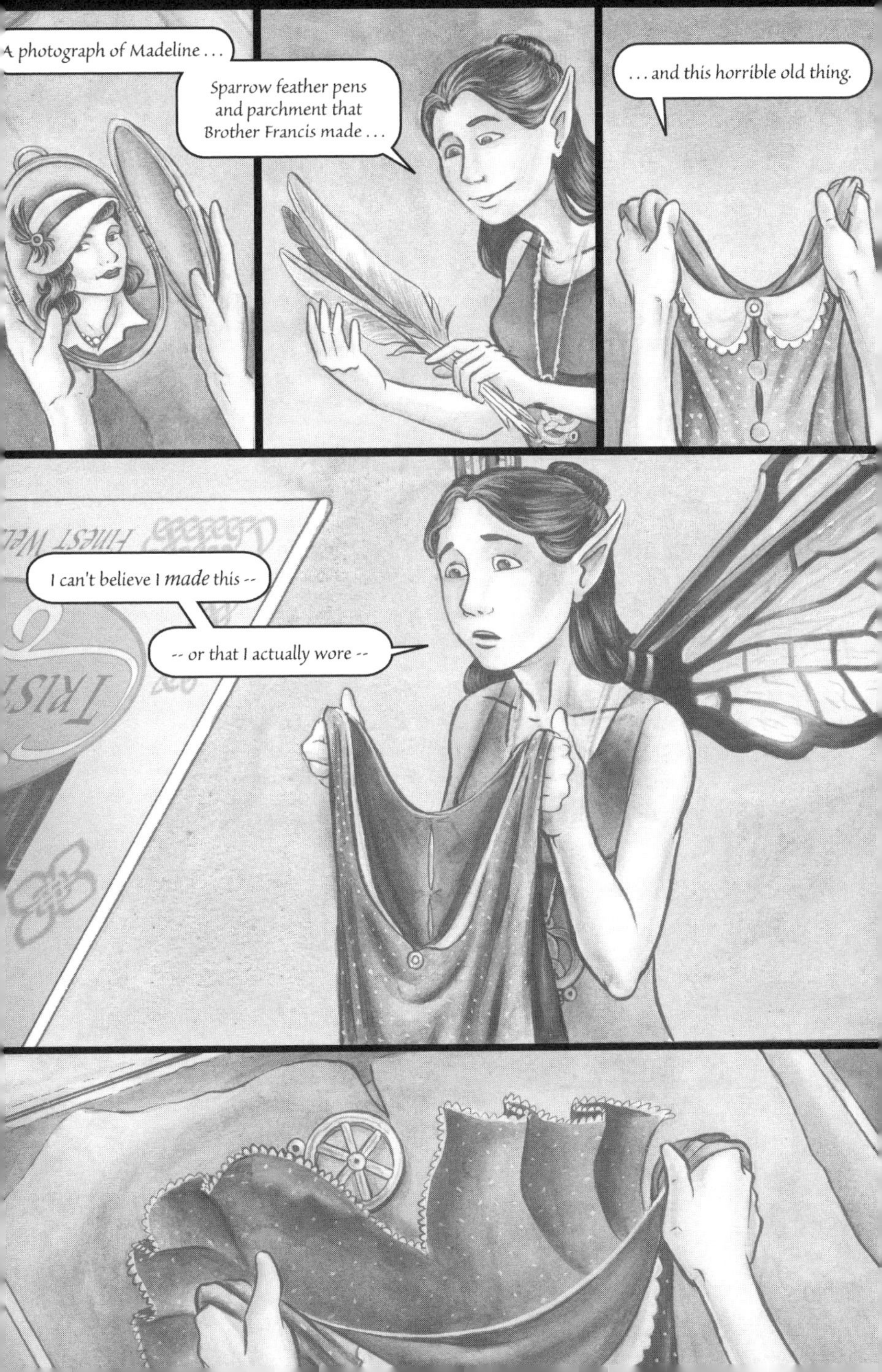
A photograph of Madeline . . .
Sparrow feather pens and parchment that Brother Francis made . . .
. . . and this horrible old thing.
I can't believe I *made* this --
-- or that I actually wore --

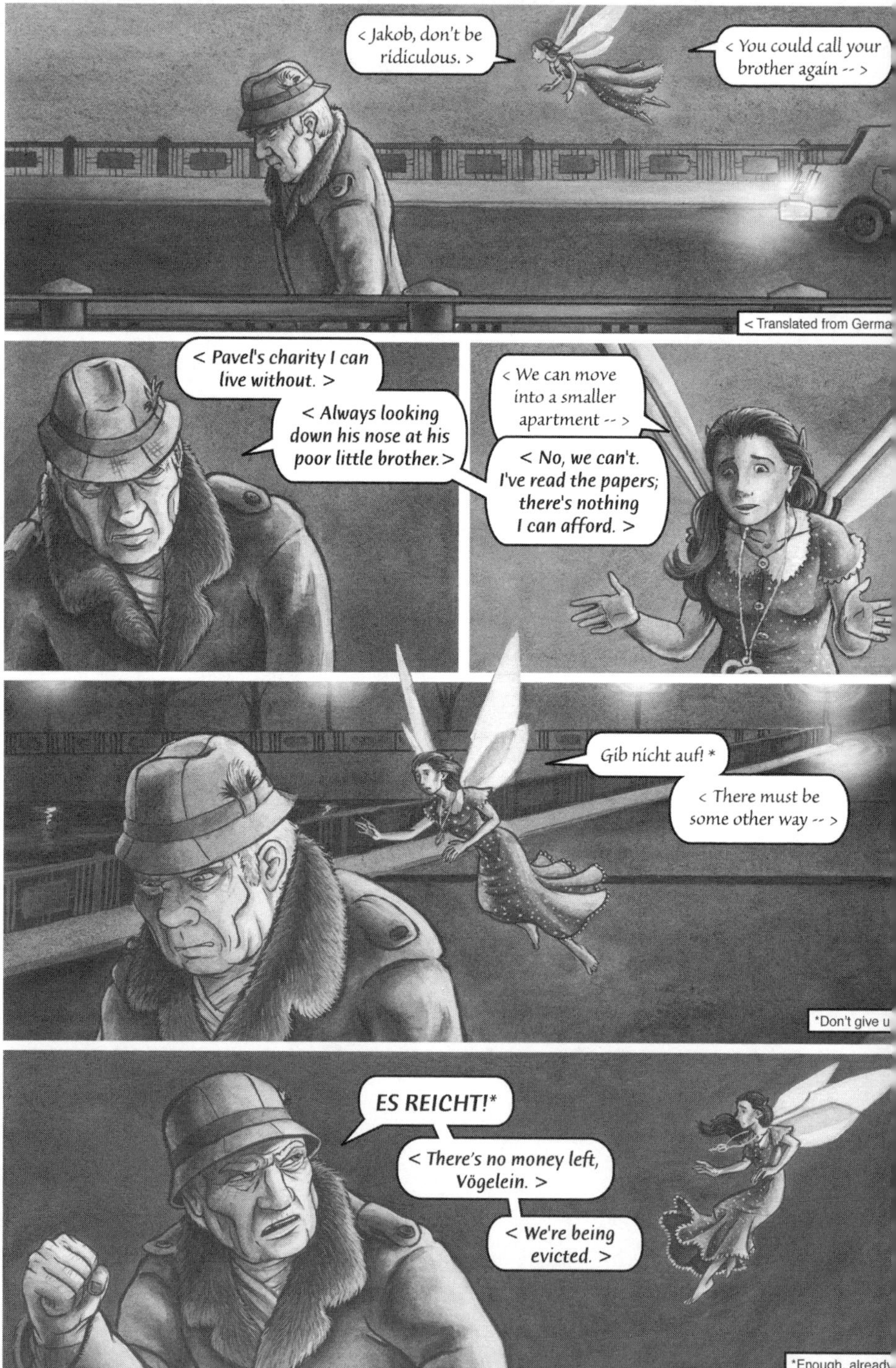
< Jakob, don't be ridiculous. >
< You could call your brother again -- >
< Translated from Germa
< Pavel's charity I can live without. >
< Always looking down his nose at his poor little brother.>
< We can move into a smaller apartment -- >
< No, we can't. I've read the papers; there's nothing I can afford. >
Gib nicht auf! *
< There must be some other way -- >
*Don't give u
ES REICHT!*
< There's no money left, Vögelein. >
< We're being evicted. >
*Enough, already

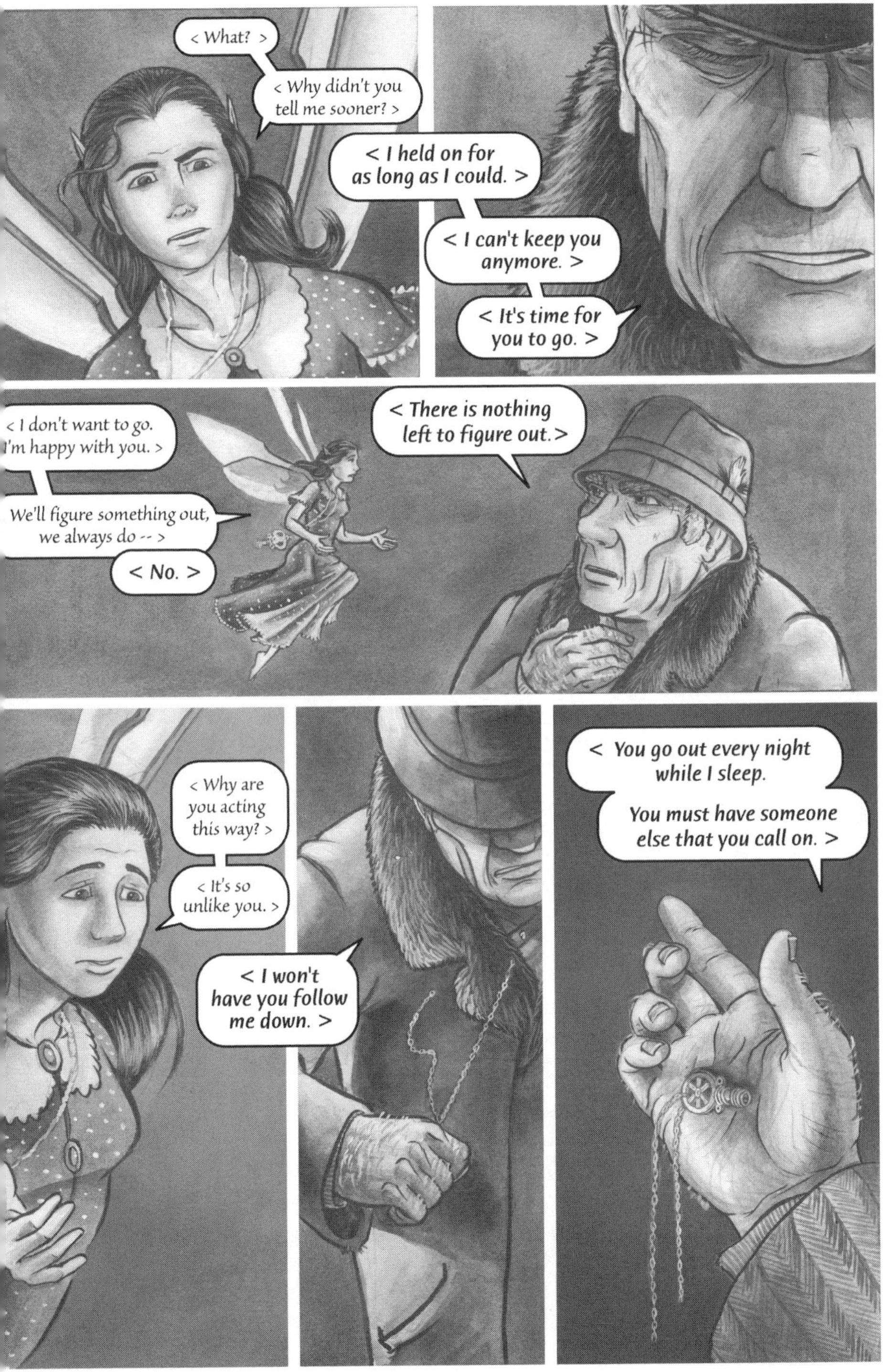
< What? >
< Why didn't you tell me sooner? >
< I held on for as long as I could. >
< I can't keep you anymore. >
< It's time for you to go. >
< I don't want to go. I'm happy with you. >
We'll figure something out, we always do -- >
< No. >
< There is nothing left to figure out. >
< Why are you acting this way? >
< It's so unlike you. >
< I won't have you follow me down. >
< You go out every night while I sleep.
You must have someone else that you call on. >

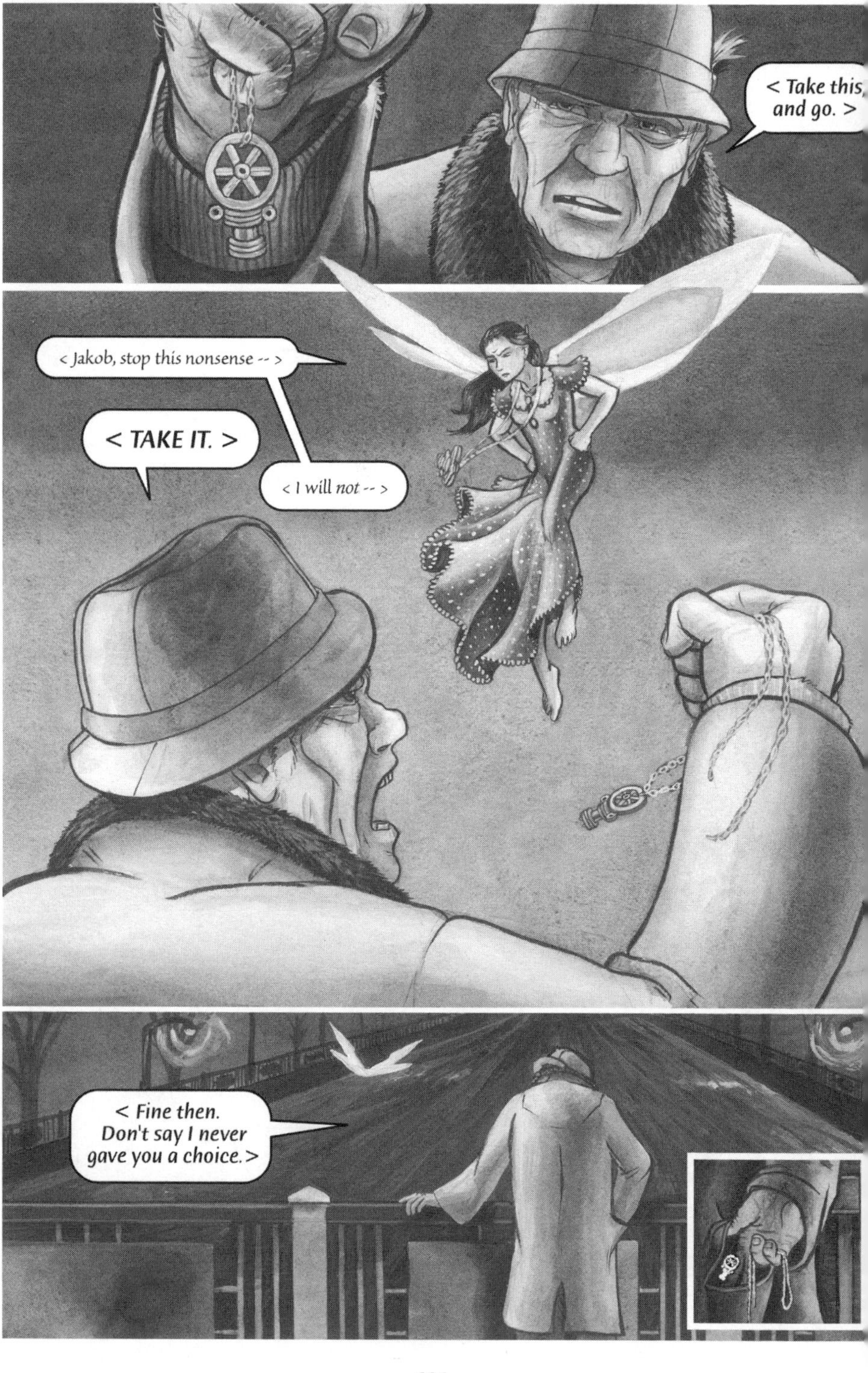
< Take this,
and go. >
< Jakob, stop this nonsense -- >
< TAKE IT. >
< I will not -- >
< Fine then.
Don't say I never
gave you a choice.>

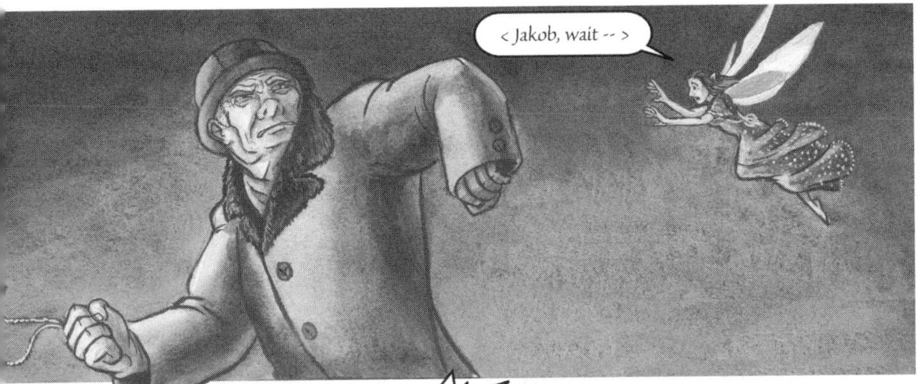
< Jakob, wait -- >

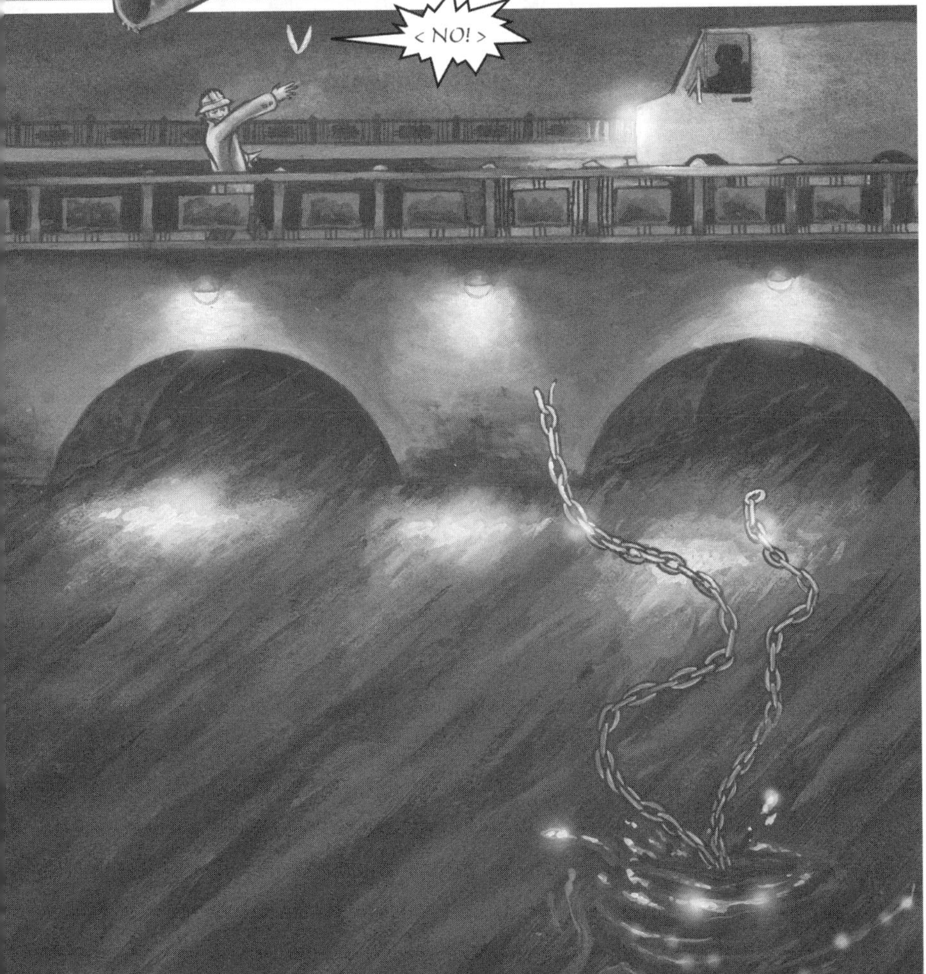
< NO! >

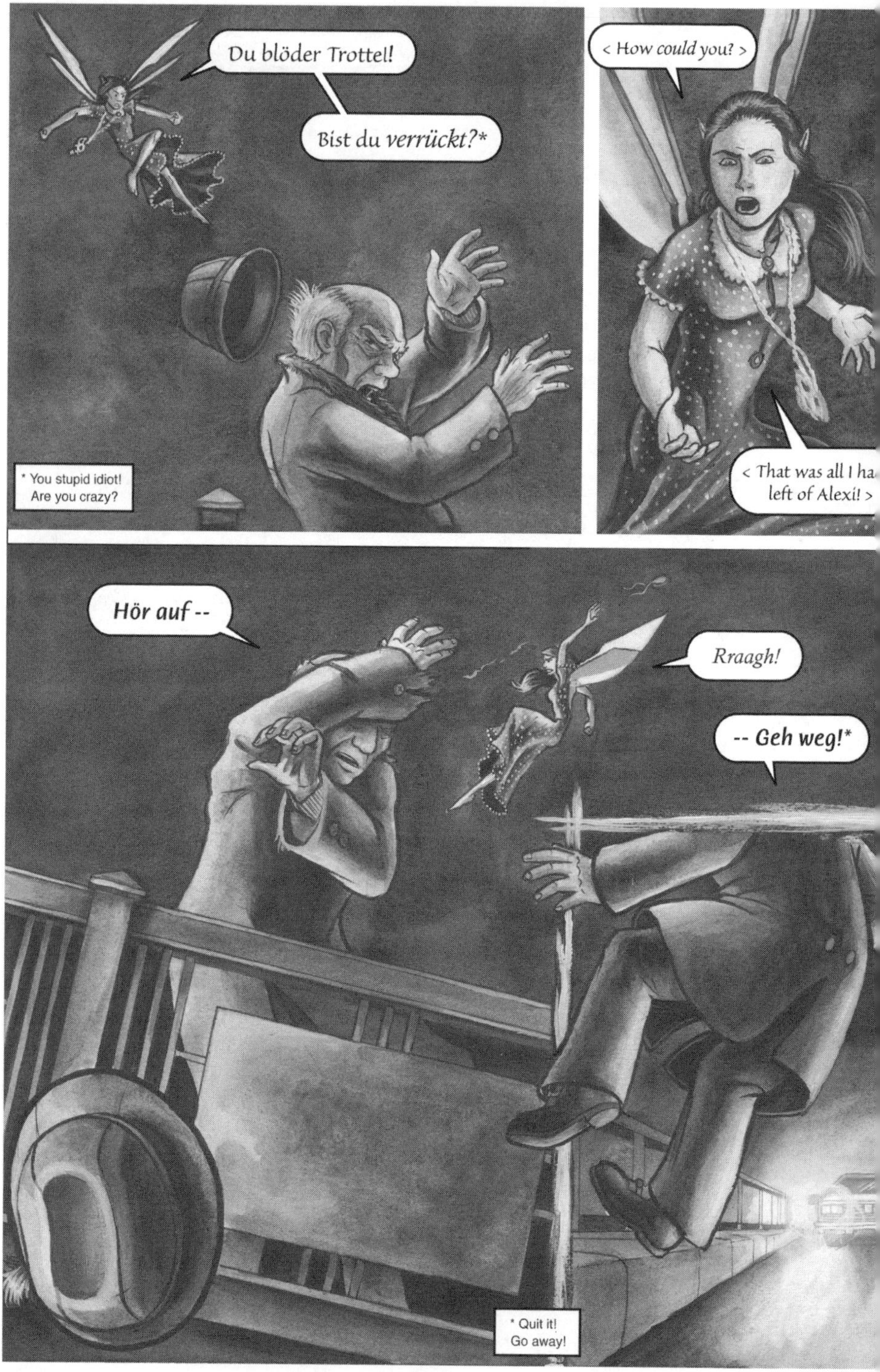
Du blöder Trottel!
Bist du verrückt?*
* You stupid idiot! Are you crazy?
< How could you? >
< That was all I ha left of Alexi! >
Hör auf --
Rraagh!
-- Geh weg!*
* Quit it! Go away!

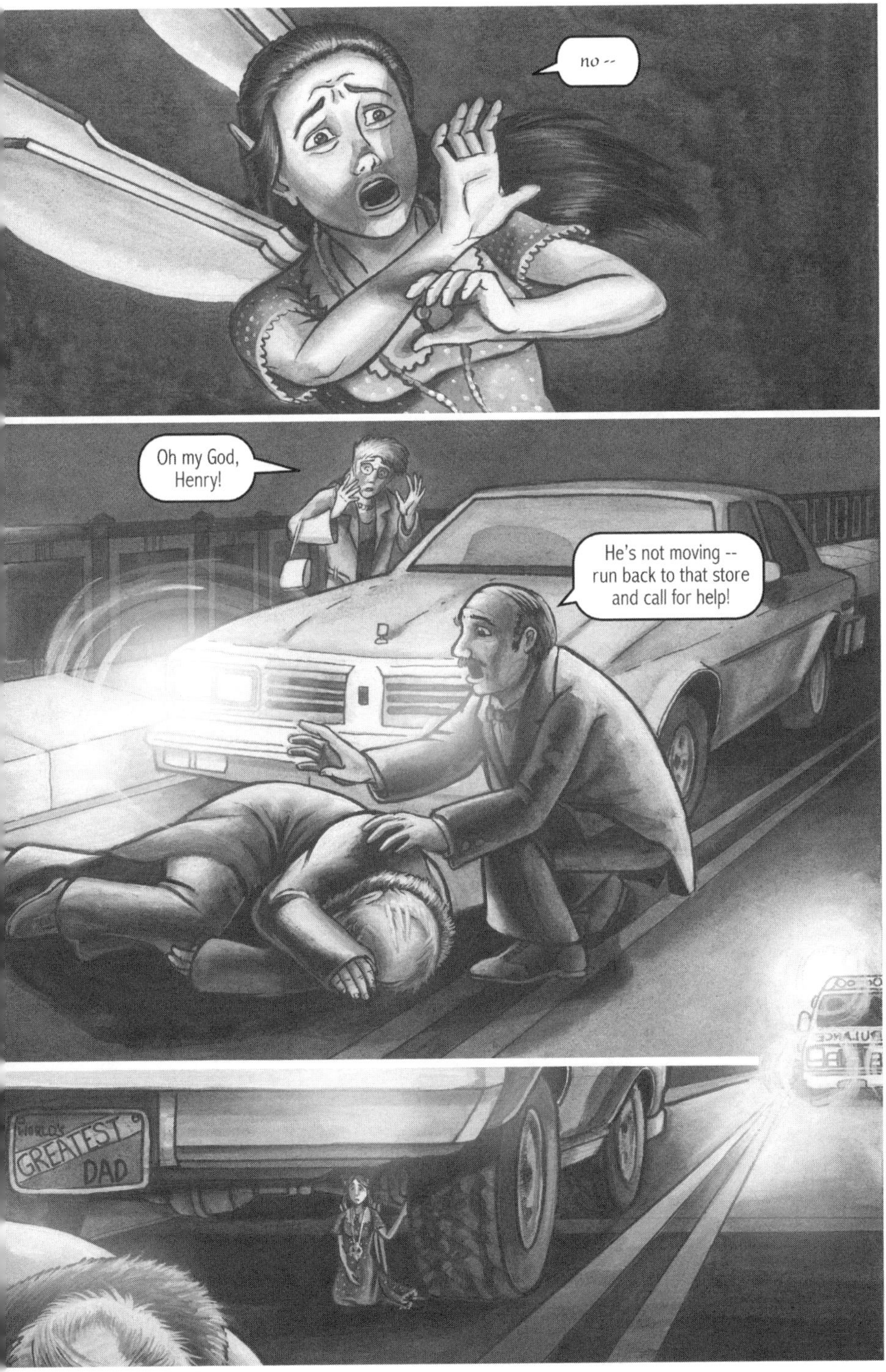
no --
Oh my God, Henry!
He's not moving -- run back to that store and call for help!
WORLD'S GREATEST DAD

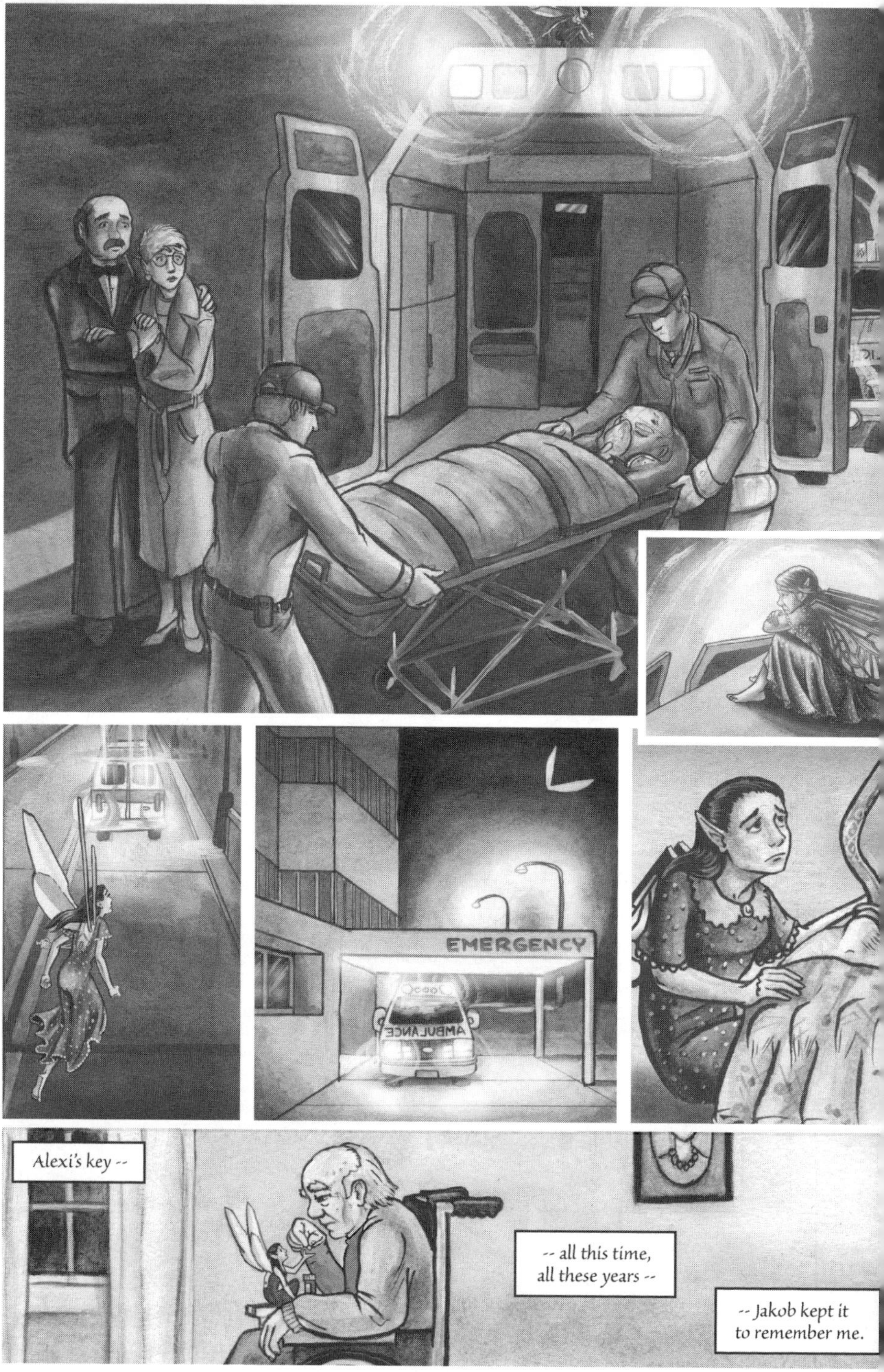
EMERGENCY
AMBULANCE
Alexi's key --
-- all this time,
all these years --
-- Jakob kept it
to remember me.

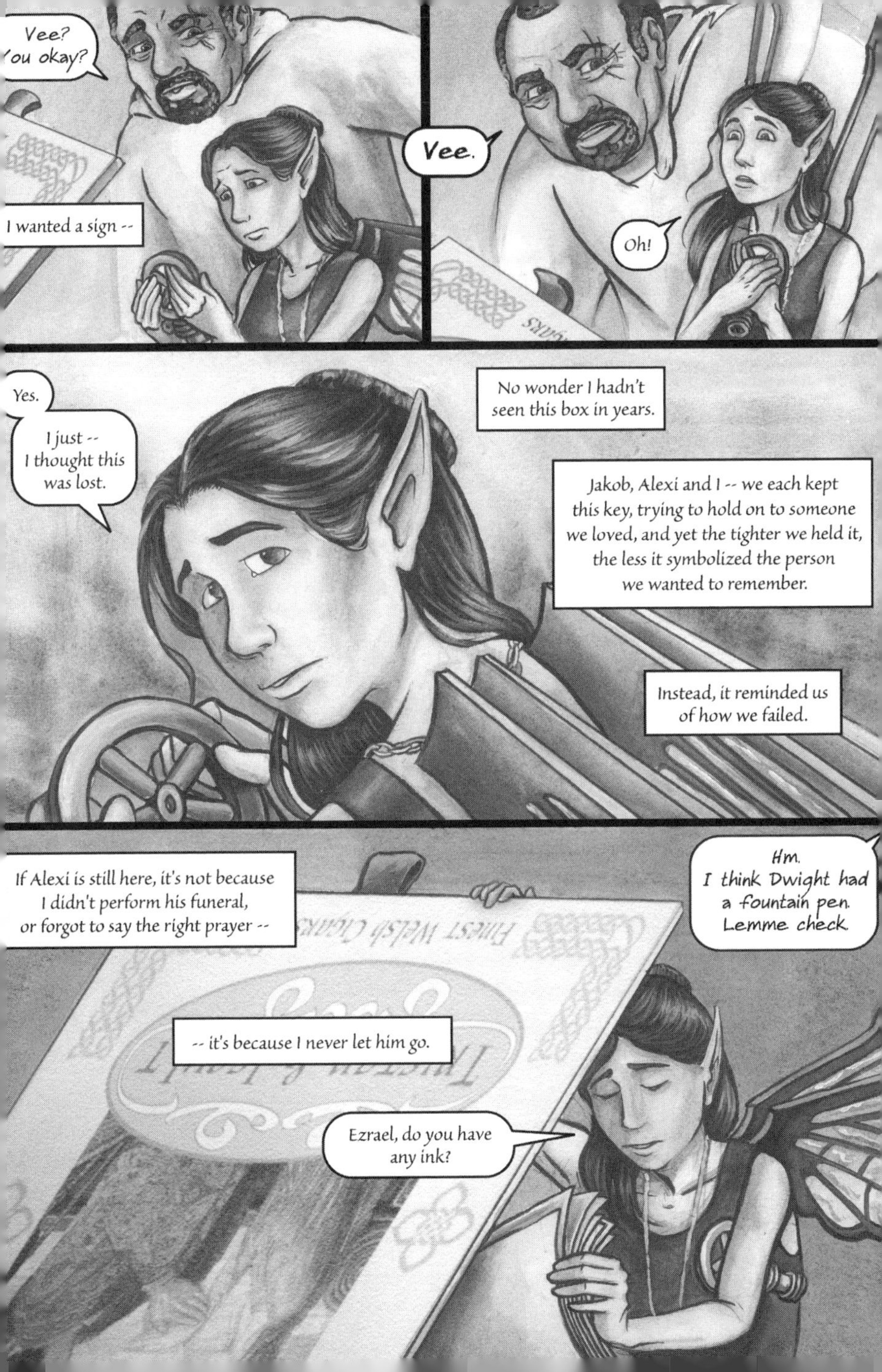

Vee? You okay?
I wanted a sign --
Vee.
Oh!
Yes.
I just -- I thought this was lost.
No wonder I hadn't seen this box in years.
Jakob, Alexi and I -- we each kept this key, trying to hold on to someone we loved, and yet the tighter we held it, the less it symbolized the person we wanted to remember.
Instead, it reminded us of how we failed.
If Alexi is still here, it's not because I didn't perform his funeral, or forgot to say the right prayer --
Hm. I think Dwight had a fountain pen. Lemme check.
-- it's because I never let him go.
Ezrael, do you have any ink?

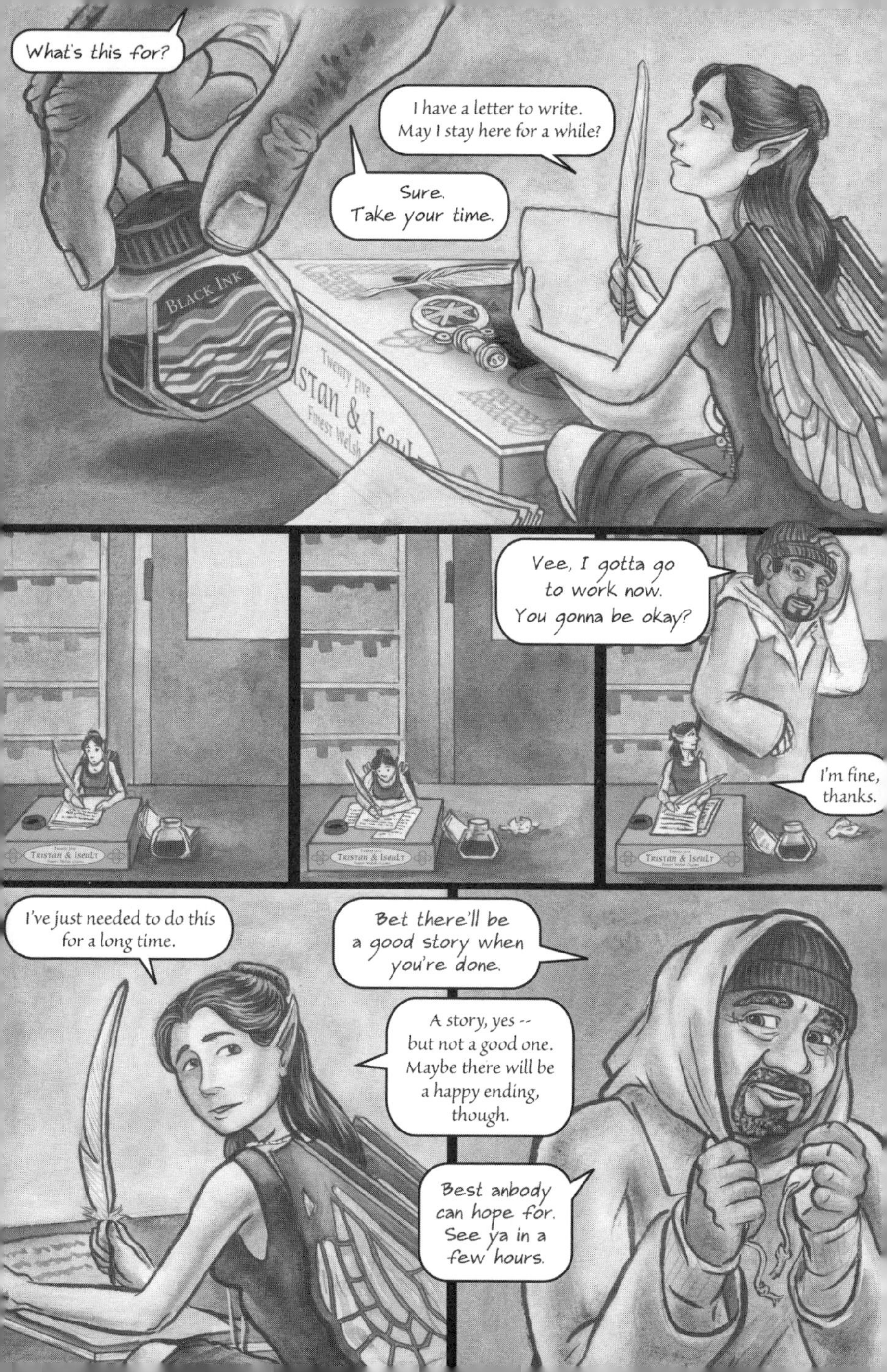
What's this for?
I have a letter to write. May I stay here for a while?
Sure. Take your time.
BLACK INK
Twenty five Tristan & Iseult Finest Welsh
Vee, I gotta go to work now. You gonna be okay?
I'm fine, thanks.
I've just needed to do this for a long time.
Bet there'll be a good story when you're done.
A story, yes -- but not a good one. Maybe there will be a happy ending, though.
Best anbody can hope for. See ya in a few hours.

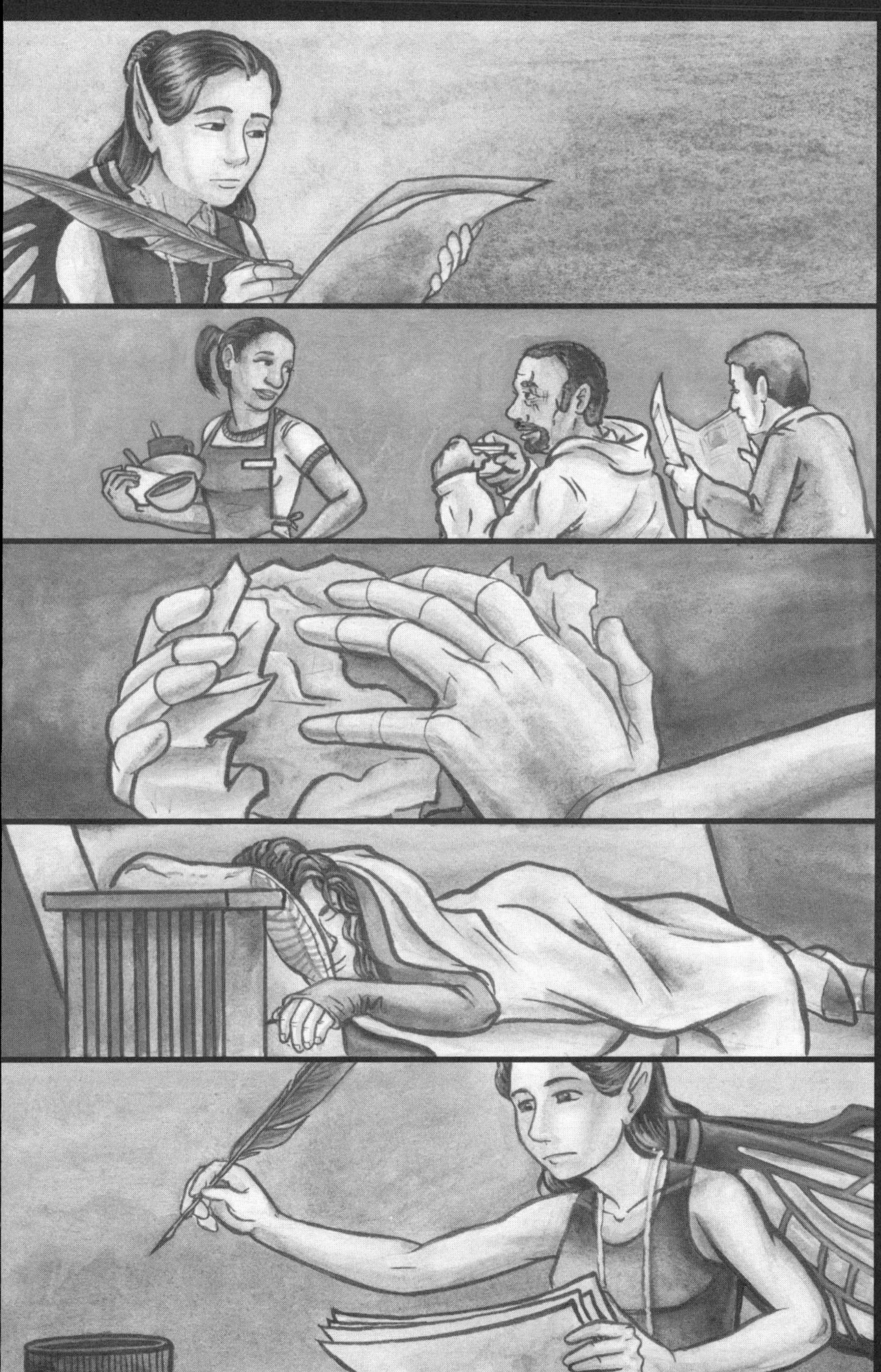

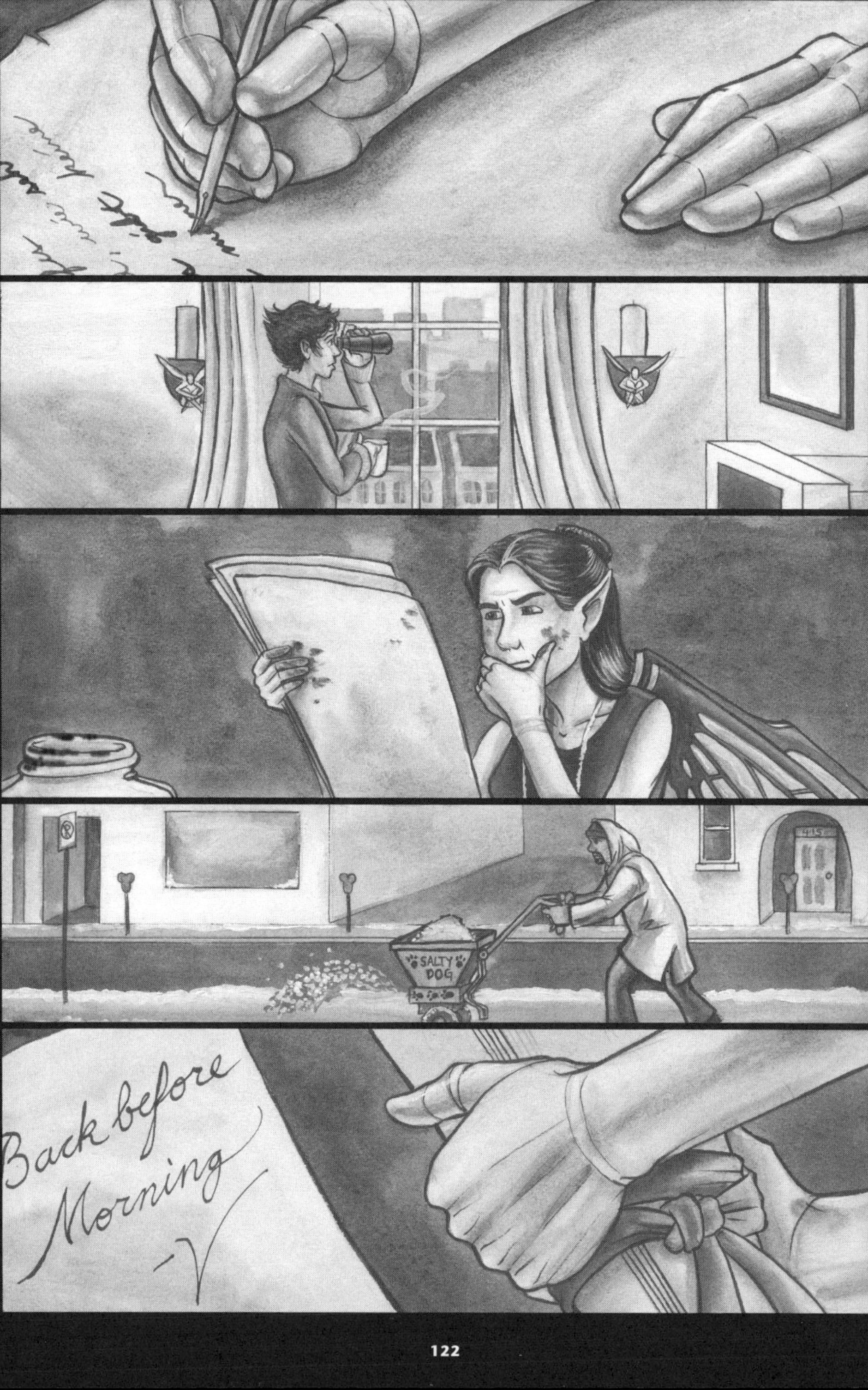
SALTY DOG
Back before Morning
-V

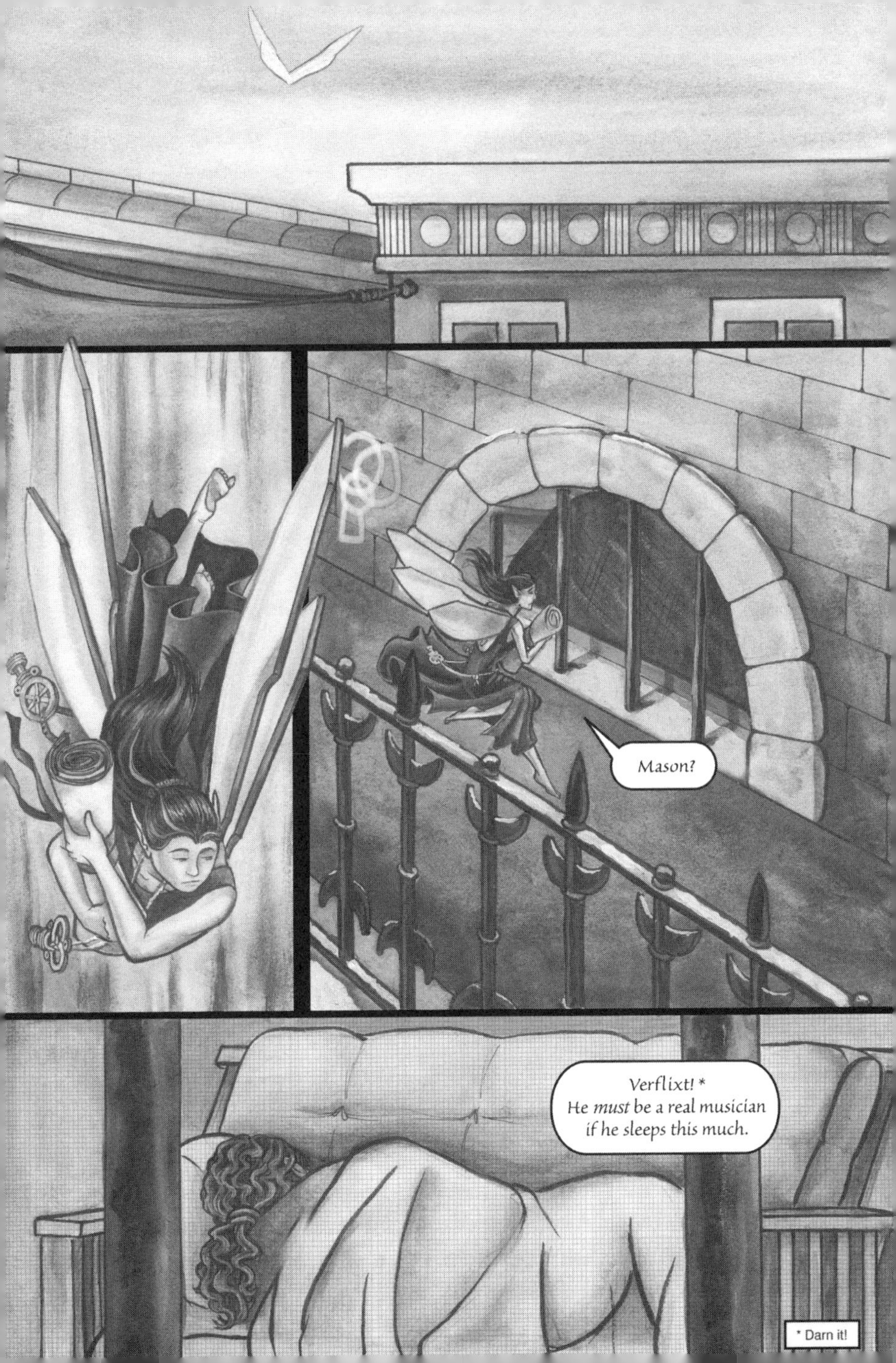
Mason?
Verflixt! *
He *must* be a real musician
if he sleeps this much.
* Darn it!

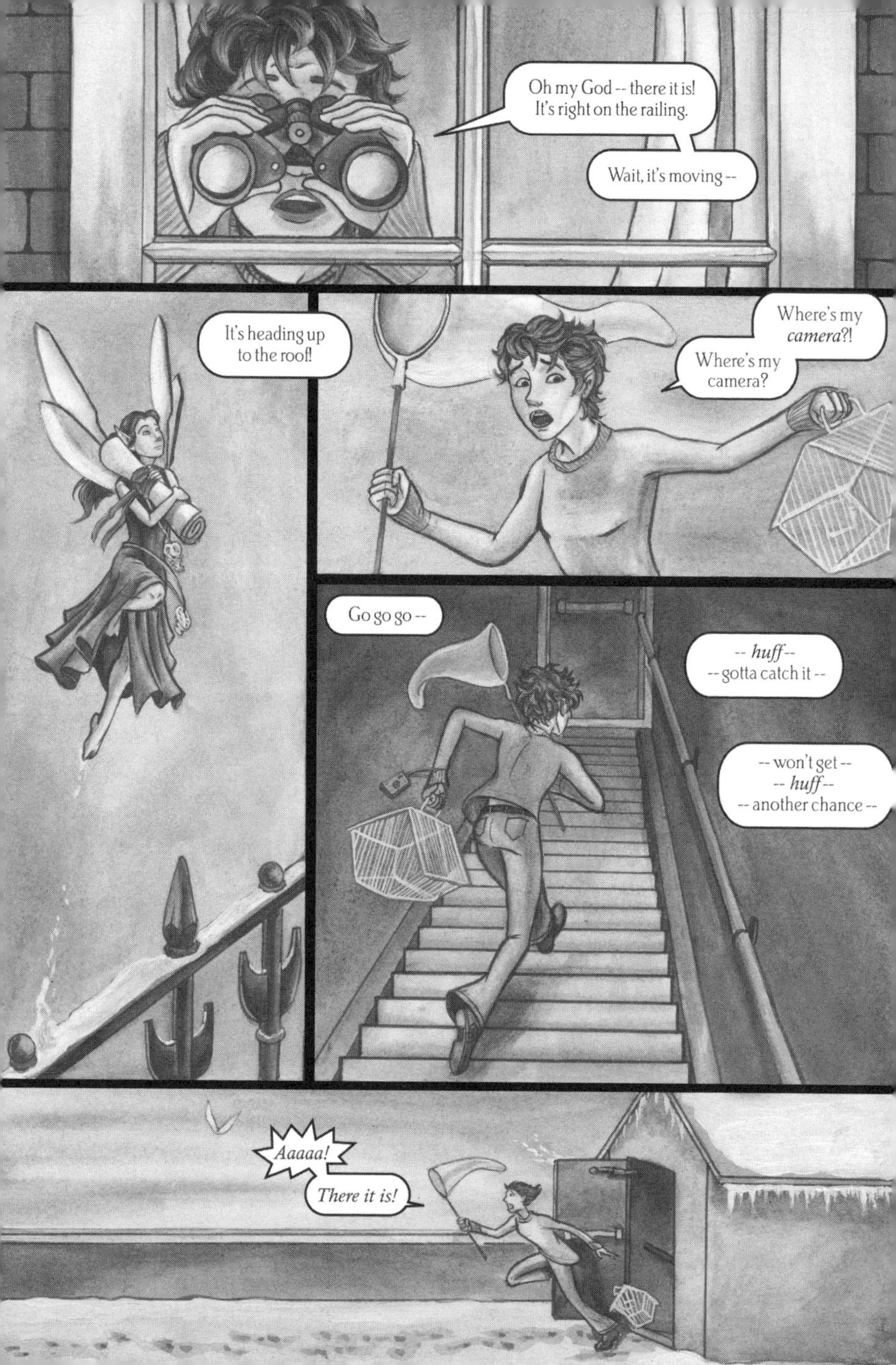
Oh my God -- there it is! It's right on the railing.
Wait, it's moving --
It's heading up to the roof!
Where's my camera?
Where's my *camera*?!
Go go go --
-- *huff* --
-- gotta catch it --
-- won't get --
-- *huff* --
-- another chance --
Aaaaa!
There it is!

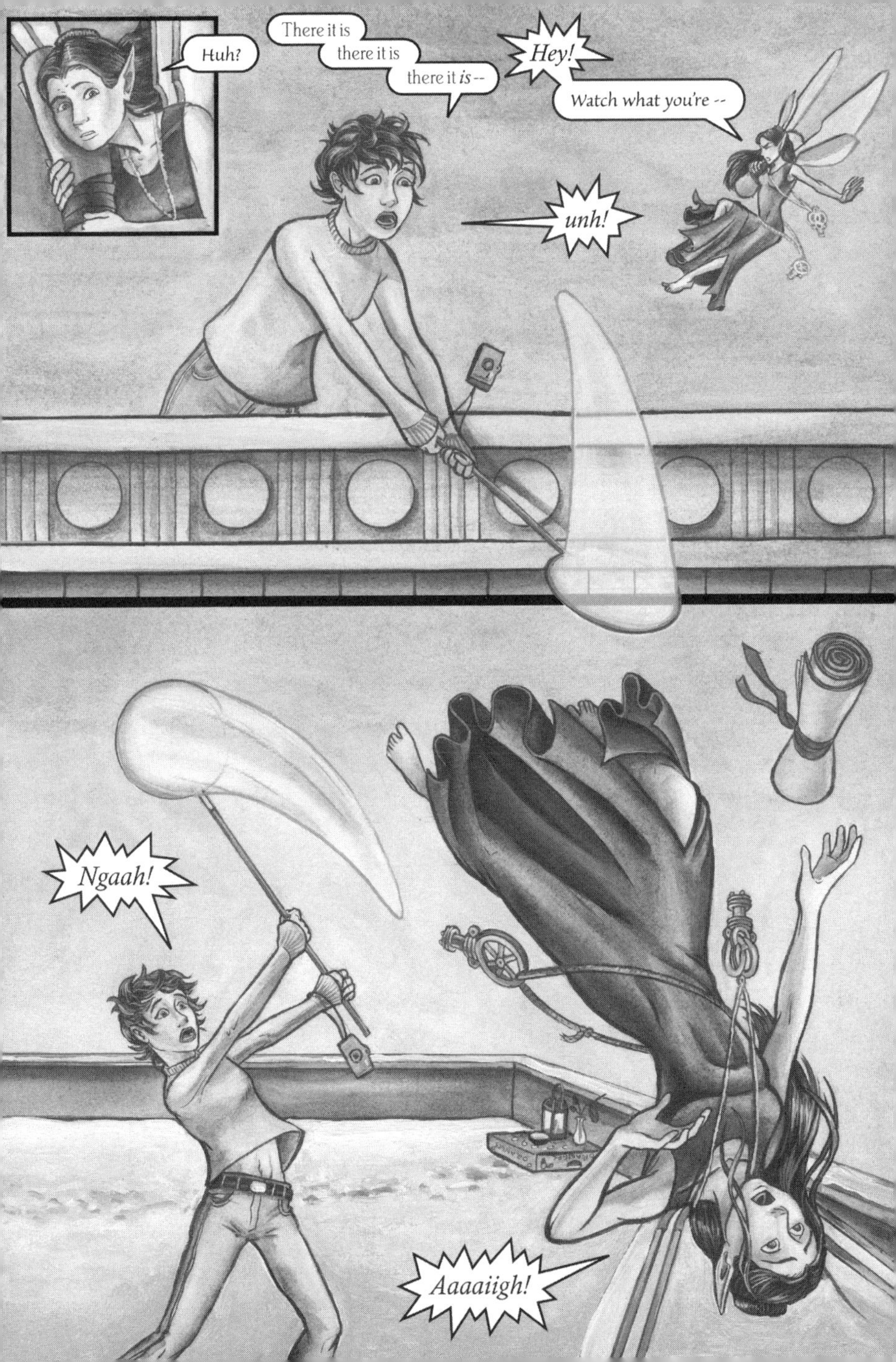
Huh?
There it is
there it is
there it *is* --
Hey!
Watch what you're --
unh!
Ngaah!
Aaaaiigh!

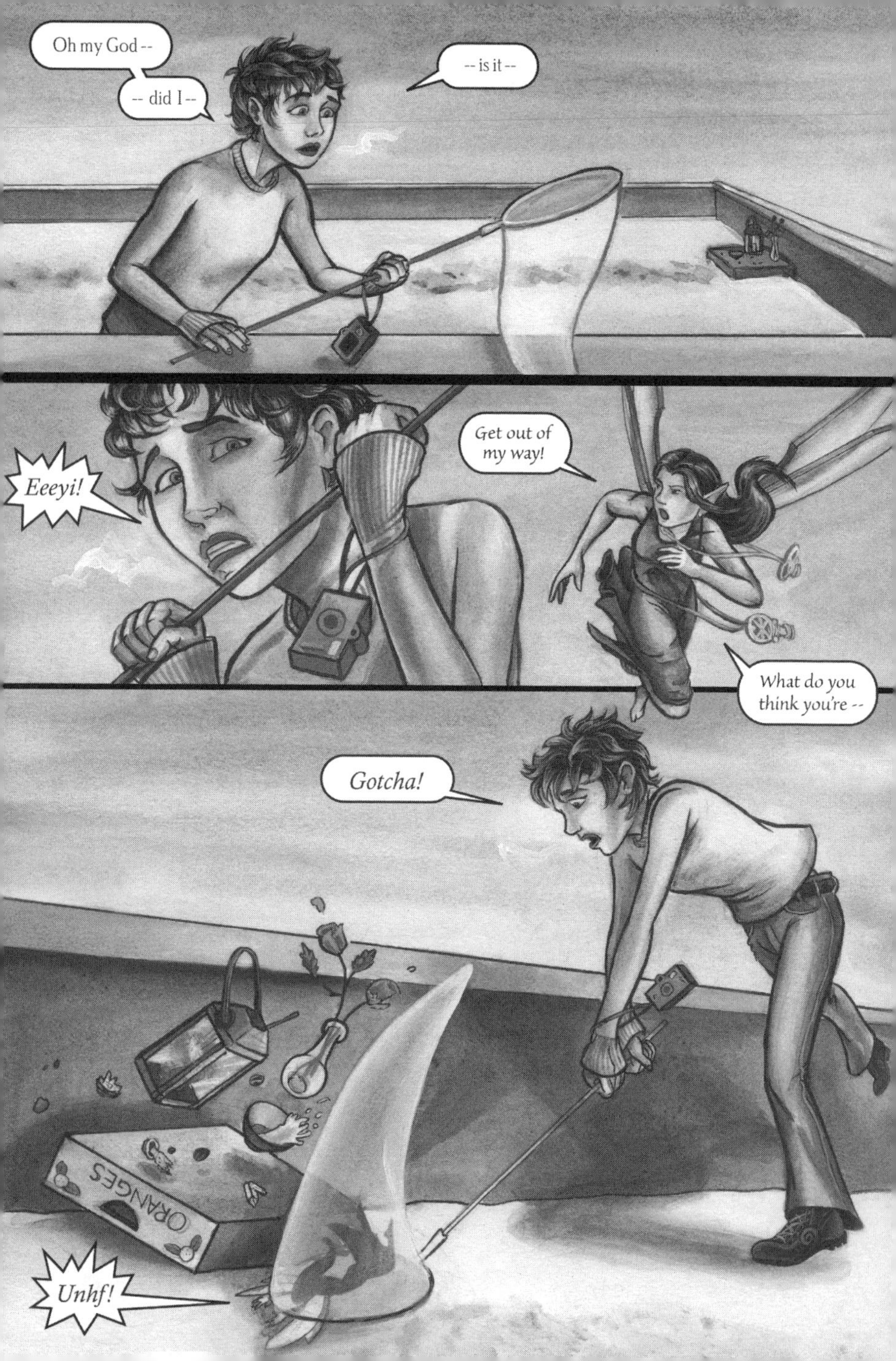
Oh my God --
-- did I --
-- is it --
Eeeyi!
Get out of my way!
What do you think you're --
Gotcha!
ORANGES
Unhf!

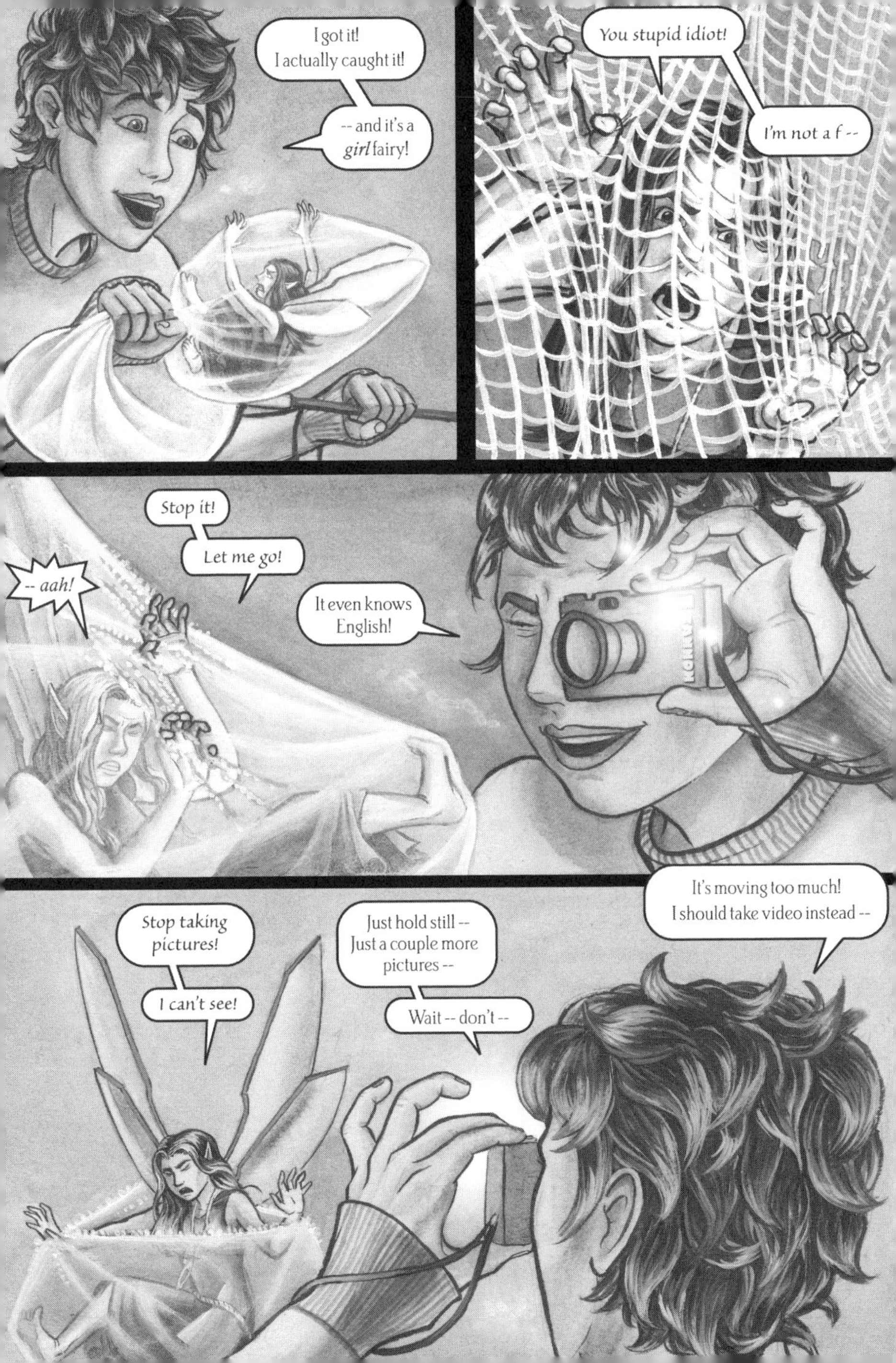
I got it! I actually caught it!
-- and it's a *girl* fairy!
You stupid idiot!
I'm not a f --
Stop it!
Let me go!
-- aah!
It even knows English!
Stop taking pictures!
I can't see!
Just hold still -- Just a couple more pictures --
Wait -- don't --
It's moving too much! I should take video instead --

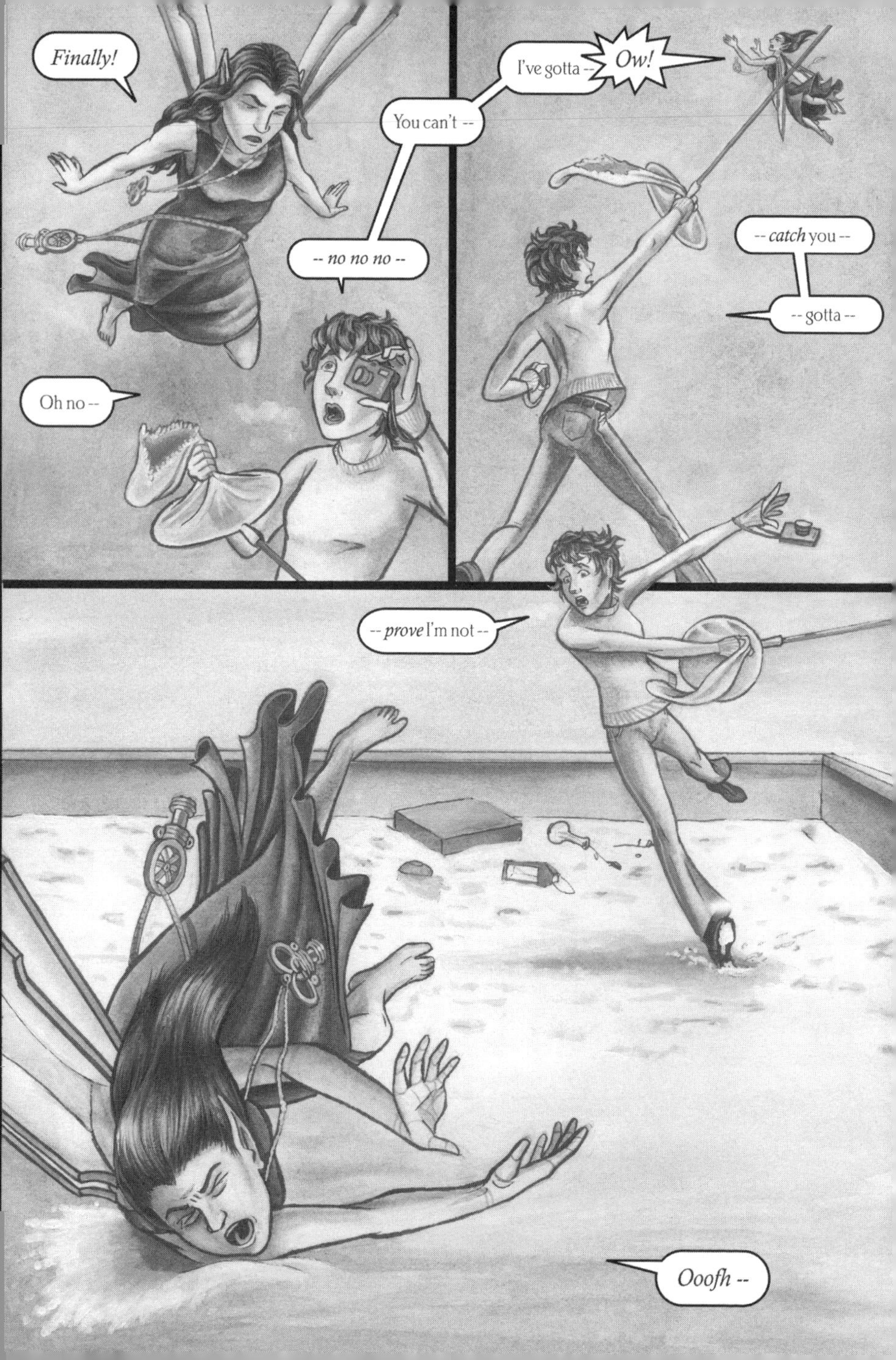
Finally!
You can't --
-- *no no no* --
Oh no --
I've gotta --
Ow!
-- *catch* you --
-- gotta --
-- *prove* I'm not --
Ooofh --

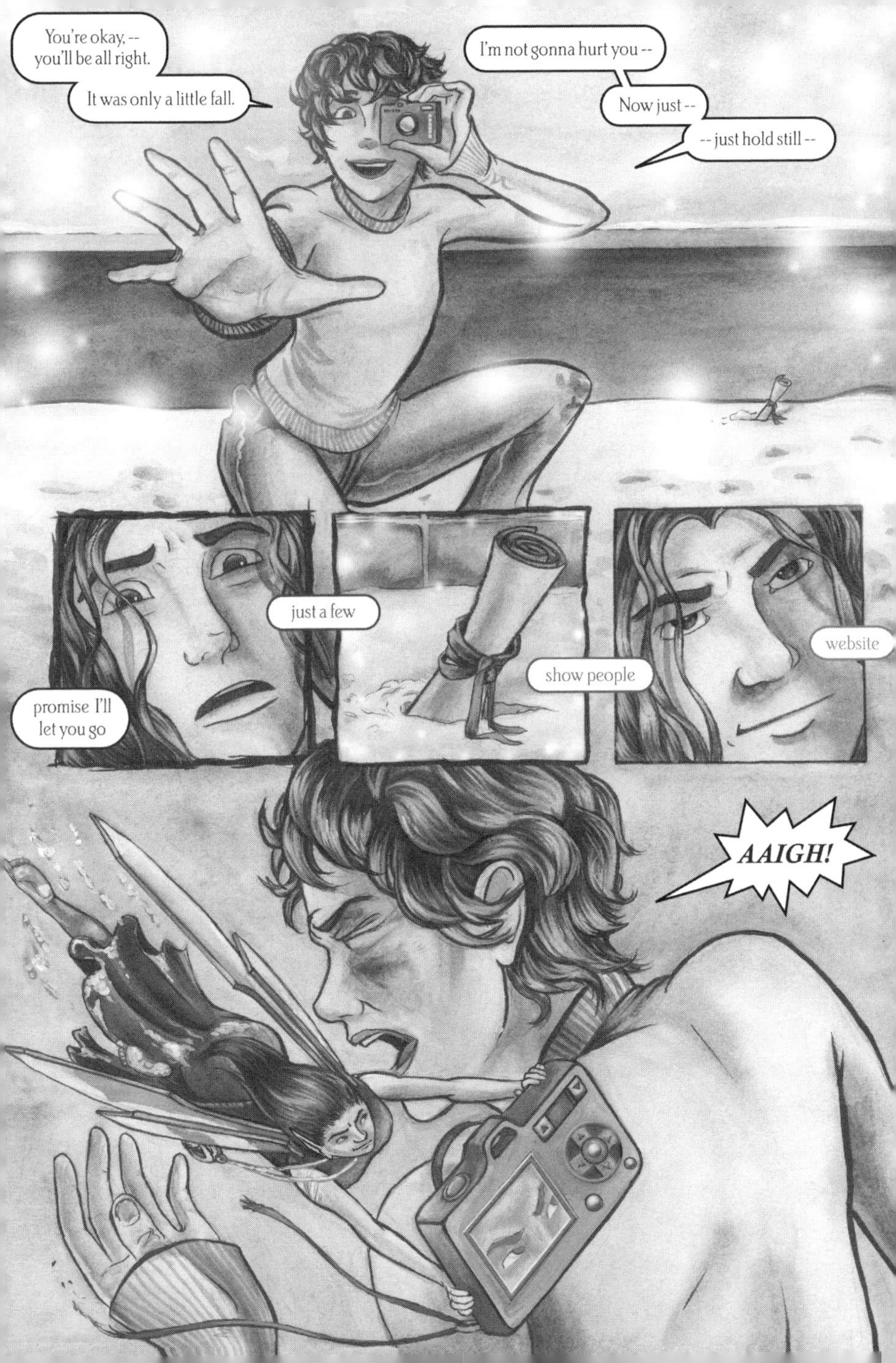
You're okay, --
you'll be all right.
It was only a little fall.
I'm not gonna hurt you --
Now just --
-- just hold still --
promise I'll let you go
just a few
show people
website
AAIGH!

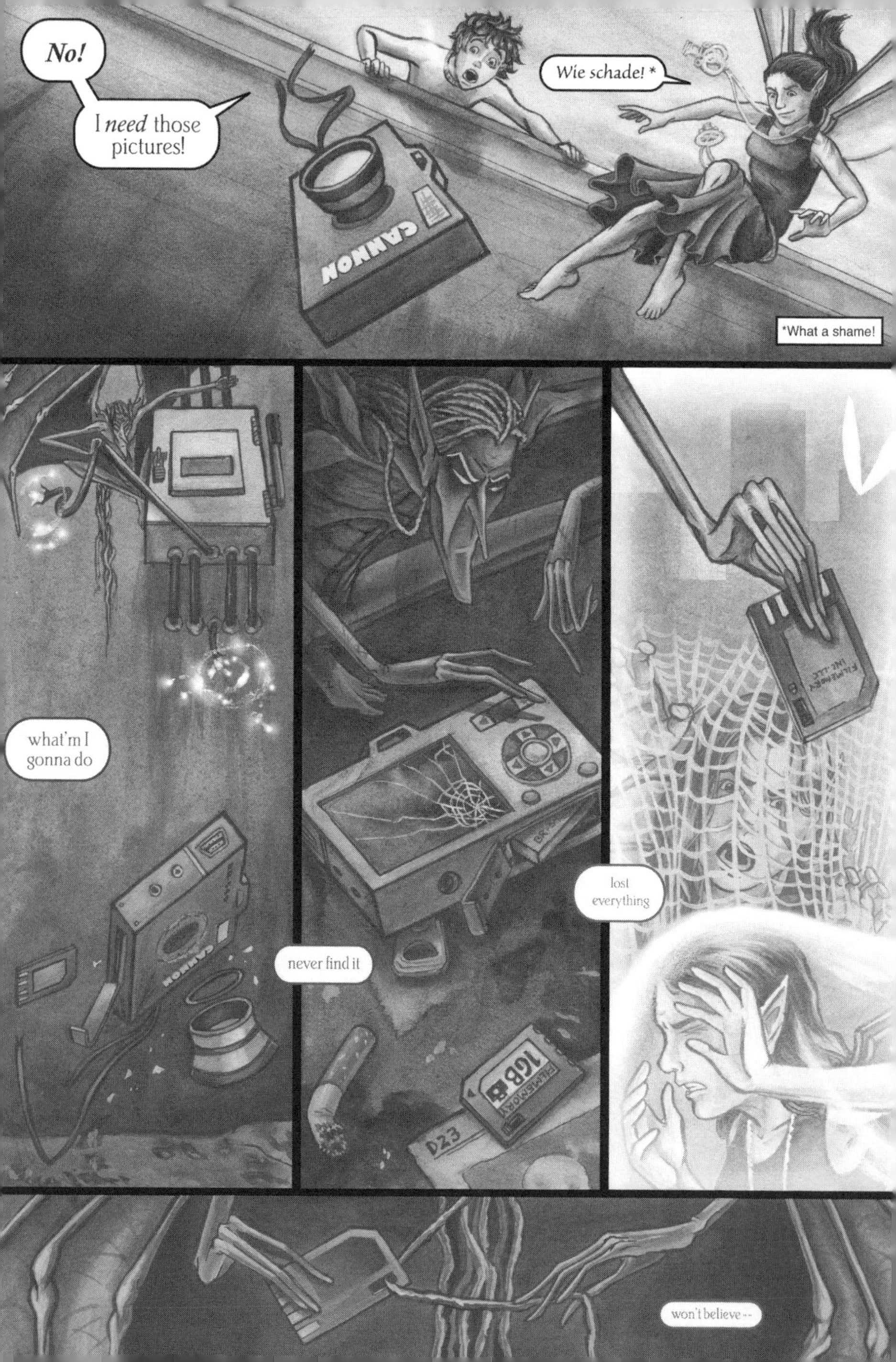
No!
I *need* those pictures!
Wie schade! *
*What a shame!
what'm I gonna do
never find it
lost everything
won't believe ...

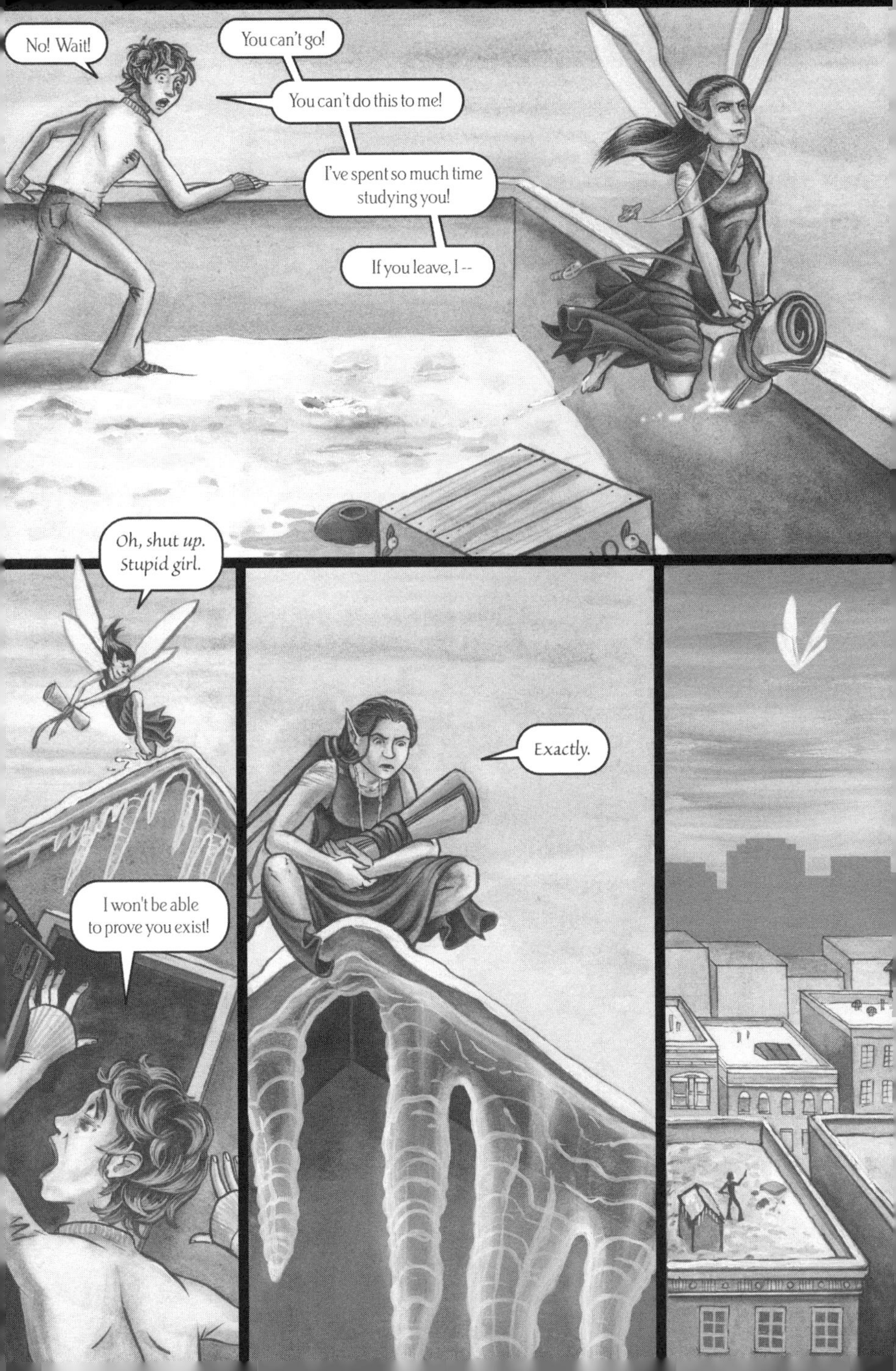
No! Wait!
You can't go!
You can't do this to me!
I've spent so much time studying you!
If you leave, I --
Oh, shut up. Stupid girl.
I won't be able to prove you exist!
Exactly.

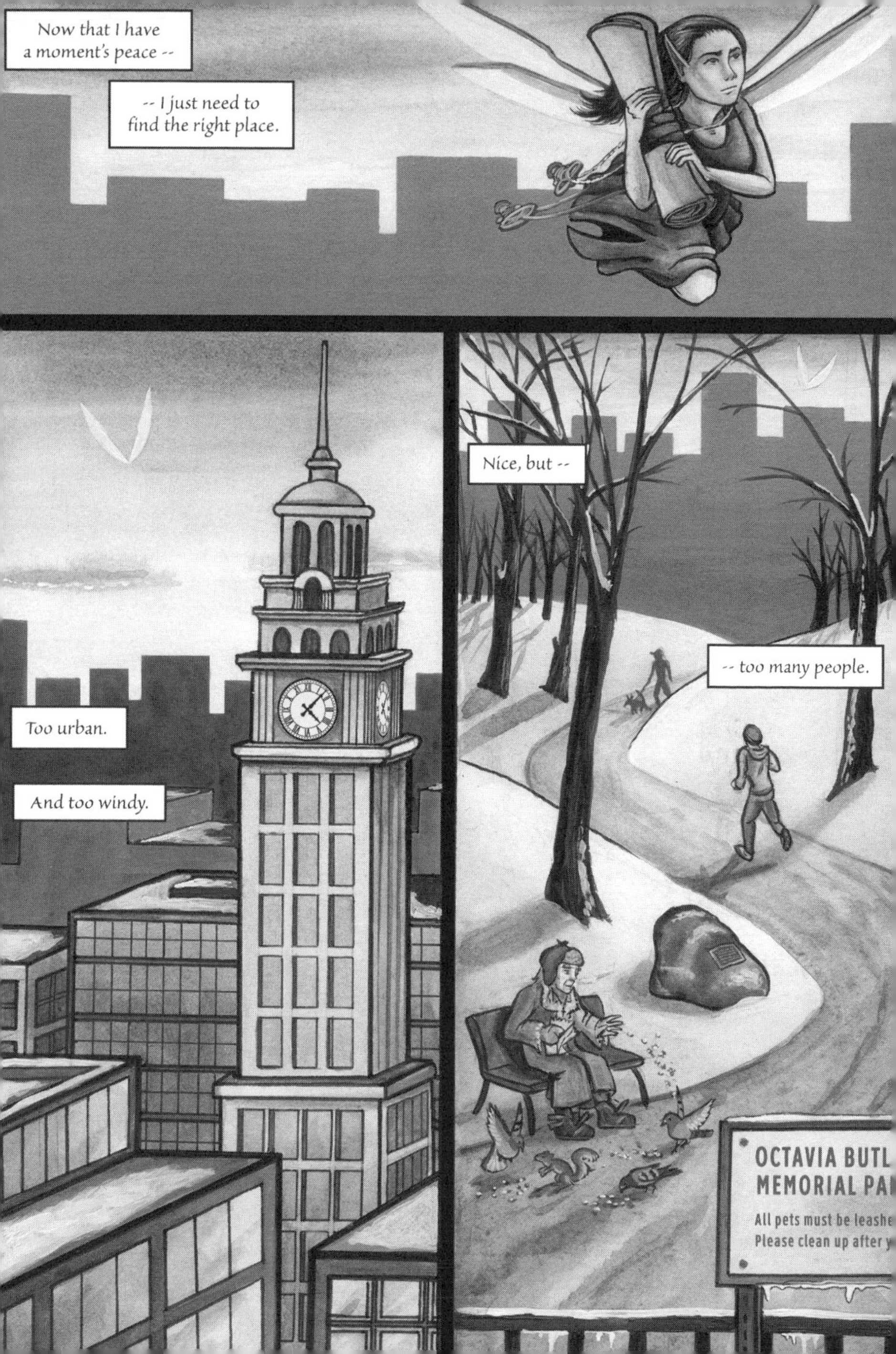
Now that I have a moment's peace --
-- I just need to find the right place.
Too urban.
And too windy.
Nice, but --
-- too many people.
OCTAVIA BUTL
MEMORIAL PA
All pets must be leashe
Please clean up after y

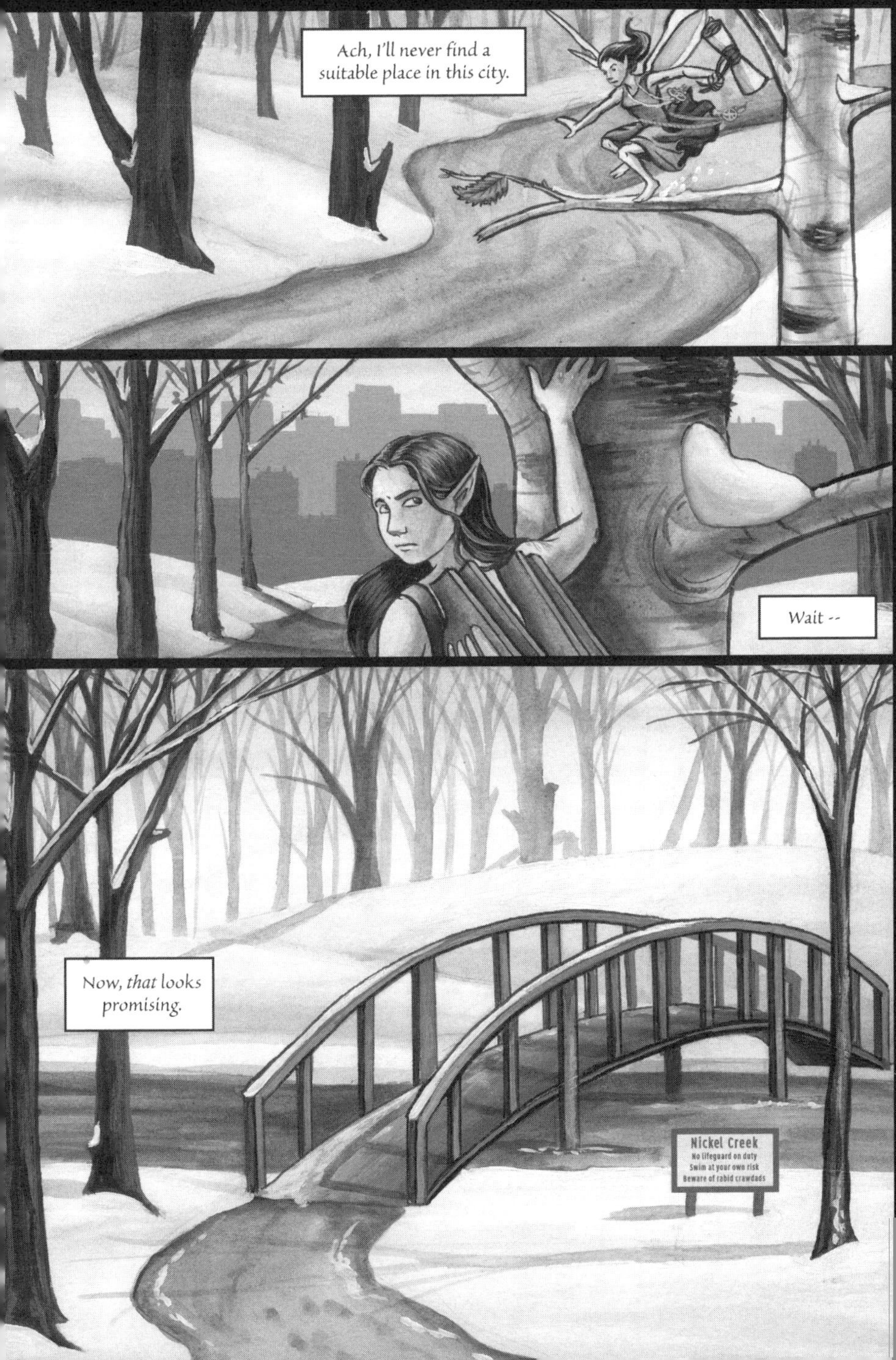

Ach, I'll never find a suitable place in this city.
Wait --
Now, *that* looks promising.
Nickel Creek
No lifeguard on duty
Swim at your own risk
Beware of rabid crawdads

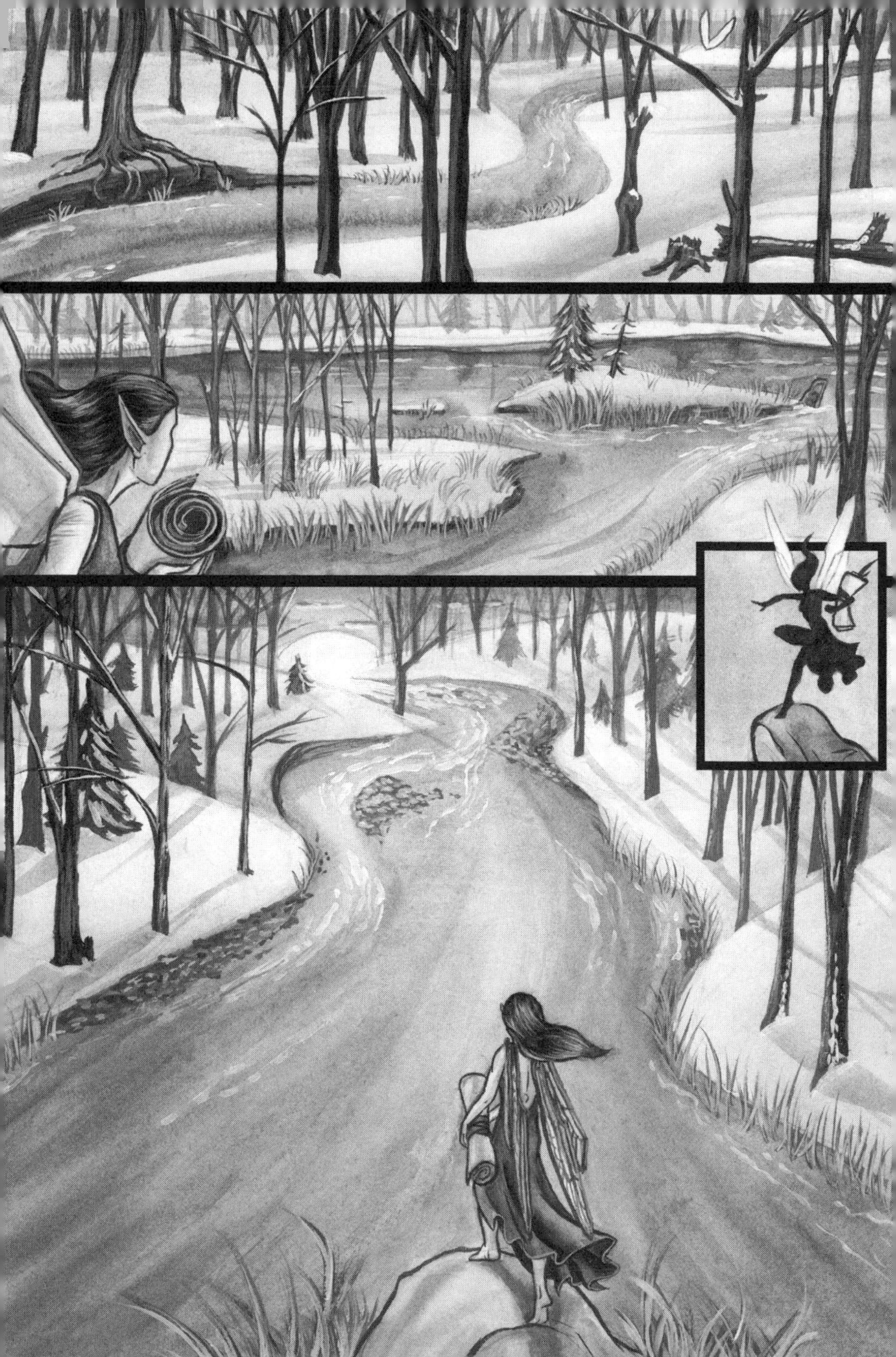

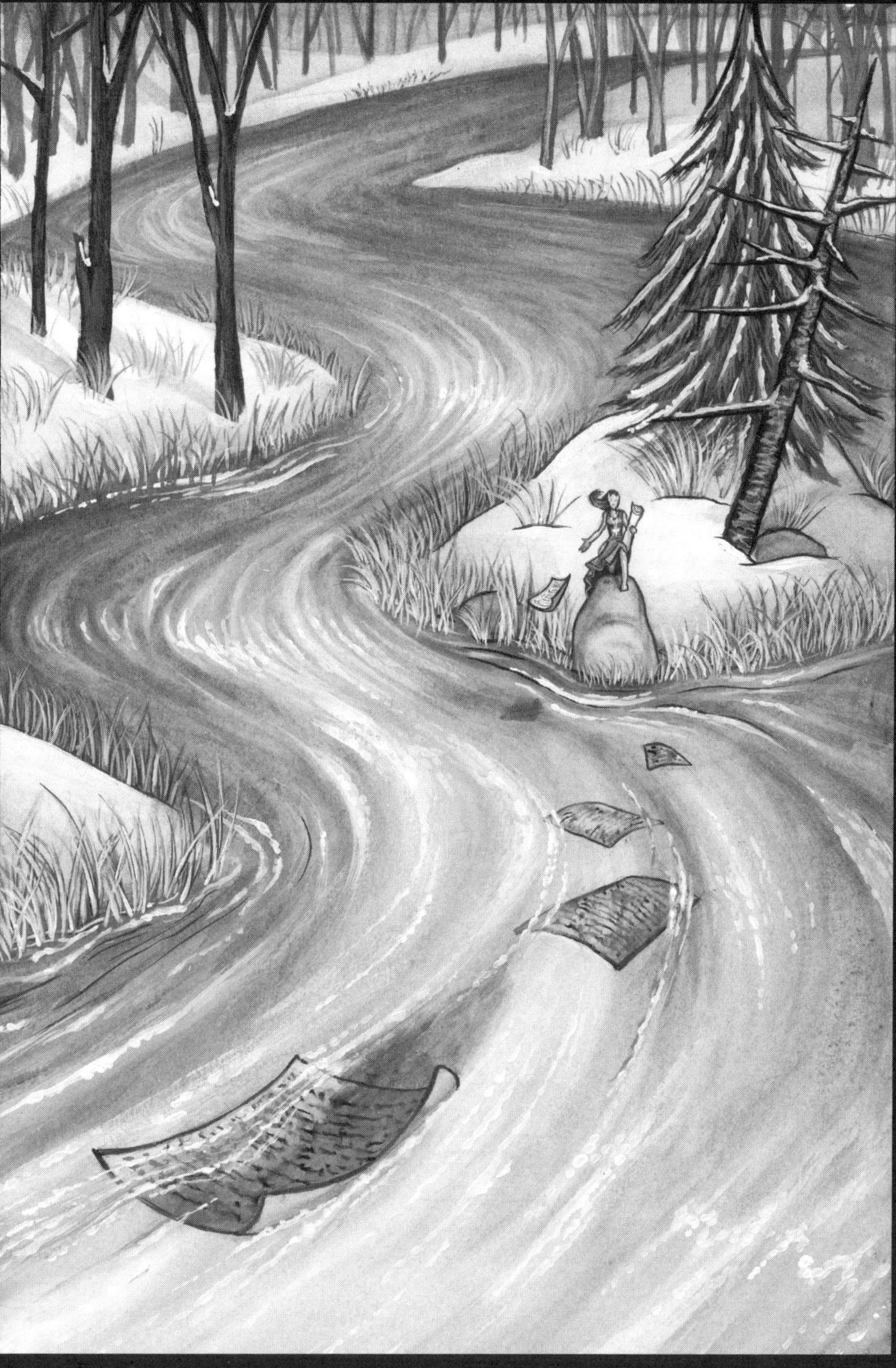

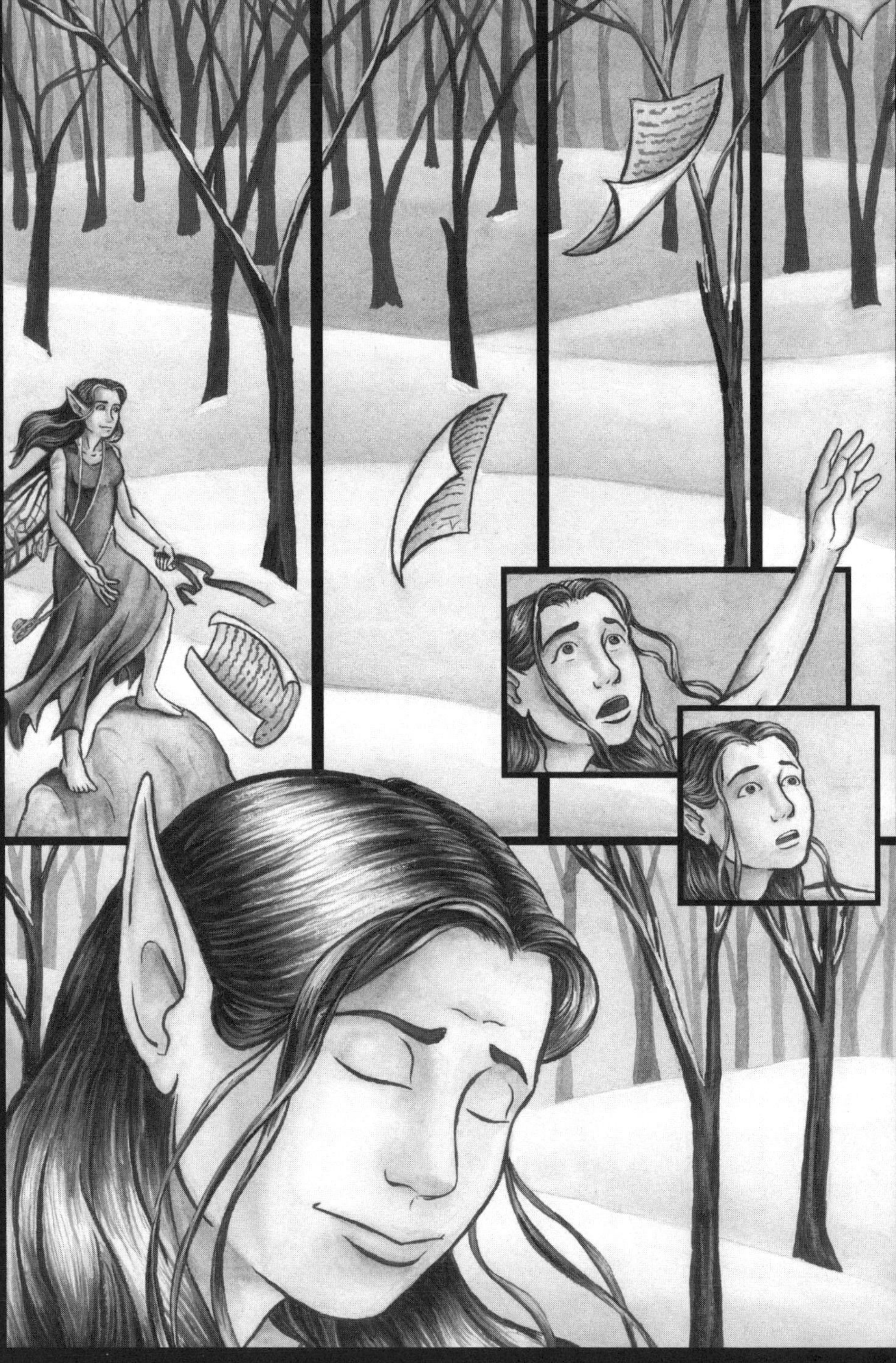

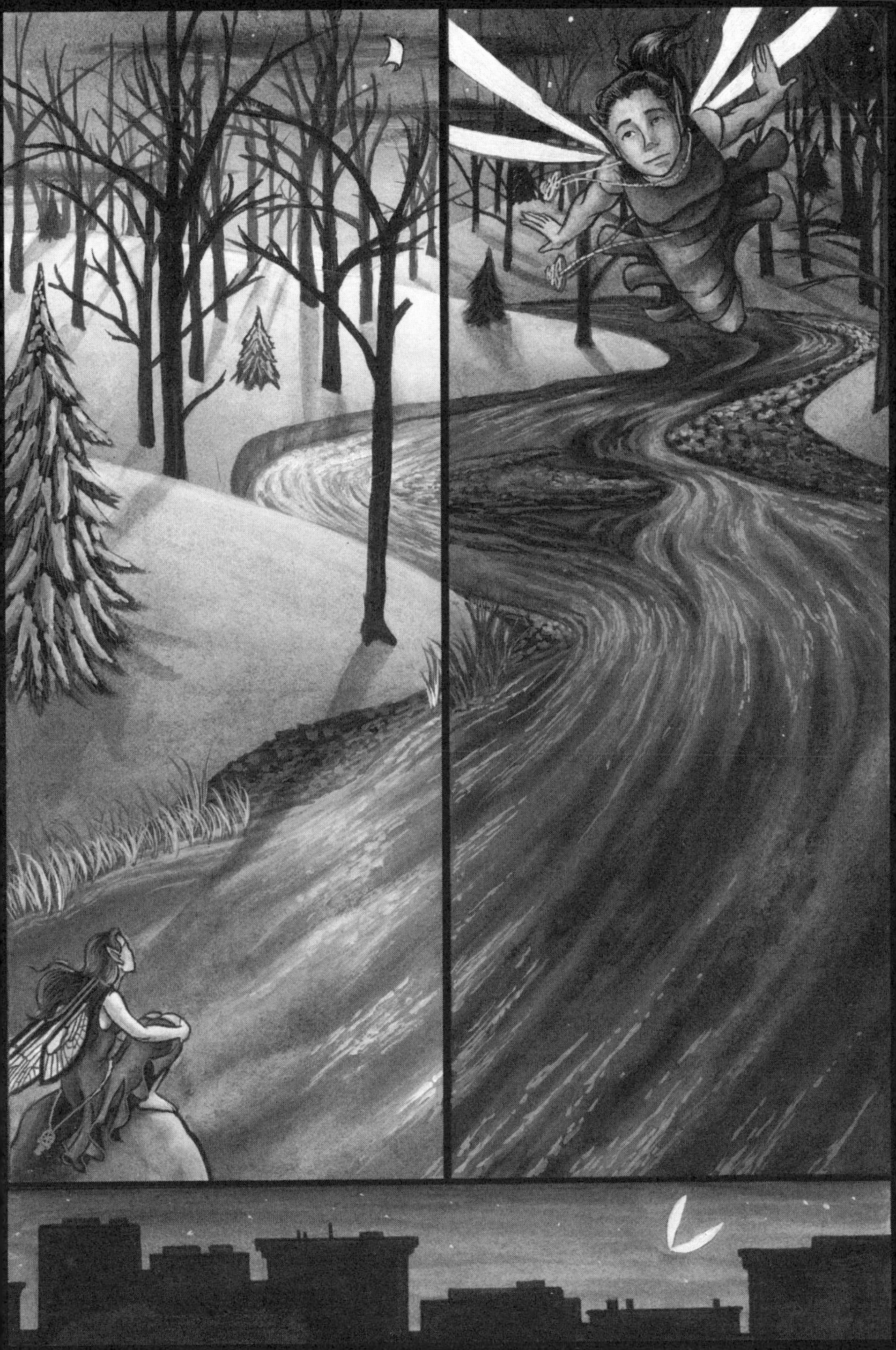

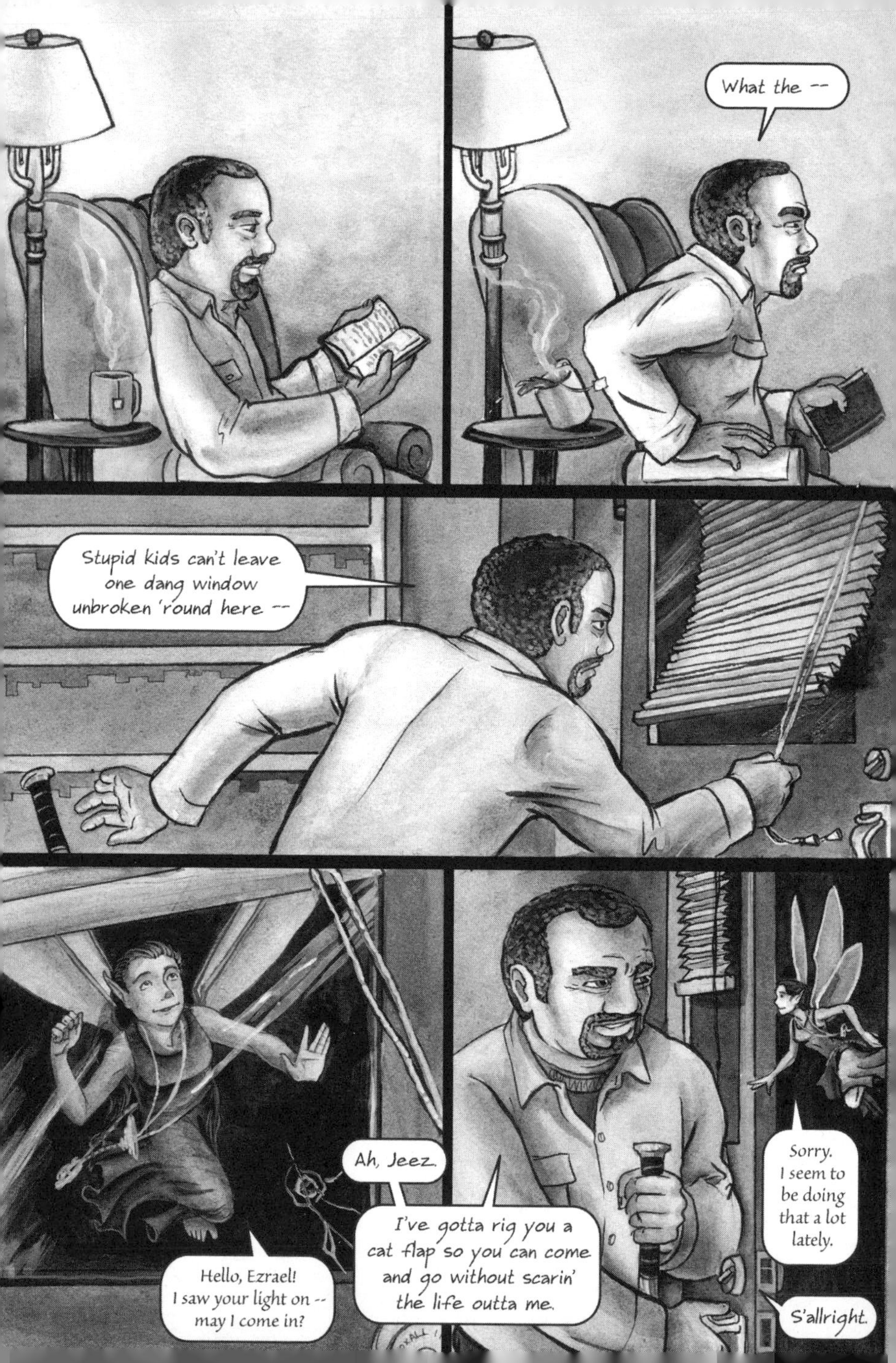
What the --
Stupid kids can't leave one dang window unbroken 'round here --
Hello, Ezrael! I saw your light on -- may I come in?
Ah, Jeez.
I've gotta rig you a cat flap so you can come and go without scarin' the life outta me.
Sorry. I seem to be doing that a lot lately.
S'allright.

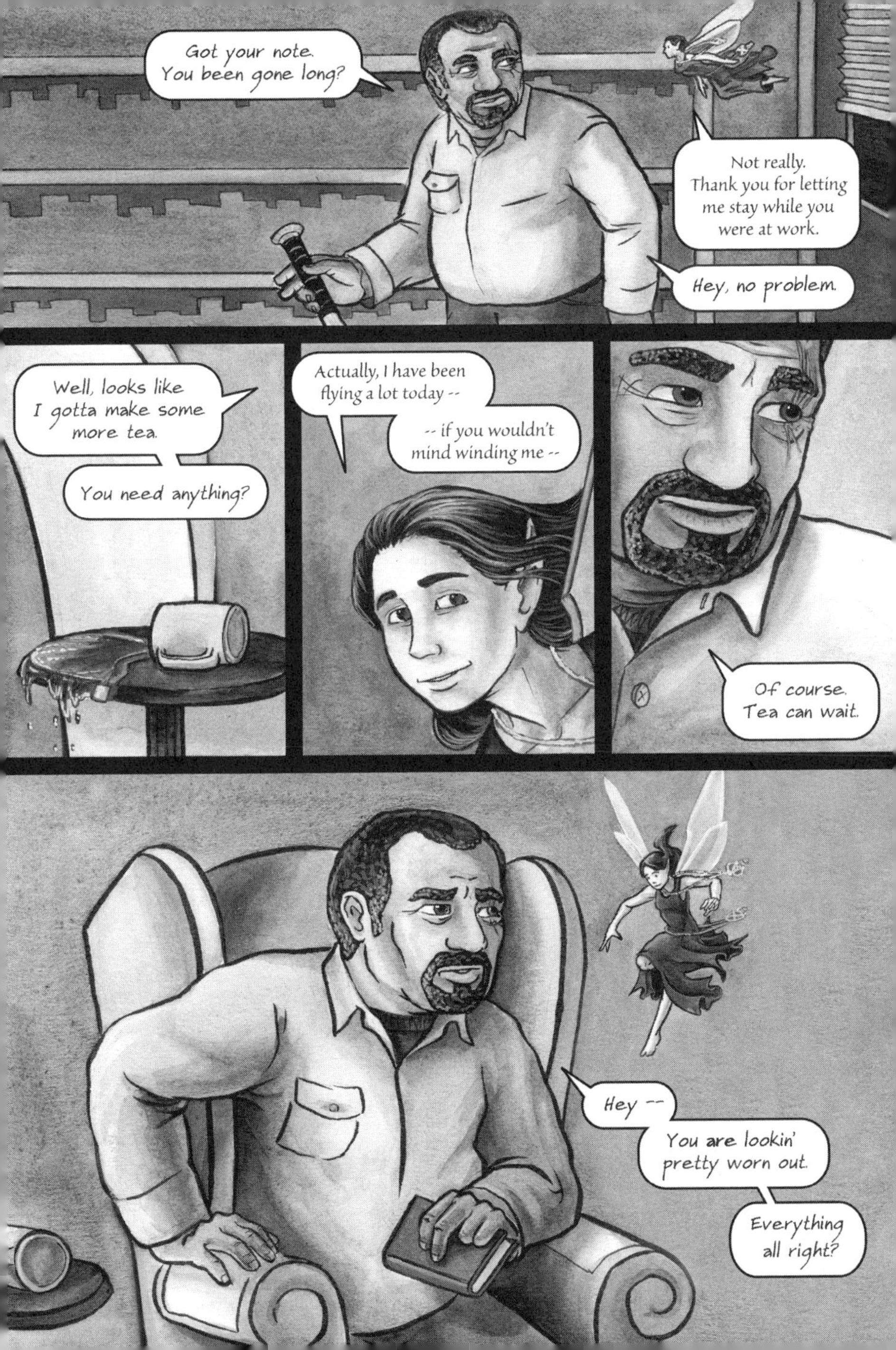
Got your note.
You been gone long?
Not really.
Thank you for letting me stay while you were at work.
Hey, no problem.
Well, looks like I gotta make some more tea.
You need anything?
Actually, I have been flying a lot today --
-- if you wouldn't mind winding me --
Of course.
Tea can wait.
Hey --
You are lookin' pretty worn out.
Everything all right?

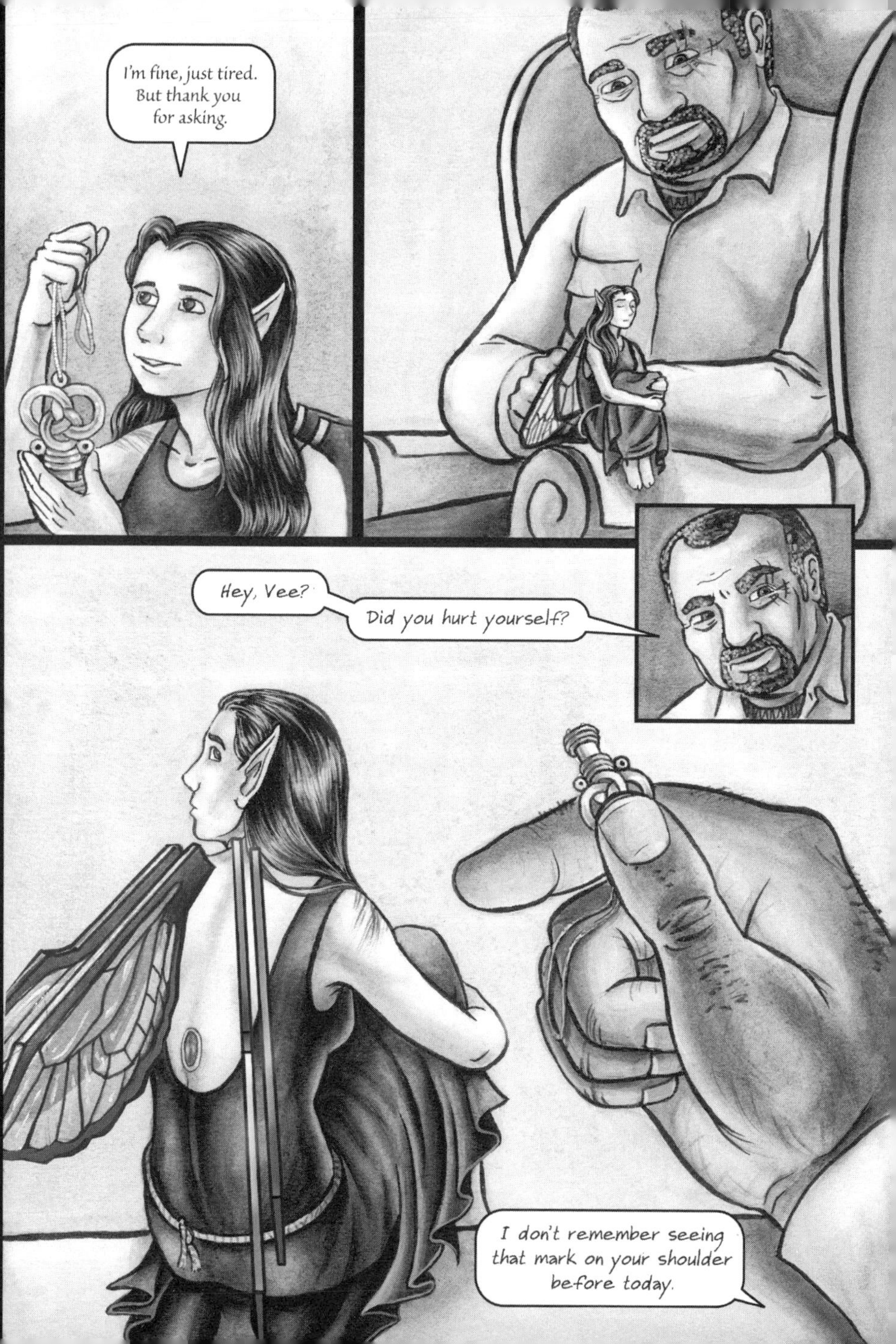
I'm fine, just tired. But thank you for asking.
Hey, Vee?
Did you hurt yourself?
I don't remember seeing that mark on your shoulder before today.

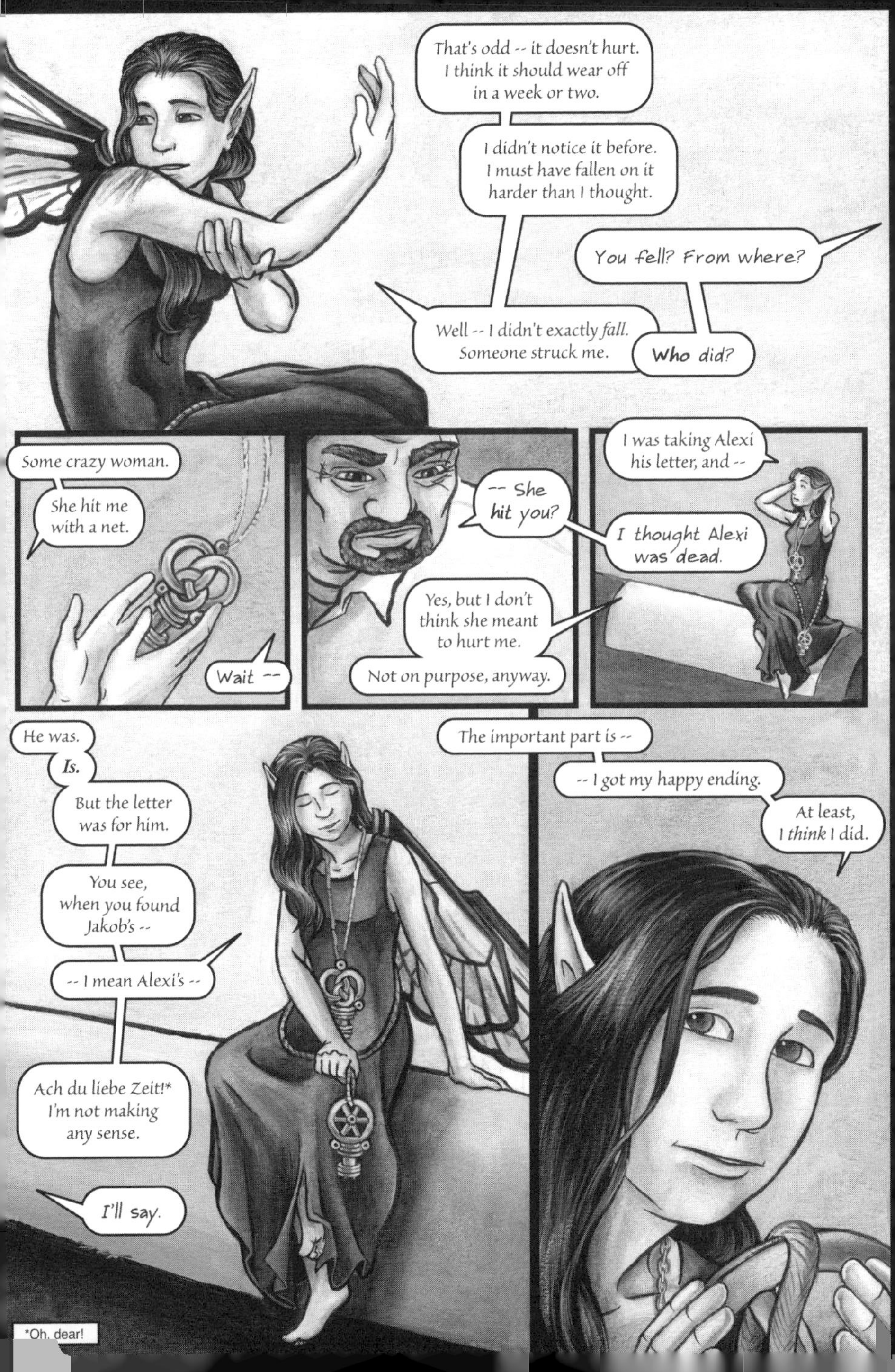
That's odd -- it doesn't hurt. I think it should wear off in a week or two.
I didn't notice it before. I must have fallen on it harder than I thought.
You fell? From where?
Well -- I didn't exactly *fall*. Someone struck me.
Who did?
Some crazy woman.
She hit me with a net.
Wait --
-- She **hit** you?
Yes, but I don't think she meant to hurt me.
Not on purpose, anyway.
I was taking Alexi his letter, and --
I thought Alexi was dead.
He was.
Is.
But the letter was for him.
You see, when you found Jakob's --
-- I mean Alexi's --
Ach du liebe Zeit!* I'm not making any sense.
I'll say.
The important part is --
-- I got my happy ending.
At least, I *think* I did.

*Oh, dear!

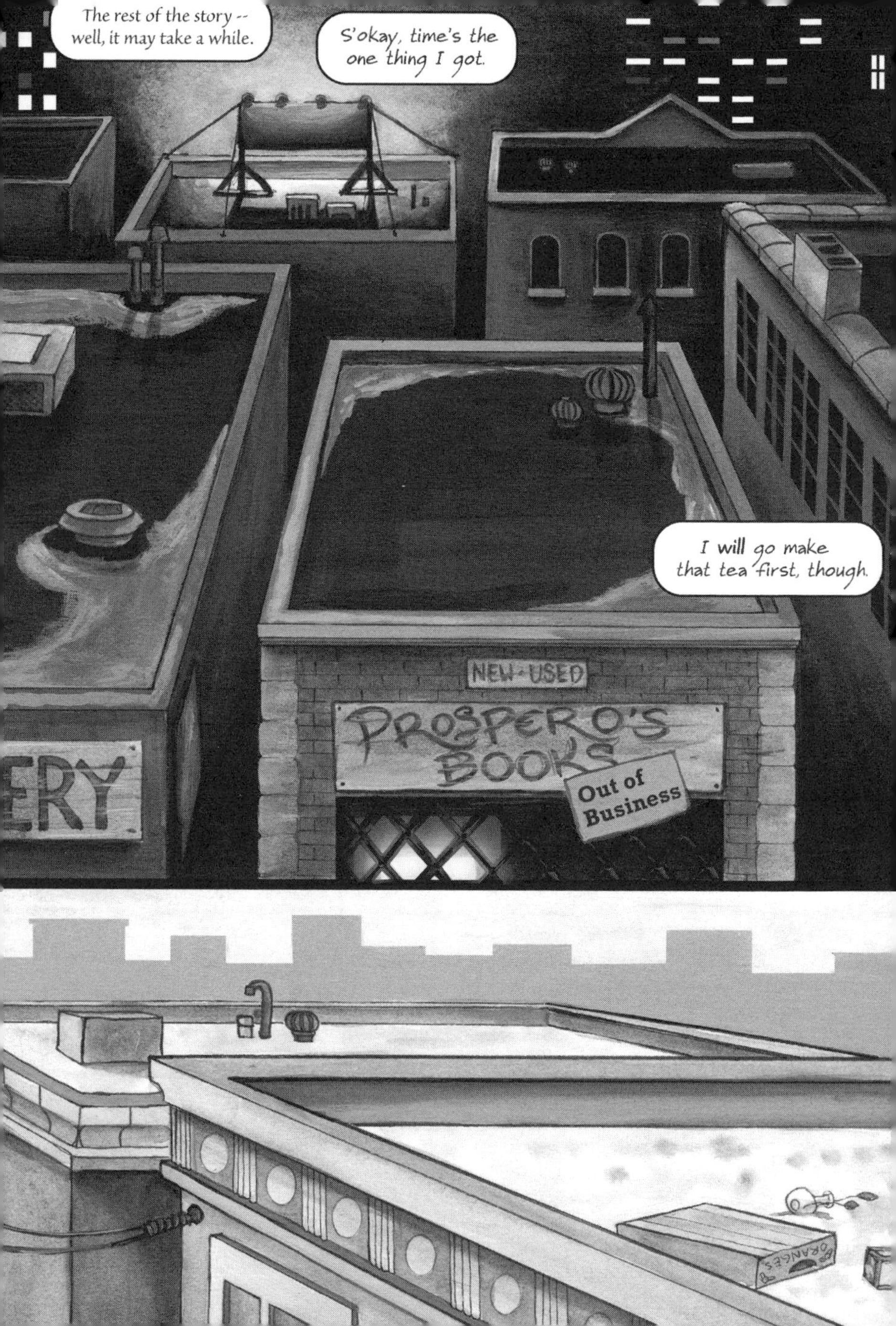
The rest of the story -- well, it may take a while.
S'okay, time's the one thing I got.
I will go make that tea first, though.
NEW-USED
PROSPERO'S BOOKS
Out of Business
ERY

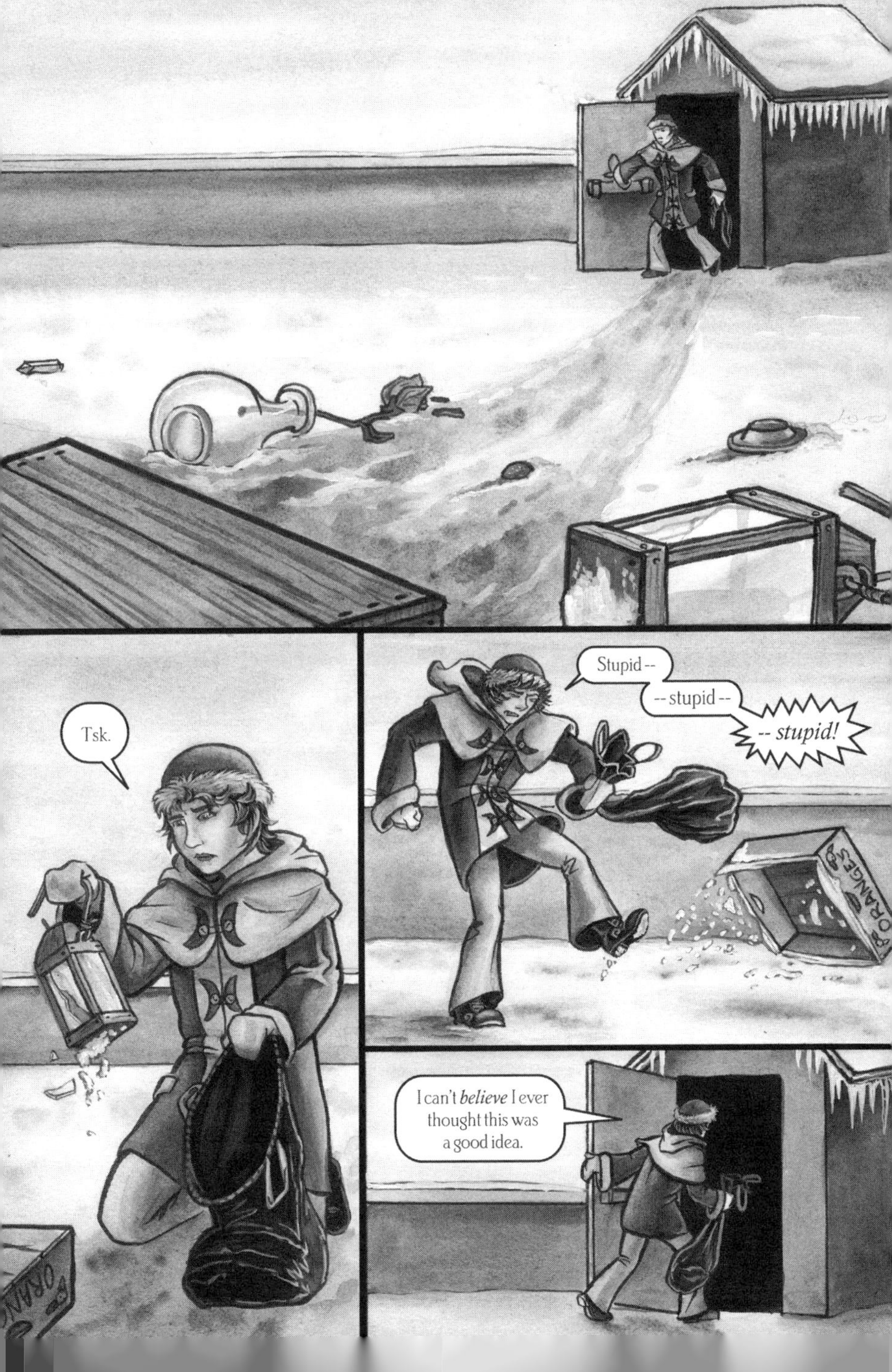
Tsk.
Stupid --
-- stupid --
-- *stupid!*
ORANGES
I can't *believe* I ever thought this was a good idea.

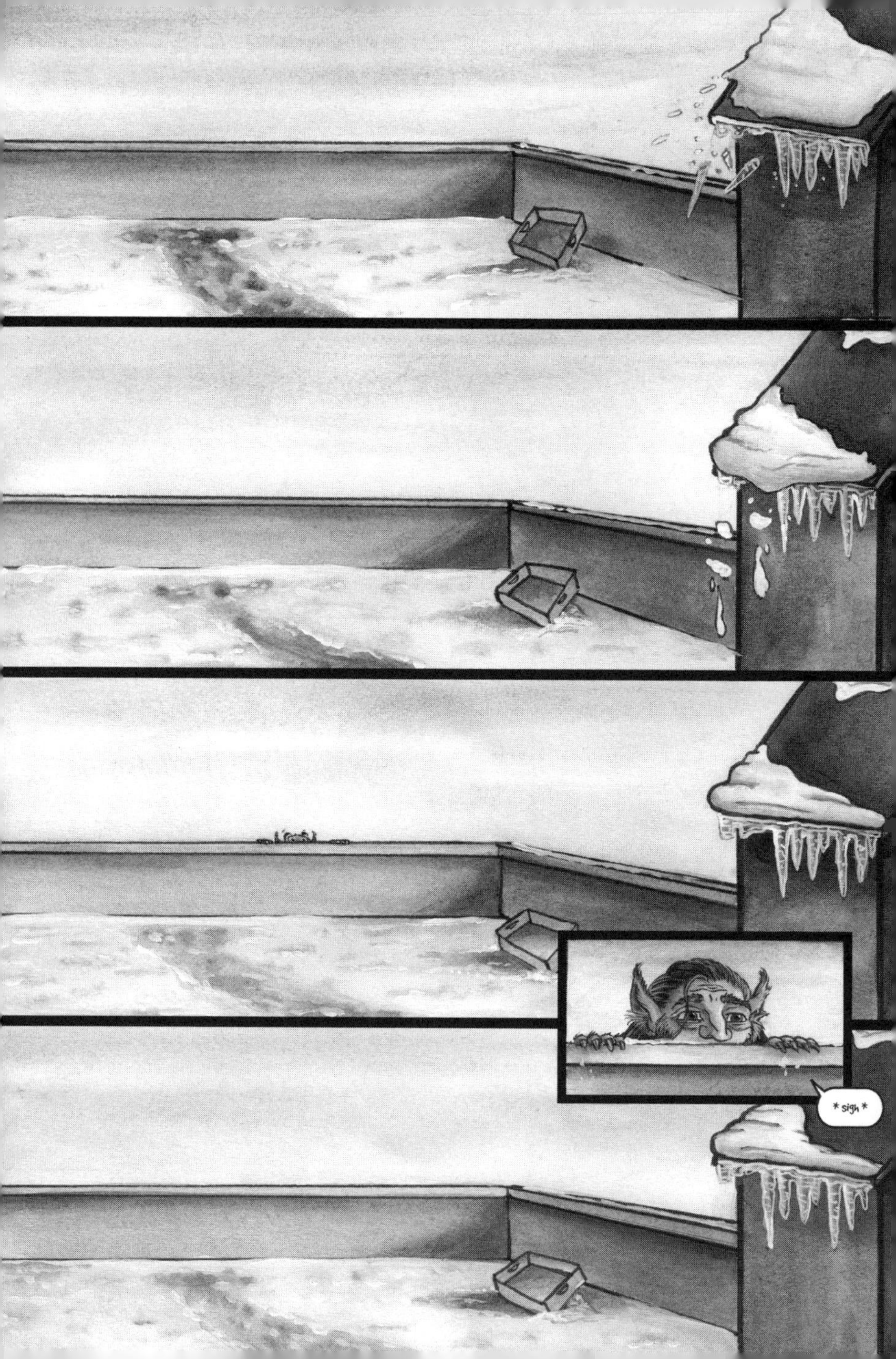
* sigh *

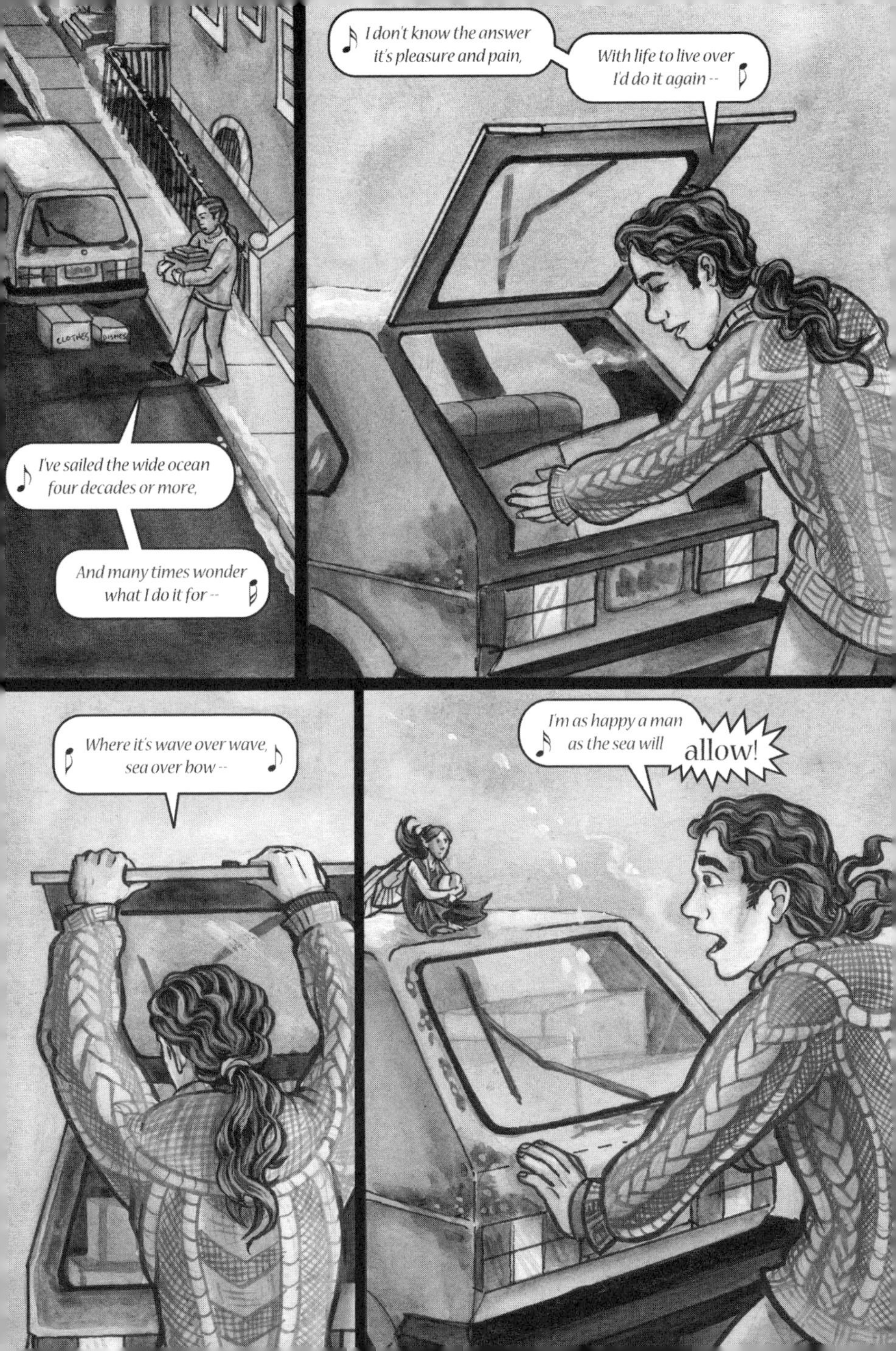

CLOTHES
DISHES
I've sailed the wide ocean four decades or more,
And many times wonder what I do it for --
I don't know the answer it's pleasure and pain,
With life to live over I'd do it again --
Where it's wave over wave, sea over bow --
I'm as happy a man as the sea will allow!

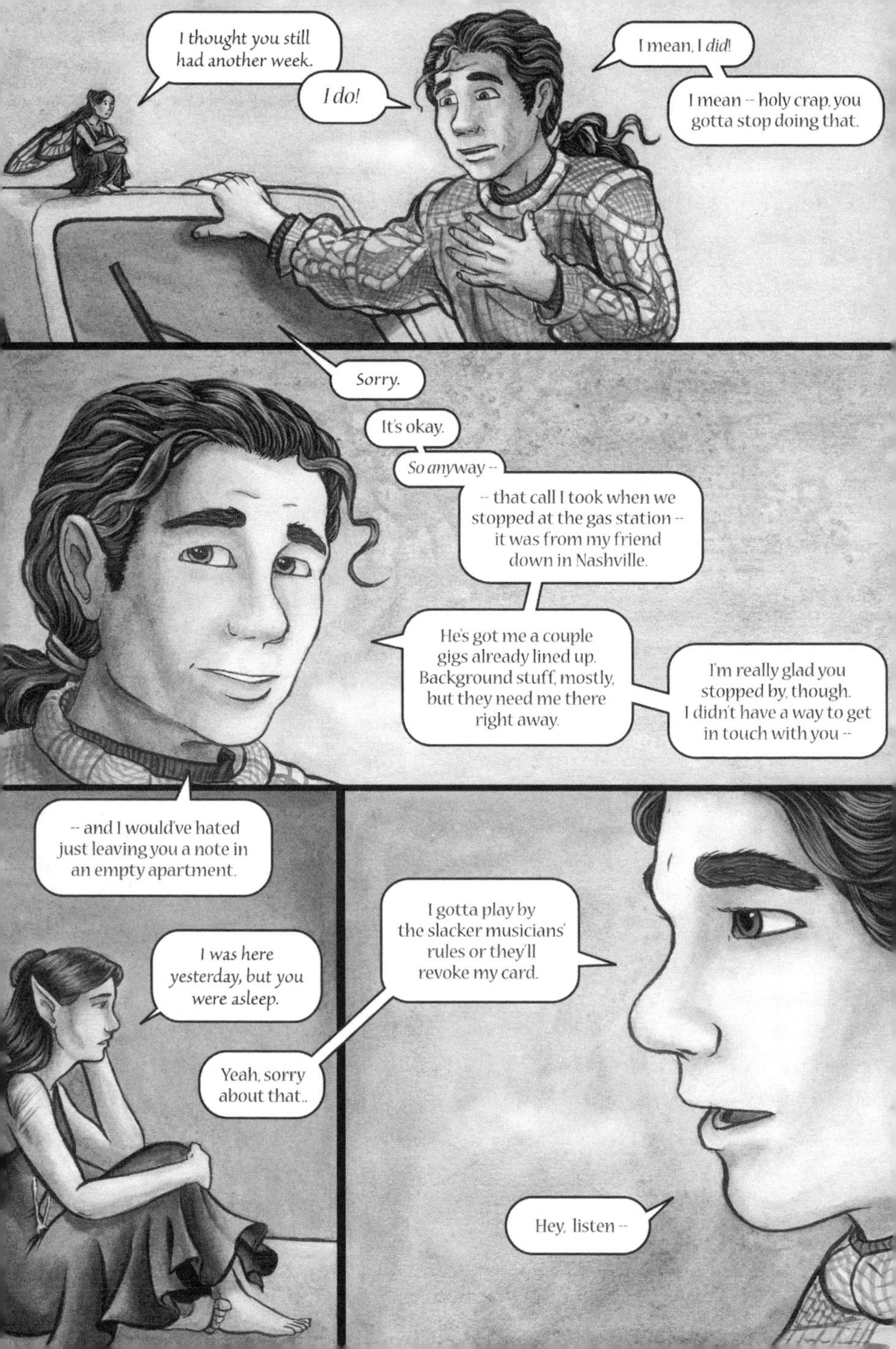
I thought you still had another week.
I do!
I mean, I *did*!
I mean -- holy crap, you gotta stop doing that.
Sorry.
It's okay.
So anyway --
-- that call I took when we stopped at the gas station -- it was from my friend down in Nashville.
He's got me a couple gigs already lined up. Background stuff, mostly, but they need me there right away.
I'm really glad you stopped by, though. I didn't have a way to get in touch with you --
-- and I would've hated just leaving you a note in an empty apartment.
I was here yesterday, but you were asleep.
Yeah, sorry about that..
I gotta play by the slacker musicians' rules or they'll revoke my card.
Hey, listen --

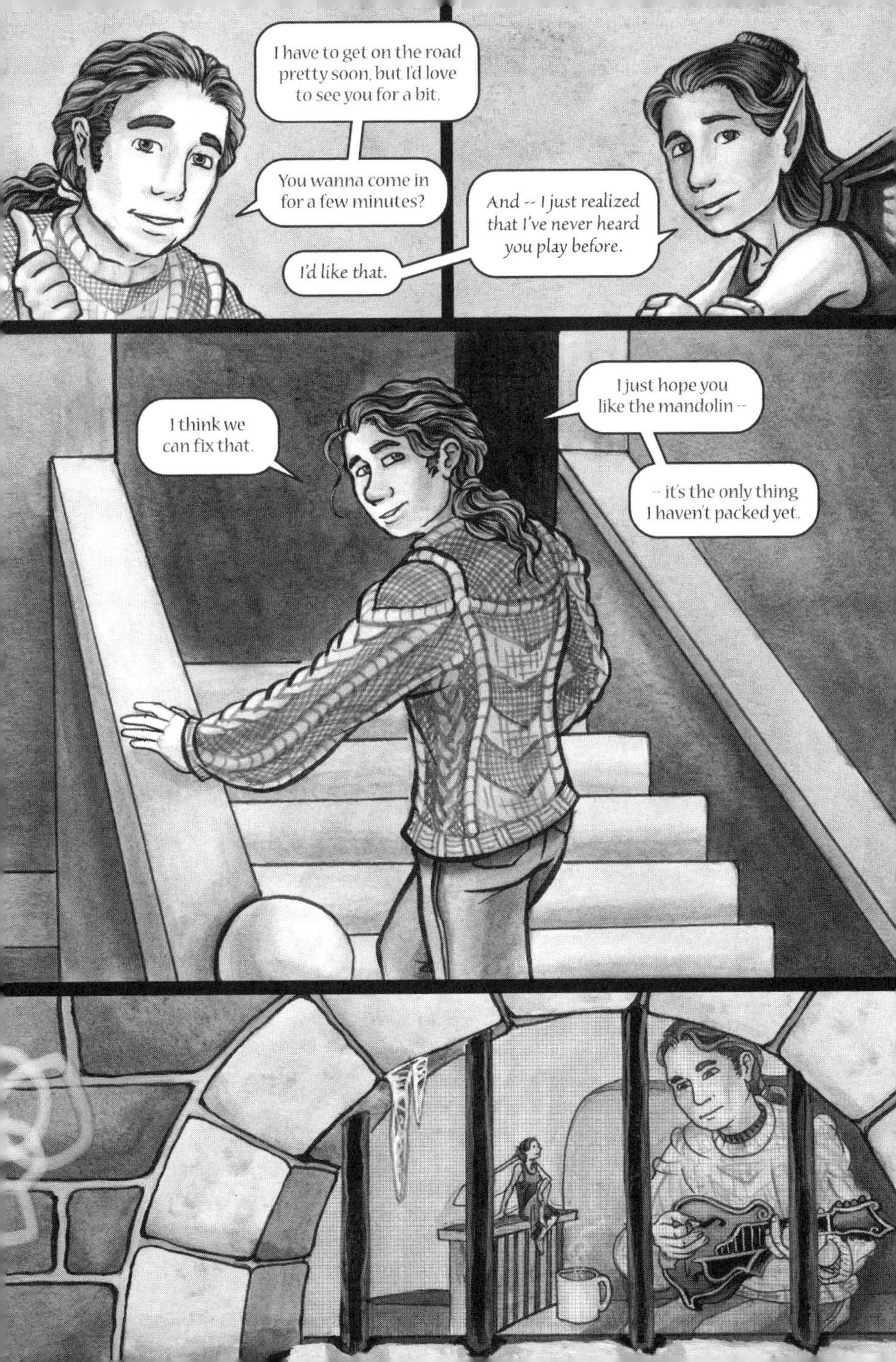
I have to get on the road pretty soon, but I'd love to see you for a bit.
You wanna come in for a few minutes?
I'd like that.
And -- I just realized that I've never heard you play before.
I think we can fix that.
I just hope you like the mandolin --
-- it's the only thing I haven't packed yet.

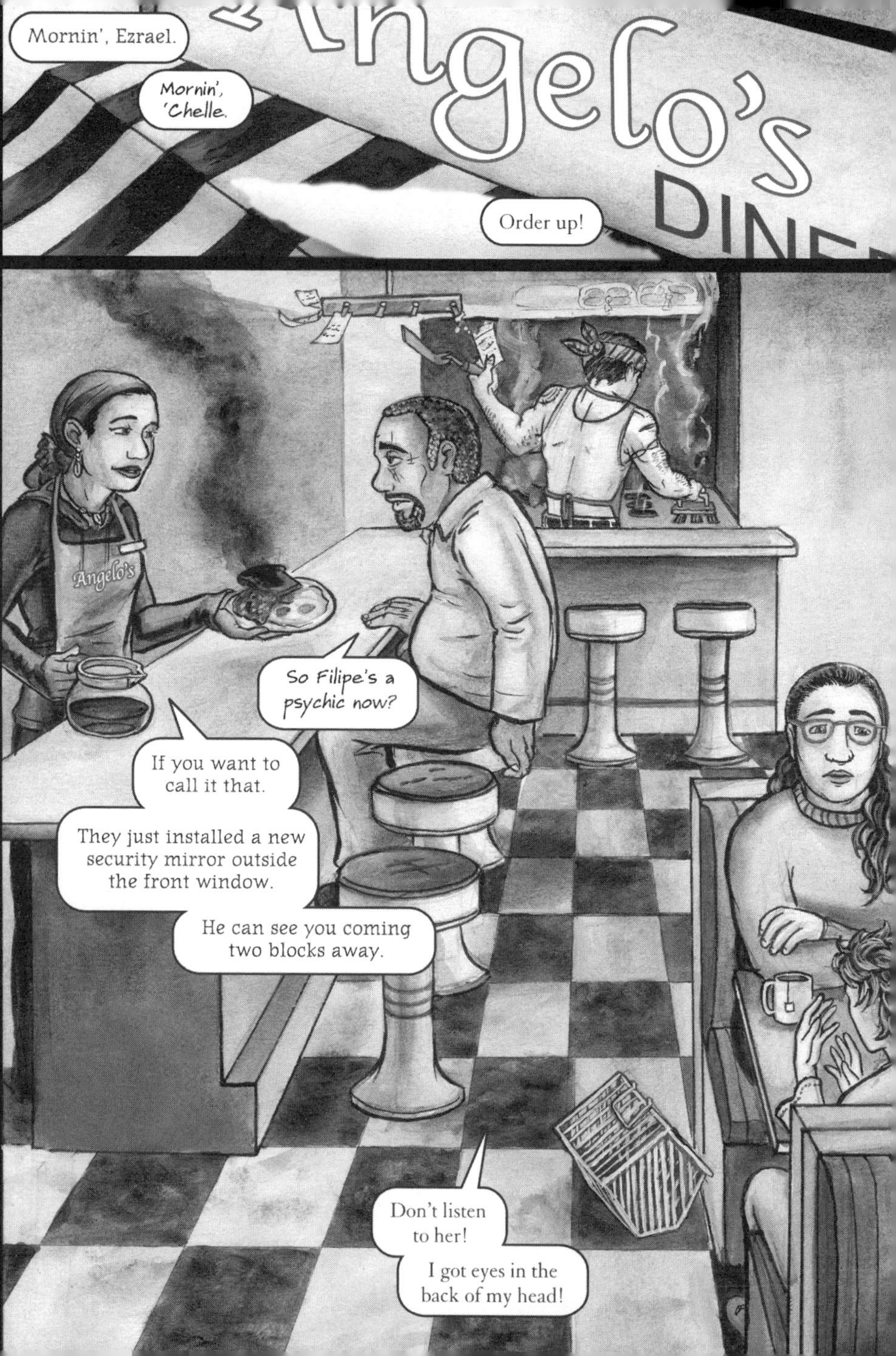
Mornin', Ezrael.
Mornin', 'Chelle.
Angelo's DINE
Order up!
Angelo's
So Filipe's a psychic now?
If you want to call it that.
They just installed a new security mirror outside the front window.
He can see you coming two blocks away.
Don't listen to her!
I got eyes in the back of my head!

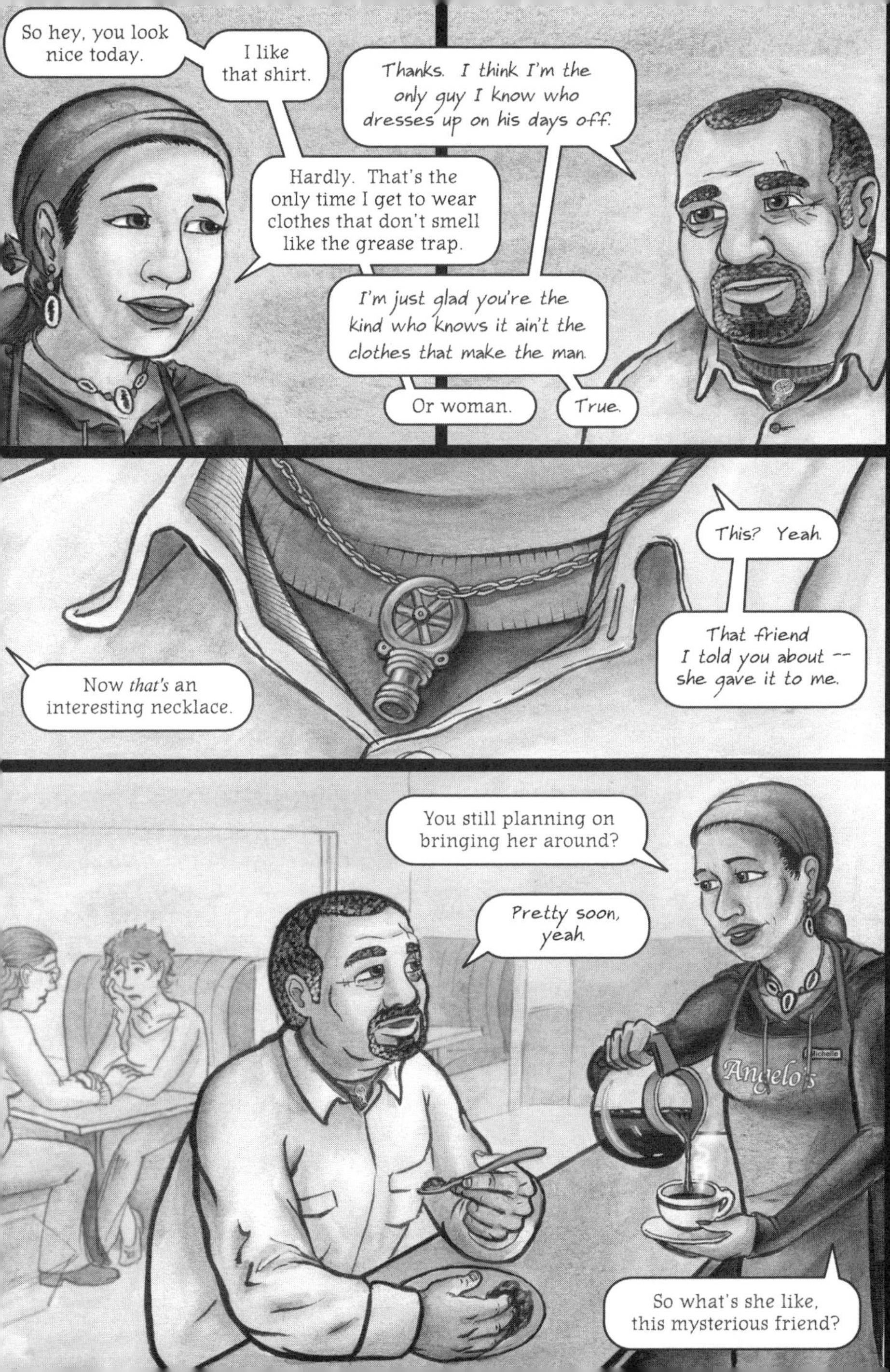
So hey, you look nice today.
I like that shirt.
Thanks. I think I'm the only guy I know who dresses up on his days off.
Hardly. That's the only time I get to wear clothes that don't smell like the grease trap.
I'm just glad you're the kind who knows it ain't the clothes that make the man.
Or woman.
True.
Now *that's* an interesting necklace.
This? Yeah.
That friend I told you about -- she gave it to me.
You still planning on bringing her around?
Pretty soon, yeah.
Angelo's
Michelle
So what's she like, this mysterious friend?

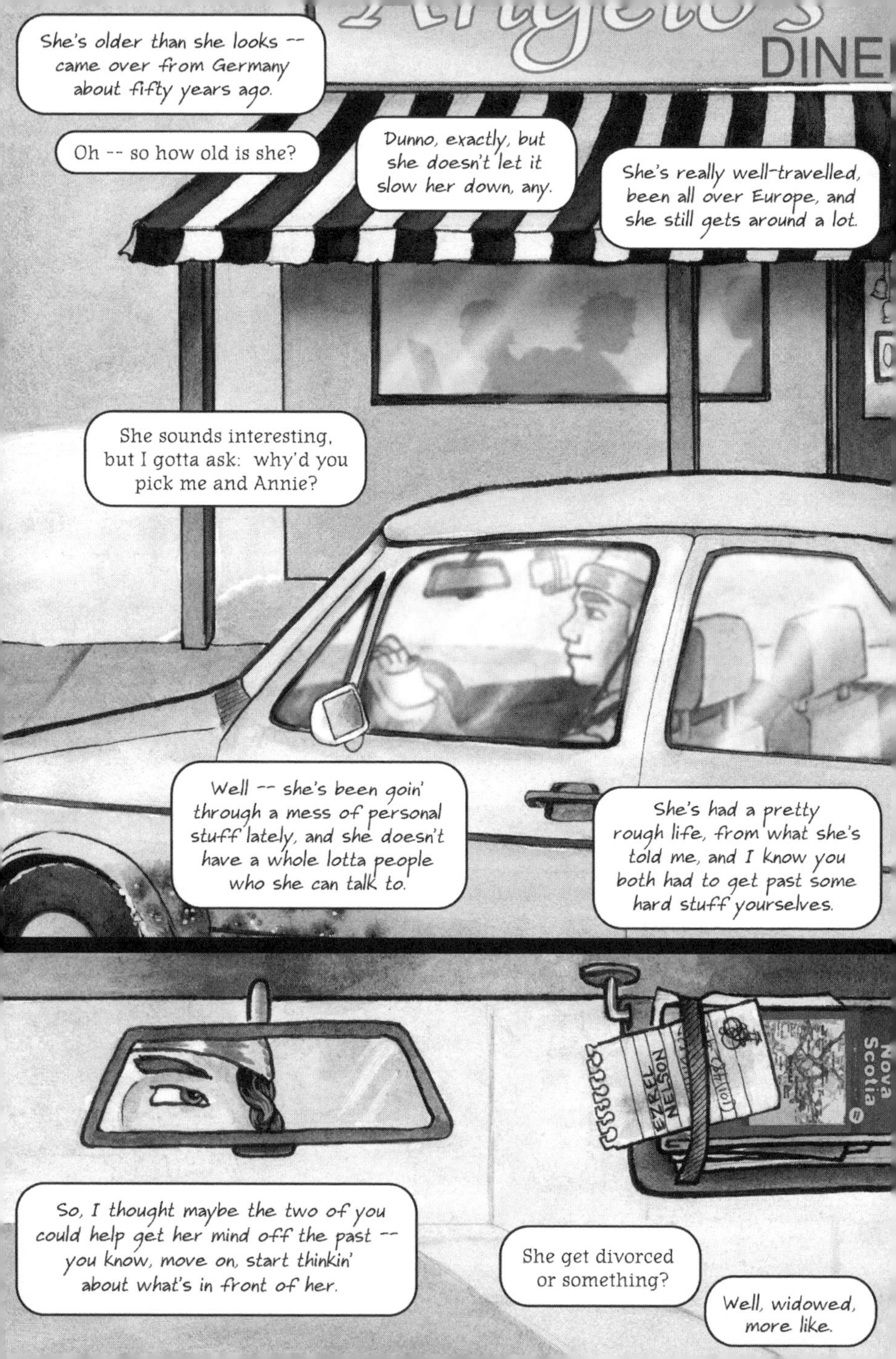
She's older than she looks -- came over from Germany about fifty years ago.
Oh -- so how old is she?
Dunno, exactly, but she doesn't let it slow her down, any.
She's really well-travelled, been all over Europe, and she still gets around a lot.
She sounds interesting, but I gotta ask: why'd you pick me and Annie?
Well -- she's been goin' through a mess of personal stuff lately, and she doesn't have a whole lotta people who she can talk to.
She's had a pretty rough life, from what she's told me, and I know you both had to get past some hard stuff yourselves.
EZREL NELSON
Nova Scotia
So, I thought maybe the two of you could help get her mind off the past -- you know, move on, start thinkin' about what's in front of her.
She get divorced or something?
Well, widowed, more like.

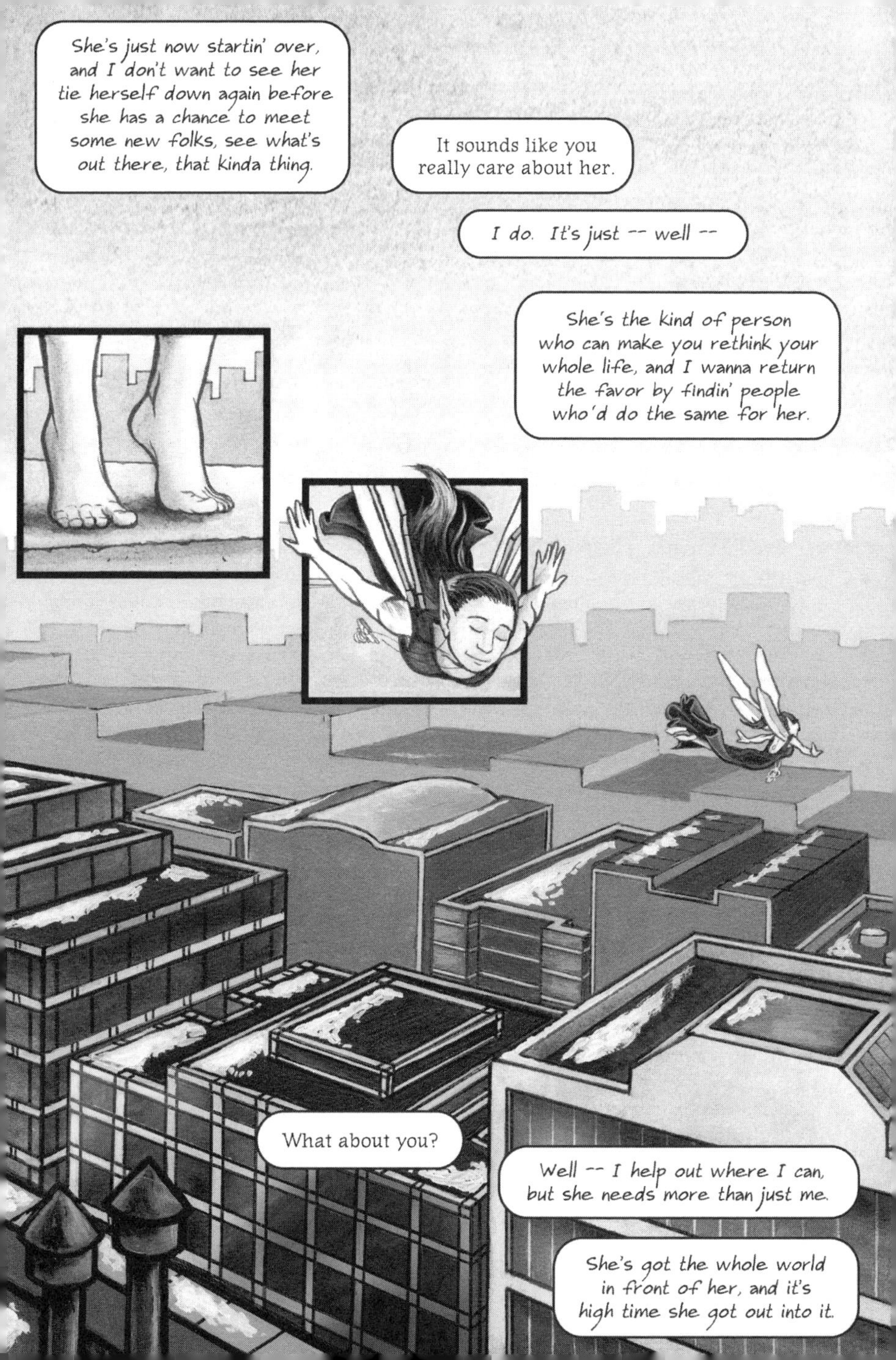
She's just now startin' over, and I don't want to see her tie herself down again before she has a chance to meet some new folks, see what's out there, that kinda thing.
It sounds like you really care about her.
I do. It's just -- well --
She's the kind of person who can make you rethink your whole life, and I wanna return the favor by findin' people who'd do the same for her.
What about you?
Well -- I help out where I can, but she needs more than just me.
She's got the whole world in front of her, and it's high time she got out into it.

ENDNOTES

Front cover, handwriting: The shadowy calligraphy you see on the front cover is actually a portion of the letter that Vögelein wrote to Alexi, and getting it on the cover required a team effort. First, I wrote the text and had it translated into German by Maryvonne Sarfati, a native speaker from the same part of Germany as Vögelein. Then, I turned the letter over to Jeff Berndt, co-creator of *Vögelein* and artist in his own right, who used an actual hand-cut quill pen to write the calligraphy. It's a superb job on all counts, and pulling my friends' talents together in interesting new ways is one of my favorite parts of creating a book.

Page 1, Vögelein's name: The pronunciation of "Vögelein" is a little tricky. The German "V" is softer than the hard, American "V" so it comes out as "PFEU-gul-ine." When you say it fast, it sounds like "Pfoo-Geline." An alternate pronunciation is "Vogue-el-ine"— she is an immigrant, after all, and that's how the Americanized version of her name would be pronounced.

Page 5, Blake's quote: My favorite story about Blake was told at his funeral. One year, Blake spent some time volunteering at a battered women's shelter. It seemed a little odd that a young man in his early twenties would donate his time to such a charity, and when asked about it, Blake replied with that quote. I found this so moving, and so descriptive of Blake's personality that I decided to use those words as the dedication.

Page 15, Chartres Cathedral: As point of reference, the cathedral at Chartres is 112 feet (34 meters) high, which means that this hotel is at least ten stories tall.

Page 19, bottom two panels: The little drawing on the bricks is Ezrael's way of showing Vögelein a safe place to visit. It's drawn with a piece of chalk, and will eventually wash away.

Page 20, pub: Kate O'Leary is a friend who played concertina in our local sessions, and we used to joke that her name would make a great name for a pub, so here it is. The interior of the pub is based on Conor O'Neill's in Ann Arbor, Michigan, where my friends and I have played many a session. They've recently expanded, and they also have a pub in Boulder, Colorado.

The session: Mason is walking in to a Irish traditional music session. Typically informal and relaxed, these gatherings are usually held in pubs or living rooms at a set time each week, and exist not just for the purpose of playing and learning traditional Irish music, but also for camaraderie between musicians — most sessions will attract at least a few listeners, but the music is first and foremost for the players themselves. Unlike a jazz jam session, active participation in a "trad" session requires foreknowledge of Irish music in general and a few tunes in specific, and often one or more musicians will act as session leader to keep the music flowing at an appropriate pace. Though each session breeds its own set of regulars, a well-versed musician is usually welcome at any Irish session anywhere in the world; Mason has been joining this session as often as he can before he leaves town.

Page 21, "busking": This term refers to the fine art of performing live in public places to entertain people, usually in hopes of earning a few bucks.

Music: The music staves you see passing overhead are those of traditional Irish tunes, the kind very likely to be played at a pub session such as this one. The first tune is a slide called "Merrily Kiss the Quaker" (or occasionally, "Merrily Kissed the Quaker's Wife") and the second is a reel called "The Wise Maid."

Page 22, music: Again, these are common

traditional session tunes. The top panel's tune is a four-part Scottish reel called "The High Road to Linton," the second tune is a jig called "Donnybrook Fair," the third tune is a reel called "Ships are Sailing" and the bottom one is a slipjig called "The Foxhunter's Jig"—a slipjig is a tune written in a 9/8 time signature.

To get complete sheet music, along with a list of albums where you can hear each of these tunes (and hundreds more), please visit www. thesession.org, an invaluable resource for sessioneers the world around.

Mason's instrument: The instrument Mason plays in the session is an Irish Bouzouki (sometimes referred to as a "'zouk" or a "'zouki"), the modern-day, flat-backed cousin of the Greek instrument. Bouzouki was introduced into Irish music in the 1960s by players like Dónal Lunny and Andy Irvine, and remains an important part of many Irish bands, including Dervish and Altan. It usually has four pairs of strings, is typically tuned GDAD or GDAE, and is used primarily for accompaniment.

"What's the difference between a bodhrán and a trampoline?": You take off your shoes when you jump on a trampoline. The bodhrán, or Irish frame drum, is a much-maligned instrument, and being a bodhrán player myself, I've heard my share of these jokes. "Bodhrán" is usually pronounced "bough-rawn," to rhyme with the sentence "There's a cow on my lawn," though some people pronounce it to rhyme with "moron" — the choice is yours.

Page 23, "craic": This modernized Irish term refers to the kind of light-hearted, mischievous fun you have when you're out with a bunch of friends at the pub, or playing music, or both. It's pronounced—and traditionally spelled—as "crack"; its "Irishized" spelling is often used to differentiate it from other, less fortunate meanings, and that's why I chose to use it here.

Page 25, "self-defense": Washburn banjos do indeed have a reputation for being heavy and well-built, though I don't believe the manufacturer would encourage this use of their product. No actual banjos were harmed during the creation of this graphic novel.

Page 26, Jess' apartment: I actually own the dress in the third panel. It's based on a 16th-century German gown, and was custom-made for me by a friend, Jackie Williams.

Page 27 "Daoine": Jess' password comes from the term *Daoine Sidhe* (pronounced "Deena Shee" or "Theena Shee"), which is an Irish Gaelic name for the faerie folk. Yeah, she's a bit obsessed.

Page 28, doll's head: Jess is hand-rooting hair into the fairy doll's head. A few years ago I made scale models of both Vögelein and the Duskie, and rooting their hair was the most time-consuming part of the entire process.

Page 30, digestive biscuits: These are semi-sweet cookies made for dunking in tea. They taste a little bit like shortbread. I have a special weakness for chocolate-dipped oatmeal digestives, and if no one's there to stop me, I will easily plow through half a packet in one sitting.

Page 31, soldiers: The war that Alexi and Vögelein are trying to escape is called the War of the Grand Alliance (1688–1697), which resulted when Karl II, Elector of the Palatinate, died without an heir. King Louis XIV of France used this opportunity to claim the Palatinate through his sister-in-law, Elizabeth Charlotte, who was Karl's sister, and therefore Princess of the Palatinate. The sack and burning of Heidelberg in March 1689 (as seen at the end of *Vögelein: Clockwork Faerie*) was one of the war's first major battles.

Roma/Romani: To quote from an essay written by Ronald Lee, "[Roma] is a common plural which includes both male and female members of the Romani people. Roma is the plural of Rom, which means an adult male member of the group. A female member of the group is called a Romni. Thus, the term Rom should not be applied to a woman. Since Roma is already a plural, the term Romas should not be used in English. The proper adjective in English is Romani not Roma as in Romani language or Romani music. The language spoken by Roma is also called Romani which in this case is a noun."

"Erich's tools": Alexi had learned enough of the blacksmithing trade to earn a little money—and make contacts—whenever it proved useful.

Page 32, *"Bi-Baxt! Avri! Avri!"*: Alexi is part of the Kalderash clan of Roma, and they believe that owls are very bad luck, and that their cry foretells death. He says "Bad luck! Out! Out!" as he chases it from the barn.

Page 37, *"Chirikli"*: This is a Romani word meaning "female bird," which is roughly what Vögelein's name means in English.

Page 49, Soldiers: The model for the soldier that takes Vögelein is Jeff Berndt. One of Jeff's hobbies is historical re-enactment, with a focus on the British side of the American Revolution. You

can find out more (and see photos of Jeff in his tricorn hat) at www.hands-onhistory.com.

Page 52, Michelle: Observant readers will remember Michelle as the college student who gave Jason so much grief in *Vögelein: Clockwork Faerie.*

Angelo's Diner: I took the inspiration for this diner from two separate restaurants in Ann Arbor. The look and feel comes from The Fleetwood Diner, the best all-night greasy spoon in town, and the name comes from Angelo's Restaurant, highly favored by locals as a fabulous place to get breakfast and lunch.

If you visit the Fleetwood, order the Hippie Hash; at Angelo's, try their homemade raisin toast.

Page 53, Ezrael's breakfast: I had originally wanted to use diner lingo in this scene, but couldn't find a way to fit it in without it sounding forced. Just so I don't feel like all that research was wasted, Ezrael's order of two over-easy eggs, rye toast, hash browns and black coffee translates as "Flop two, whiskey down, sweep the kitchen and draw one in the dark."

Page 57, Bibi Zhuzha: *Bibi* is a Romani term of respect and endearment, meaning "Aunt" and used in affectionate, respectful reference to any Romani matriarch, not just a family relative.

Zhuzha is the Hungarian form of "Susan," so "Bibi Zhuzha" translates as "Aunt Susan."

Page 66, Mami: *Mami* is the Romani word for "Grandmother." *Mami* and *Bibi Zhuzha* both refer to the same woman; Gina's grandmother and Mason's "Aunt."

Page 70, *"raklo"*: This Romani word means "(non-Romani) boy."

Page 82, candle: The Chinese character on the candle reads "tranquility" or "stillness."

Page 83, the Brown Man: This fellow is most likely a form of Scottish or Irish brownie—they're usually harmless, though they do enjoy a bit of mischief now and again. In an ideal world, he'd probably be secretly finishing a farmer's chores in return for gifts of food, but here in the city he's pretty lost.

Page 91, Brenda: The model for Brenda is Jennifer Contino, a comics journalist who wrote the foreword for *Vögelein: Clockwork Faerie. (Photo courtesy of Alexandra Duff.)*

Page 92, "The Monster Slayers": This refers to a group of young adventurers in Mark "M'Oak" Oakley's *Thieves and Kings* series of graphic novels. In Vögelein's world, they have their own animated television series. Sadly, in our world they do not.

Page 95, "kleinblitzen": This German word translates as "tiny lightnings," and is the term that Vögelein uses to refer to the static electricity that allows her fine motor control over her fingers and toes.

Page 103, Ezrael's conversation: In the last few months, Ezrael has introduced Vögelein to several people he deems trustworthy; Mason is only one of her current Guardians.

Pages 104-105, Prospero's Books: The interior of Ezrael's home is based in part on the Cross Street Bookstore, a wonderful bookshop in Ypsilanti, Michigan. Sheridan, the proprietor, sold me many of the reference books I used when writing *Vögelein*. The store will probably never have a website, but that's for the best. It's the kind of place you can only truly experience in person, and I encourage everyone to shop there.

Page 110, cigar box: Vögelein's life seldom lent itself to acquiring many possessions; most of the time, the only items she owned were the clothes on her back and her two keys. As she mentions earlier in the story, her previous transitions between Guardians were often abrupt and violent, and did not allow her to save mementos, but after Jakob rescued her in Paris during World War Two, she had time to gather a few keepsakes from the wreckage of Madeline's house before he shipped out.

Page 112, flashback: Jakob was Vögelein's last "full-time" Guardian; his death occurred at the beginning of *Vögelein: Clockwork Faerie*. This scene takes place approximately ten years before the time of the current story.

Page 133, Nickel Creek: You'd be amazed how many places like this exist right within, or just outside, an average city. If Vögelein followed this stream a little further to where it joins the nearby river, she'd find herself surrounded by factories, industrial pollution and heavy boat traffic, but this little creek is protected from commercialization by its diminutive size, the surrounding swamp, and a thin strip of park land.

The name of the stream comes from an excellent bluegrass band. You can find out more about them at www.nickelcreek.com.

Page 145, song lyrics: The song Mason is singing is "Wave Over Wave," with lyrics by Jim Payne and Janis Spence, and music by Jim Payne. The chorus, in its entirety, goes:

> *Where it's wave over wave, sea over bow*
> *I'm as happy a man as the sea will allow.*
> *There's no other life for a sailor like me*
> *But to sail the salt sea, boys, sail the sea.*
> *There's no other life but to sail the salt sea.*

In addition to its appearance on Jim Payne and Fergus O'Byrne's album of the same name, "Wave Over Wave" gained further popularity after it was recorded by fellow Newfoundland artists Great Big Sea, and has become a favorite among folksingers worldwide.

For more information, please visit Jim Payne's website at www.singsong.nfld.com.

ONE FINAL BLAKE STORY

Just a few weeks prior to the printing of this book, I was having lunch with my husband's father, who was a high-school English teacher for over thirty years. He asked me how progress on the book was going, and so I mentioned the very positive conversations I'd had with Blake's grandfather, Lowell "Jerry" Mason.

It turns out that my father-in-law not only knows Blake's grandfather, but that Blake's late mother was one of his best-remembered and dearest students. Stranger than fiction, indeed.

About Blake Mason

The character of Mason is based on a very real person, Martin Blake Linell, but when I knew him, he went by Blake Mason. We met shortly after he moved back from Halifax to his former home in the Lansing area. He had returned to help his mother pass away with dignity, easing her struggle through her final months with terminal cancer.

Blake began attending the same Irish music sessions that my friends and I frequented, guitar in hand, always eager for tunes and conversation. He quickly gained a reputation as a skilled and empathic rhythm guitarist, the highly-coveted type capable of drawing together the disparate melodic lines of session instruments to create a whole greater than the sum of the parts.

It wasn't long before he and two other session regulars started a band. Aptly named with the Irish Gaelic word for "sweet," Millish played an exhilarating combination of traditional and modern, Jazz and folk and pure-drop Irish music.

Millish, taken in 2001. (l-r): Blake Mason, Jeremy Kittel, Tyler Duncan, Glenn Bering. Photo by Doug Coombe.

Millish began to play out more often, and quickly landed some high-profile gigs, including the Detroit Festival of the Arts. Blake was a consummate bandmate, never late for practice — and when he didn't show up for rehearsal one night, everyone immediately knew something was wrong.

On November 8th, 2001, Blake passed away at his mother's home in Laingsburg, Michigan. The cause of death was a brain aneurysm, the same illness that had also afflicted his father and his aunt.

Though I didn't know Blake as well as I would have liked, I found myself deeply struck by his loss. He was a passionate, kind and loving soul, removed from this life with breathtaking abruptness. Every time I was around Blake, I was moved by his compassion and his ability to be present in each moment. Despite his young age, he seemed to have a deep understanding of the world, and always seemed fully aware — he truly listened to life, observed it in a way that most of us don't.

When I started gathering ideas for the second Vögelein book, I felt a need to memorialize Blake in some way, to let him stick around here a little longer, and influence more people with his personality. After talking to his bandmates and friends, and later, his relatives, I decided to base one of the main supporting characters on Blake.

The most difficult part of doing so was creating some flaws for Mason that Blake didn't have; I felt that if I portrayed Mason exactly like Blake, people wouldn't think he was a realistic character! (One such addition: to the best of my knowledge, Blake was never abused as a child.)

Today, Blake is fondly remembered by his friends and family, and Millish continues to perform. Their self-titled first album is dedicated to his memory, and the final track features a short clip of Blake playing guitar on "Kirstie's Weather Hair," a tune he taught the band. For more information, including sample tracks from their album, please visit www.millish.com.

MEET THE MUSICIANS

All the musicians playing at the pub session are real people. Here's a bit about each one.

Stephanie Cornelius is a mechanical engineer from western New York. At the turn of the century,  her Life Journey passed through Ann Arbor, where she found Irish fiddling and the best friends she's ever known. Her life is blessed and full—she's back home working as a private consultant, and enjoying the adventure with her young nephews and her partner Tim.

 **Dale Dahl** is a flute and whistle player who plays a host of other instruments, including guitar. He makes his own bodhráns out of snare drums, practices flute while driving on the highway, and plays in sessions and pubs all over the world, at all hours of the night.

Emily Peterson is a laser and x-ray physicist, trad-musician, and occasional food artist living in Chicago's Pilsen neighborhood.  On the average evening, one can logically expect to find her in the lab, at the pub, and/or eating Mexican food. She is thrilled to see herself immortalized in paint and print.

Colleen Shanks started playing the highland pipes when she was 12, then shortly after moved on to Irish music and took up the whistle. A few years  later she heard the Irish pipes and thought that's what she'd really like to do, so she started taking lessons from Al Purcell and later Terence McKinney. She currently attends Eastern Michigan University, where she majors in Elementary Education.

 If librarian **Jennifer Foster** had known at age 15 that she would play a banjo at her wedding, she would have stepped in front of a CSX train, thereby causing a massive chemical spill and the evacuation of her hometown. She lives in Michigan with her husband Solomon, who defends himself with accordion and tin whistle.

Alison Perkins is one of the brightest young stars on the Detroit Irish music scene. She is a three-time Midwest Irish fiddle champion in the 15-18 category, and is currently a member of Finvarra's Wren,  where she plays Irish, Scottish and Celtic-American folk music. Find out more about Allison at www.finvarraswren.com.

NOTES ON ALEXI

Since I am not an expert in Romani history and culture, I contacted Mr. Ronald Lee, who teaches a course on the Romani Diaspora at the University of Toronto and is also the author of *Learn Romani*, a Romani language primer, and *Goddam Gypsy*, an autobiography.

After reading *Vögelein: Clockwork Faerie*, Mr. Lee's first comment was that I needed to include a footnote in this volume explaining why Alexi traveled alone. He explained that in modern times, a solitary lifestyle would not be terribly unusual, but in Alexi's time, one Rom living by himself would be extremely rare, and would require a backstory. Originally, I'd left Alexi's history unwritten, daunted by the amount of research an accurate depiction would require, but thanks to Mr. Lee's knowledge and suggestions, I was finally able to solidify Alexi's history, clan and origins:

Alexi was born in Wallachia, a principality in Eastern Europe which is now part of Romania. The Holy Roman Empire and the Ottoman Empire fought constantly over this territory, but the lords in closest contact with their subjects were the powerful aristocrats known as boyars. These feudal landowners frequently owned Romani slaves to work in their fields and homes, similar to African-American slaves in the United States, and among these slaves existed a class of skilled laborers called *laieshi*. Though the *laieshi* possessed a small amount of freedom to travel within their lord's estate, they were still considered property and had to give a portion of whatever they earned back to their owners. Alexi's parents were among these *laieshi*, and worked as *kovachi*, or blacksmiths.

During one of many skirmishes involving their lord's estate, Alexi's parents took advantage of the chaos and escaped west, continuing their flight until they came to Augsburg, the same town in which there lived a young watchmaker's apprentice named Heinrich Uhrmacher. Before they could continue further west, Alexi's parents both died of fever, leaving their young son to fend for himself.

Heinrich and Alexi eventually became business partners of a sort; they were kept apart by class and society, but Heinrich's eccentric clockworks demanded obscure materials that only a proficient trader like Alexi could locate. When Heinrich set up his Master's shop in Heidelberg, Alexi followed, and continued his trading missions, returning with everything Heinrich needed to create Vögelein.

FURTHER READING

Learn Romani by Ronald Lee
University Of Hertfordshire Press, 2005
ISBN: 978-1902806440

We are the Romani People by Ian Hancock
University Of Hertfordshire Press, 2002
ISBN: 978-1902806198

The Pariah Syndrome by Ian Hancock
ISBN: 978-0897200790
Karoma Publishers, 1987

Amalipen:
www.amalipen.net
A meeting place for Roma and friends of the Roma. *Amalipen* means "friend" in Romani.

The Patrin Web Journal:
www.geocities.com/~patrin
A collection of articles and links about the Roma.

Romano Kopachi (The Romani Tree):
home.cogeco.ca/~kopachi
A site for Roma, about Roma and by Roma. Includes many articles by Ronald Lee.

PINUP GALLERY

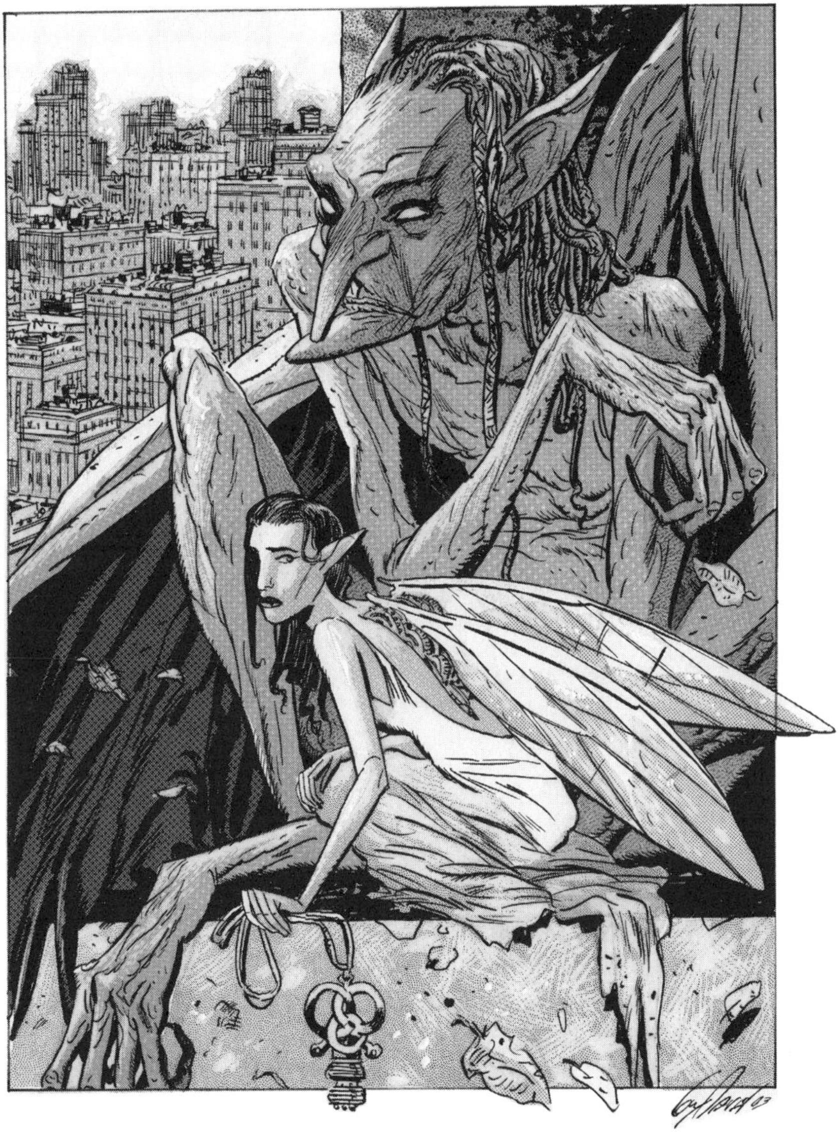

Michigan-based artist **Guy Davis** has been sketching and drawing as long as he can remember and has been content to go where his art would take him. Currently Guy is illustrating Mike Mignola's ongoing *B.P.R.D.* series, the serial *The Zombies That Ate The World* for *Metal Hurlant* and continuing with his creator owned series *The Marquis* for ONI Press. You can see his work at www.guydavisartworks.com

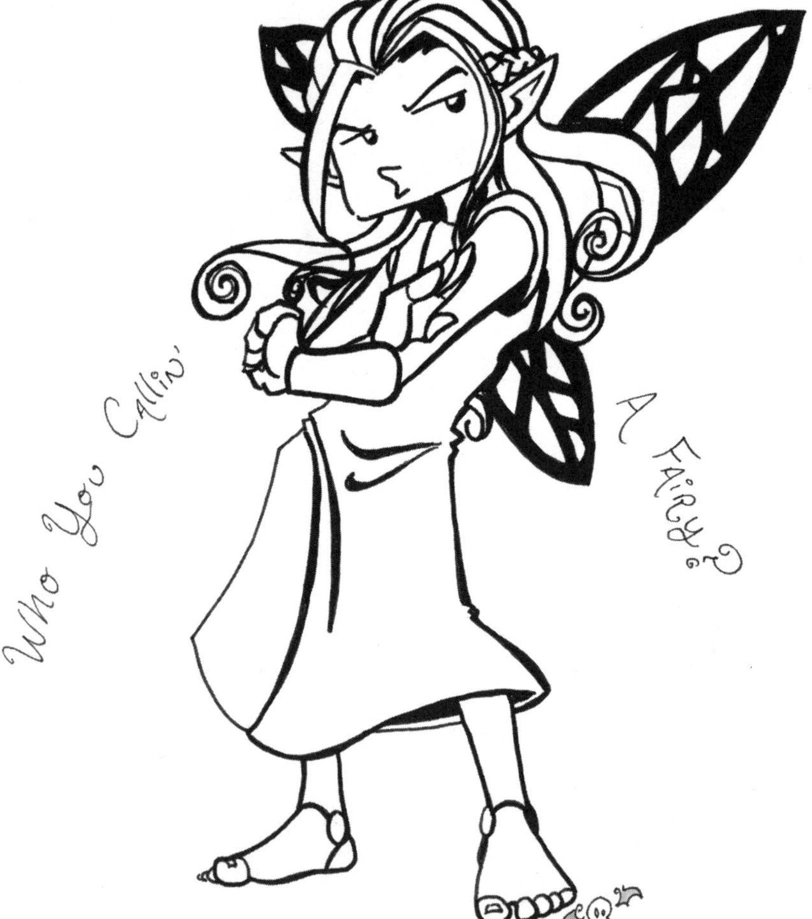
Who You Callin'
A Fairy?
MIA

Mia Paluzzi likes robots and strawberry applesauce, but not on the same plate. She is currently working on her masters degree in Sequential Art at the Savannah College of Art and Design.

Soon, she'll have a big official website, but in the meantime, her artwork can be found at rocketshoes.deviantart.com

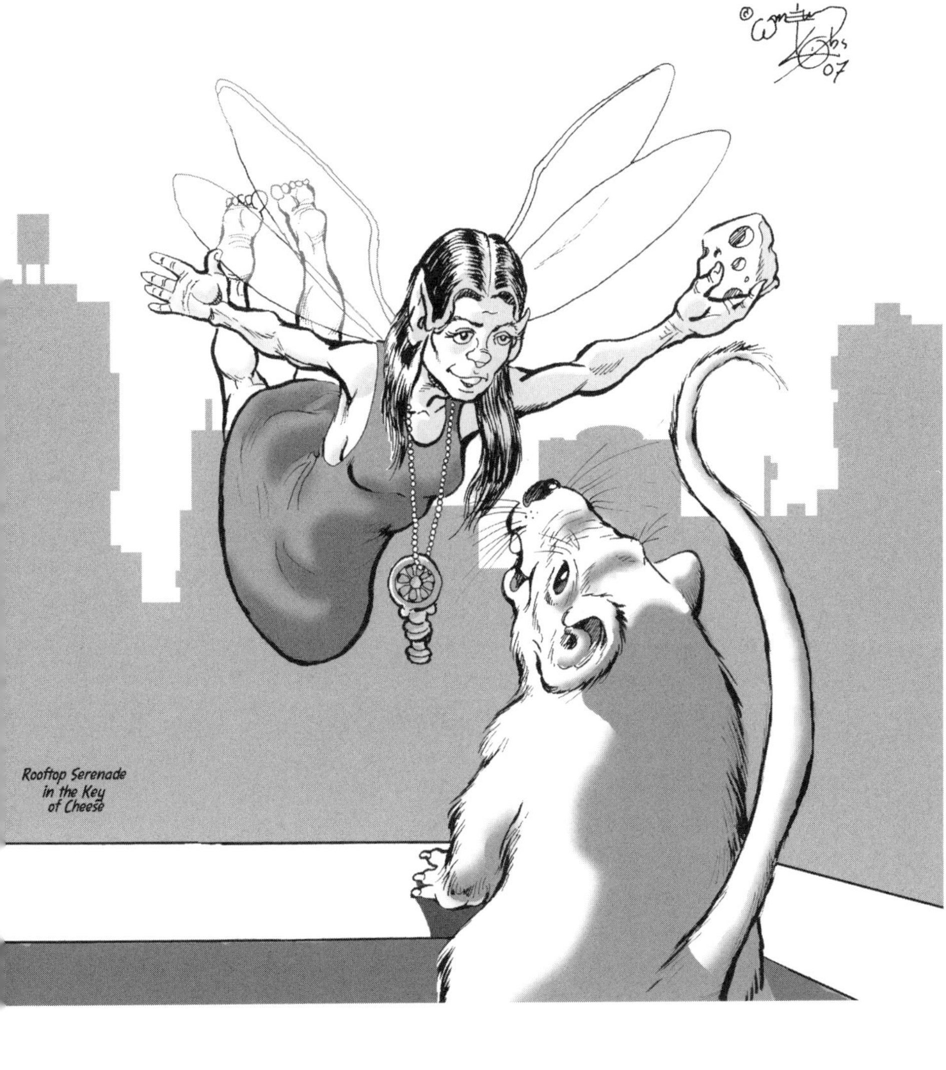
Rooftop Serenade
in the Key
of Cheese

Raised by Zen Shepherds in Ferndale, Michigan, **Bill Messner-Loebs** began drawing comic books as soon as they were made legal. He created *Journey* and *Bliss Alley*. He inked *Mr. Monster*, and wrote *Flash*, the *Batman* newspaper strip, *Jaguar*, *Dr. Fate*, *Superman*, *Green Arrow*, *Thor* and *Wonder Woman*. *Welcome to Heaven, Dr. Franklin*, his first professional work, has been collected by About Comics and *Three Tenors* was lately published by Aardwulf. He is just finishing a short novel, *Toltec*, for Actionopolis.

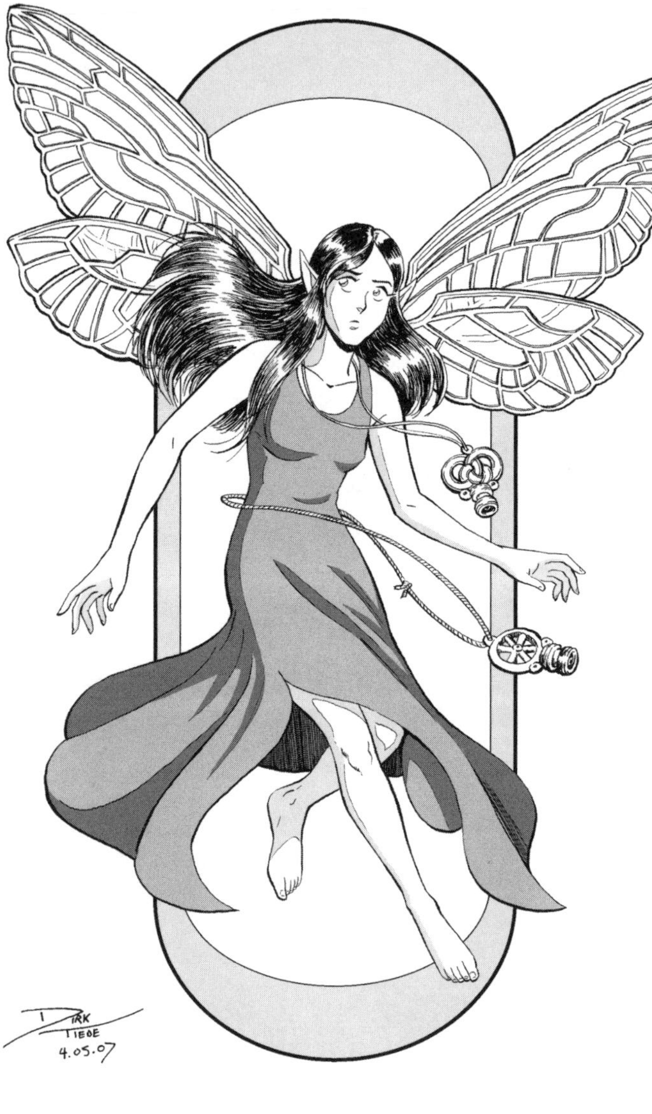
DIRK TIEDE
4.05.07

Dirk Tiede draws and writes *Paradigm Shift*, a paranormal cop story set in Chicago, where he makes his home. Having recently printed his second graphic novel, he's delighted to see Jane do the same. Dirk hosts Art Night, a community gathering for local artists, web comickers, and graphic novelists. For police procedurals, mystery, action and drama in Chicago neighborhoods, and a hint of the supernatural, see his third book online at www.dynamanga.net or www.webcomicsnation.com/dirktiede.

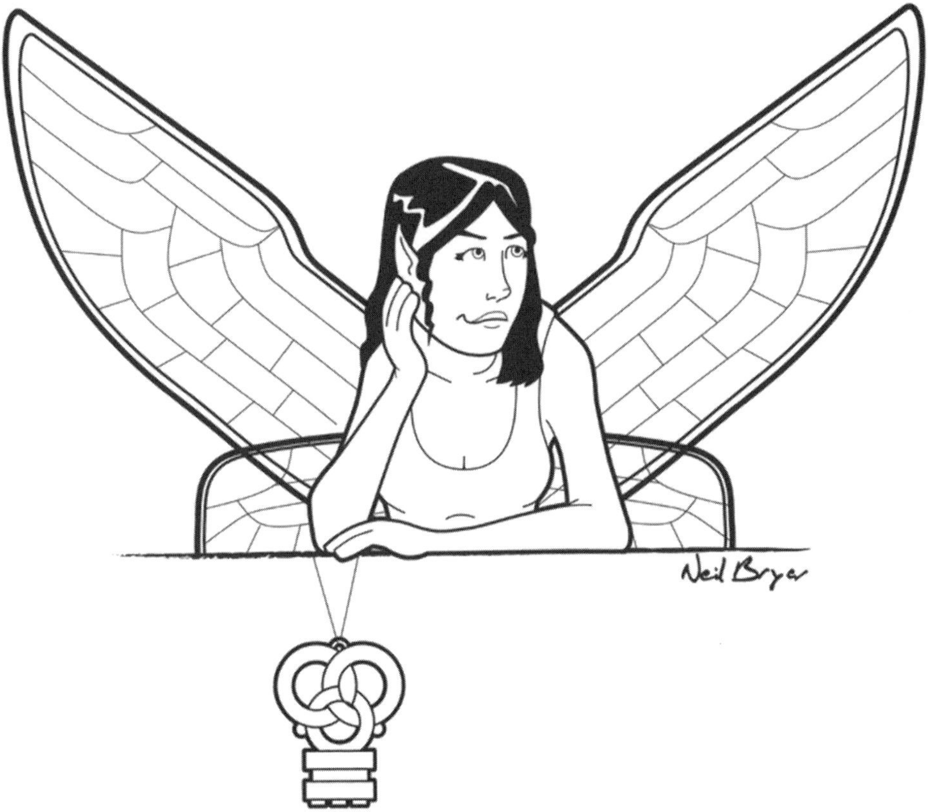
Neil Bryer

Neil Bryer fancies himself a talented artist. He also fancies himself as a gourmet cook and fantastic lover. It's nice in Neil's little fantasy world.

Neil is also the creator behind *The Crime Fighting Monk* and *Wombat*. You can find out more about both at wombatone.deviantart.com.

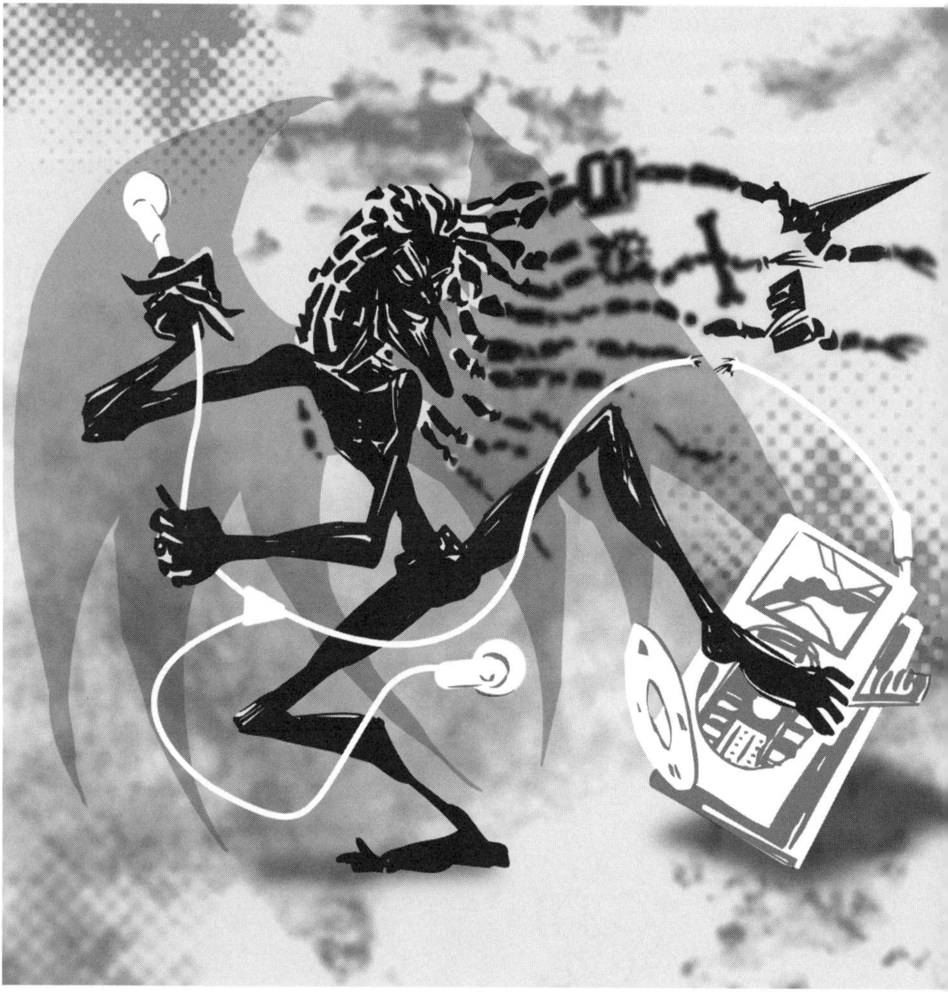

Sean Bieri has been (sporadically) making mini-comics since meeting Matt Feazell and Matt Madden in 1990, but his first full-length comic was a *Mad*-style *Star Wars* parody drawn when he was in 5th grade. He works as the art director, illustrator and occasional comics reviewer for Detroit's free weekly paper, *Metro Times*. Inspired by NYC illustrator Molly Crabapple, he organizes the local Dr. Sketchy life drawing sessions, and is a founding member, with Feazell, cartoonist Suzanne Baumann and others, of the local arts collective Hatch. He lives with his wife Sophia Raptis and a porchful of cats in the small, strangely named and strangely cartoonist-rich city of Hamtramck, Michigan.

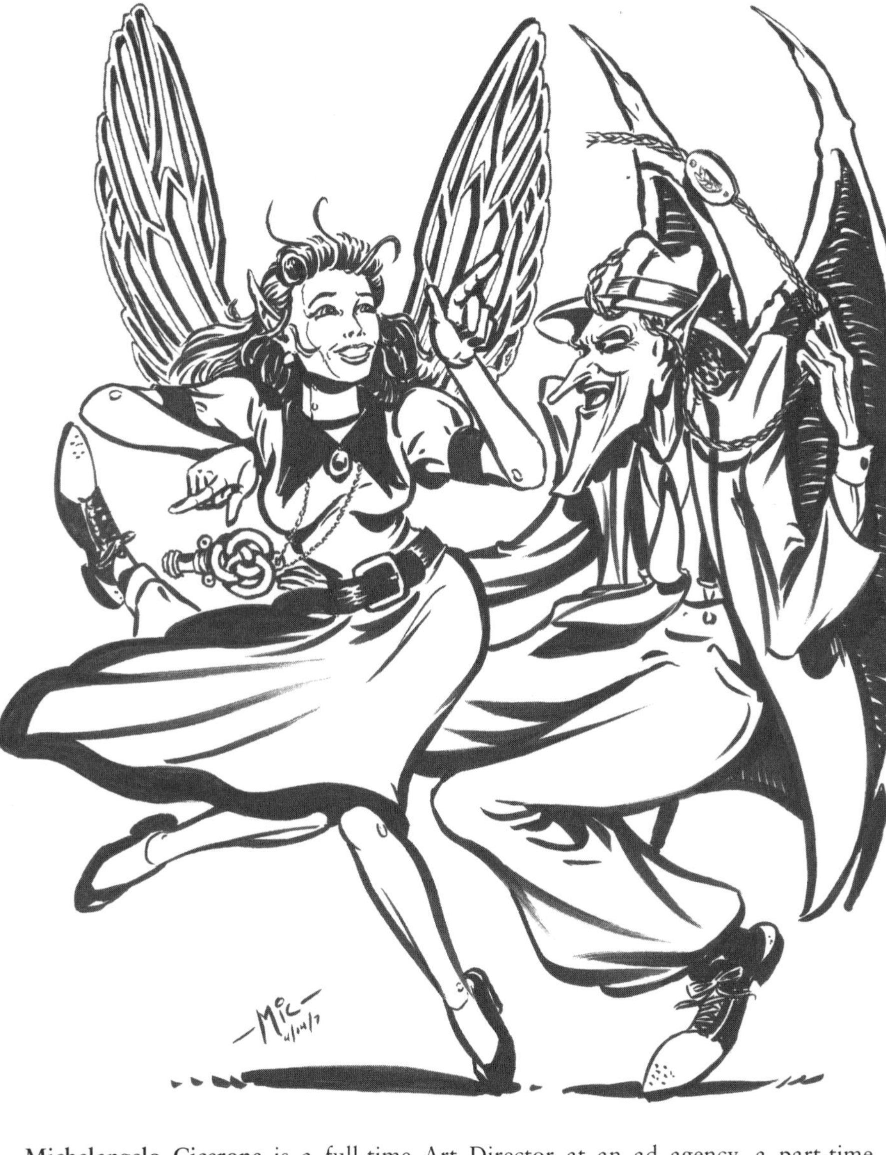

Michelangelo Cicerone is a full-time Art Director at an ad agency, a part-time cartoon art instructor and an unemployed cartoonist. On occasion, he writes and draws *The Adventures of Ozone Jones*, which is difficult to describe but a lot of fun to read. He has also been known to sell a gag or two to *Disney Adventures*. You can see more of Michelangelo's work at www.ozonejones.com.

WWW.WANDERINGPILOT.COM

PAULIK.07

Mark Paulik is a freelance illustrator, animator and comic artist who has produced illustrations and animations for clients such as Nike, Intel, Hewlett-Packard, and many newspapers and magazines. Mark is planning to move to the San Francisco Bay area for a new job working in the online social gaming industry for newly formed company Bunchball.

Until recently Mark was stored in a glass jar in some mean person's basement. He would explain his method of escape, but he was told to keep his bio short. You can see more of his work at www.wanderingpilot.com.

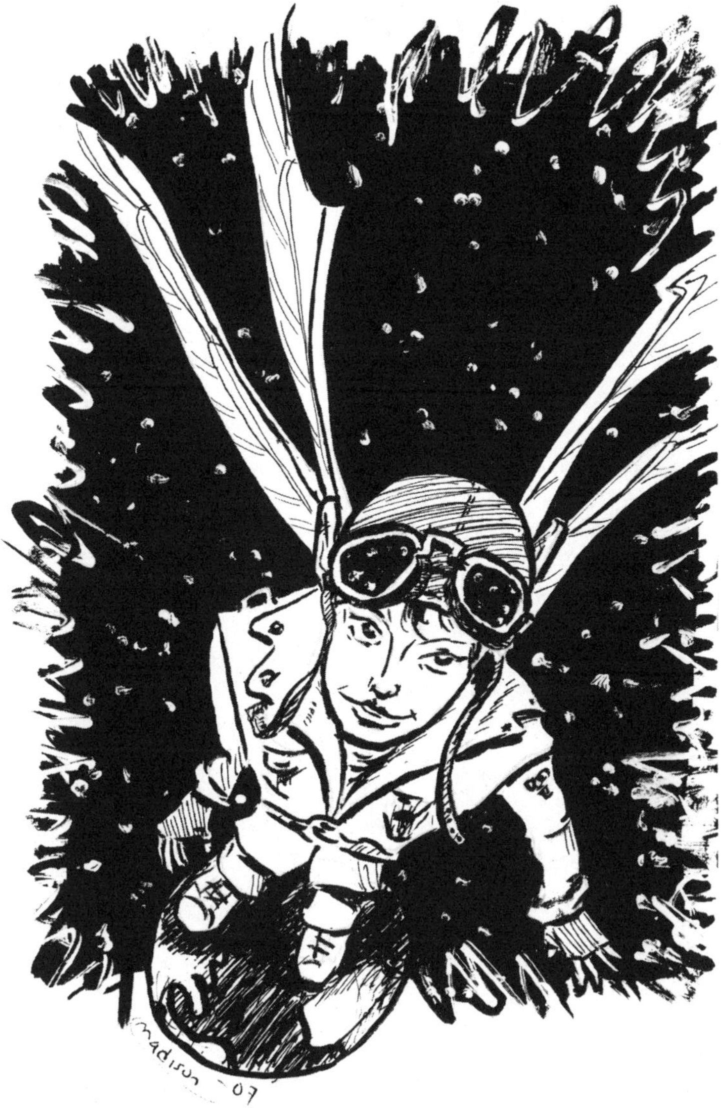

Madison Clell has turned down movie adaptations of her life, and you can find out why at www.multiples.net. Listed as a career steamboat historian in her high school reunion book, in reality she's published 13 single issues and one trade paperback of her acclaimed comic *Cuckoo*. Madison's artwork has appeared in various venues, including Chicago Cultural Center's 2006 "Humans Being" show. In 2006, Jump! Theatre [www.jumptheatre.org] recruited Madison to turn *Cuckoo* into a full length play, and they won a C.A.S.H. Grant to develop it. In addition to writing awkward bios in the third person, Madison loves to make big colorful pastels and paints yellow rubber duckies on her surfboards. Find *Cuckoo* at comic stores and bookstores, and www.multiples.net.

ACKNOWLEDGEMENTS

Work on *Vögelein: Old Ghosts* began in late 2003, right after the graphic novel edition of *Vögelein: Clockwork Faerie* hit store shelves. As with all my creative endeavors, I have been blessed time and time again with the help and generosity of a great many good people. Grateful acknowledgements to:

Jeff Berndt, for calligraphy and poetry and music and song, and for helping create Vögelein in the first place.

The family and friends of Blake Mason, for their time, approval, support and encouragement.

Maryvonne Sarfati, who checked my German (so that no one got called a corset in this volume) and did translation for the writing on the cover. Maryvonne is also part of the Bessenberg Bindery team who created the lovely special hardbound editions. Please visit them at www.bessenberg.com.

Mr. Ronald Lee, Instructor at the University of Toronto, who helped me immensely with Romani facts, history, and translation. Without his help, knowledge and guidance the book could not have been finished on time.

All my Editors and Proofreaders: Becky Cooper, Jeff Berndt, Eric Braun, Allison Frame, Emily Peterson, Jennifer Foster, Dirk Tiede, Dave Glide, Logan Kelly, Neil Bryer, Pam Noles, Maryvonne Sarfati, Layla Lawlor, Rachel Hartman, Jim Ottaviani, Kat Hagedorn, and especially Dennis Wenzel, who is a Quality Assurance Super Genius.

Rollande Krandall, who has been attempting to replicate Vögelein's key in hand-carved wax and sterling silver—for the last *four years*.

Layla Lawlor, the first person to hear this story in its entirety and deem it worth telling. Way back in 2003, she listened to me explain the plot over tea and brown bread in Conor O'Neill's, the same pub you see depicted in the session. Layla has been instrumental in its completion, from plot to dialogue to imagery, and my grateful thanks to her for fresh ideas, reality checks, Alaskan oddity tourism, and many long phone calls.

Dan Sugalski, who continues to provide me with web hosting and a blog platform from which to vent my spleen.

Matthew "Virus" Messana, for stuffed daikon, proper coffee, patient ears and kind friendship.

The scores of fans who waited patiently for the next book, and who keep reminding me that they care. You give me a reason, and the confidence, to keep creating.

<u>But most of all:</u> Infinite thanks and love go to Paul Sizer, who married me, and who continues to be the single best thing in my entire life. He puts my world into perspective, on paper and off.